GH00762334

SOUNDS GOOD 2
Music for the new Junior Cycle

Laura Lynch

The Educational Company of Ireland

First published 2019

The Educational Company of Ireland

Ballymount Road

Walkinstown

Dublin 12

www.edco.ie

A member of the Smurfit Kappa Group plc

978-1-84536-841-8

 The paper used in this book comes from Managed Forests in Northern Europe For every tree felled, at least one new tree is planted

Project Editor: Lucy Taylor

Editor: Kilmeny MacBride

Proofreader: Janice Baiton

Music Setting: Peter Nickol, Compuscript

Design: EMC Design

Layout: Compuscript

Cover: EMC

Cover Photography: Shutterstock

Illustrations: Global Blended Learning, Compuscript

Studio recordings: Sonic Studios, Stoneybatter, Dublin

The author would like to extend her thanks to all in Edco – particularly Declan Dempsey, Lucy Taylor, Kilmeny MacBride and Peter Nickol for their dedication and generous support and assistance in the completion of *Sounds Good 2: Music for the new Junior Cycle*. I would like to thank my students, past and present, your enthusiasm for music remains an inspiration, and it has always been my pleasure to be your teacher. I wish also to thank my parents for their sacrifice, support and infinite love. Deepest gratitude to Brien for his unconditional support and encouragement, and to Freddie and Pearl, the melody in my life.

Thanks to: Kevin Donnelly and Rosa Downey for their contribution to the audio CD; Al Cowan in Sonic Studios; Comhaltas; Ronan Guilfoyle.

03M20

Contents

Introduction v

   A Guide to *Sounds Good 2: Music for the new Junior Cycle*....................................... vi

   Your *Sounds Good 2* CDs x

Acknowledgements xii

Unit 1 – My Music Passport 1

  1 Me and My Music 2

  2 Film Music 7

  3 Music in Advertising 11

  4 Music and Community 16

Unit 2 – Elements of Music 24

  5 Pulse and Tempo 25

  6 Dynamics 29

  7 Pitch and Timbre 31

  8 Mood and Expression 37

  9 Rhythm 42

  10 Melody 48

Unit 3 – Listening Lab 56

  11 Active Listening 57

  12 Silent Films 76

  13 Listening and Analysing 82

  14 What is Jazz? 88

  15 Unit 3 Round-up 96

Unit 4 – Ensemble Lab 102

  16 The Renaissance 105

  17 The Baroque Period 111

  18 Conducting Lab 128

  19 The Classical Period 131

  20 The Romantic Period 140

  21 Irish Composers: Our Neglected Treasures? 145

Chapters

Chapters

Chapters

Chapters

Chapters

Unit 5 – Composing Lab **155**

22 Responding to and Reading Rhythm 157

23 Listening to and Performing Rhythm 163

24 Composing with Rhythm 166

25 Complex Metres 170

26 Composing with Melody 172

27 Composing Illustrative Motifs and Melodic Ideas 187

Chapters

Unit 6 – Creative Lab **192**

28 Harmony 194

29 Chord Progressions 204

30 Adding Chords to Melodies 212

Chapters

Unit 7 – Performing **220**

31 Getting Ready to Sing 222

32 Sight-Reading 225

33 Body Percussion! 230

34 Group Performances 235

35 Recorder Performance 247

36 The Performance Process 251

Chapters

Unit 8 – The Ukulele **254**

37 Getting Started 257

38 Playing Major Chords 260

39 Using Chords 265

40 Minor Chords 272

41 Bringing Together Our Skills 277

42 End of Unit Learning Tasks 283

Revision Lab 288

Action Verbs 322

Classroom Based Assessment 1 (CBA1) – The Composition Portfolio 325

Classroom Based Assessment 2 (CBA2) – Programme Note Guidelines 331

Glossary 333

Introduction

Welcome!

Welcome to *Sounds Good 2: Music for the new Junior Cycle*, your textbook designed to complete your study of Junior Cycle Music. *Sounds Good 2: Music for the new Junior Cycle* is an engaging and innovative textbook which places you at the centre of your learning and provides you with a suite of resources to guide you through the Junior Cycle Music Specification. As you engage in all these learning experiences I hope you will remember that music has been a part of your life for a long time. Music is a language that our hearts and minds recognise and respond to. Music has been a good friend which has been with you always.

Sounds Good 2: Music for the new Junior Cycle will provide you with an opportunity to explore your relationship with music and develop many important skills that will serve you well throughout your life. This textbook will support your learning as you engage with the Learning Outcomes set out in your subject specification. Throughout this book the concepts central to the teaching and learning of music are covered in the eight Units of Learning. New concepts are revisited, directly and indirectly through the various units, whilst developing important skills and assessing your learning experience. A Revision Lab has been added to help you revisit your learning through assessment tasks.

Development of Keys Skills, supporting your Wellbeing, and opportunities for meaningful Assessment have been embedded in the Units of Learning set out in this textbook. Investigating, evaluating and reflecting on information whilst collaborating with your classmates will provide you with important opportunities to engage with each other and learn from each other. Most importantly, you learn about yourself too!

It's important to take these opportunities to think, discover, research and explore as they will provide you with creative space to express your ideas and showcase the creative individual you are! Your *Sounds Good 2: Music for the new Junior Cycle* textbook has been designed to seek out your individual talents of creativity, innovation and enterprise. This book will help you to build on your own musical knowledge and experience to date, whilst supporting you in progressing as you imagine, compose and perform music. I hope you will be inspired by the creativity of other creative people you meet throughout this book.

I hope your *Sounds Good 2: Music for the new Junior Cycle* will be a valued companion on your learning journey. Enjoy the adventure!

Laura Lynch

A Guide to *Sounds Good 2: Music for the new Junior Cycle*

We hope you enjoy using *Sounds Good 2: Music for the new Junior Cycle*.

The *Sounds Good 2* package includes:

Three CDs – a wide range of music that links to the book to help you to learn about and appreciate music

Ukulele Fingerings Cover Flap – has been designed to help you identify and learn how to play the chords you will meet in Unit 8. Remember to keep the flap open alongside your pages when you are working through Unit 8.

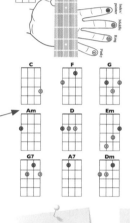

Self Assessment Post-its – at the end of each chapter for you to gather evidence of your learning, new key words and music you have listened to in each chapter

Music Glossary – musical terms you will encounter in this book, gathered and explained

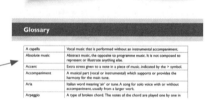

As you work through this book, there are important easy-to-follow symbols to help you. Below is an outline of what these symbols mean:

Self Assessment

 Listen to a track on the CD   Present in class   I need help

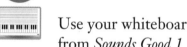 Use your whiteboard from *Sounds Good 1*   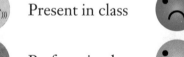 Perform in class   I'm getting there

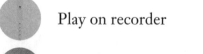 Play on recorder   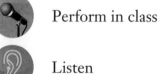 Listen   I can do this

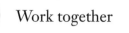 Work together   Report   I can explain or teach this to others

 Success Criteria

Learning Outcomes

Learning Outcomes identify the knowledge and skills that you should acquire through your learning experiences during the three years of the junior cycle. You will develop your knowledge and skills gradually as you engage and explore the content and learning experiences set out in your *Sounds Good* textbooks. The tables on pages vii to ix contain the official 36 Learning Outcomes for Junior Cycle Music and identify where they are met in *Sounds Good 2*. (A list of Action Verbs can be found on page 322.)

LO	Learning Outcome	UNIT
	Strand One: Procedural knowledge	
	Creating and exploring	
	Students should be able to:	
1.1	**compose** and perform or play back short musical phrases and support these phrases by creating rhythmic/melodic/harmonic ostinati to accompany them	2, 6, 7
1.2	**create** and **present** a short piece, using instruments and/or other sounds in response to a stimulus	5
1.3	**design** a harmonic or rhythmic accompaniment, record this accompaniment and **improvise** over this recording	2, 5, 6
1.4	**indicate** chords that are suitable to **provide** harmonic support to a single melody line	6, 8
	Participating and music-making	
	Students should be able to:	
1.5	read, **interpret** and play from symbolic representations of sounds	7
1.6	listen to and **transcribe** rhythmic phrases of up to four bars and melodic phrases of up to two bars	2, 5
1.7	perform music at sight through playing, singing or clapping melodic and rhythmic phrases	4, 7, 8
1.8	**rehearse** and perform pieces of music that use common structural devices and textures	4, 7
1.9	**demonstrate** an understanding of a range of metres and pulses through the use of body percussion or other means of movement	4, 7
	Appraising and responding	
	Students should be able to:	
1.10	**discuss** the characteristics and defining features of contrasting styles of music represented in the local school or community	1
1.11	**illustrate** the structure of a piece of music through a physical or visual representation	3
1.12	**indicate** where chord changes occur in extracts from a selection of songs	6, 8
1.13	**compare** different interpretations or arrangements of a piece of Irish traditional or folk music, paying attention to musical elements and other influences	2, 4, 6
1.14	**compare** pieces of music that are similar in period and style by different composers from different countries	3, 4

LO	Learning Outcome	UNIT
	Strand Two: Innovate and ideate	
	Creating and exploring	
	Students should be able to:	
2.1	**experiment** and **improvise** with making different types of sounds on a sound source and notate a brief piece that incorporates the sounds by **devising** symbolic representations for these sounds	2, 7, 8
2.2	**create** a musical statement (such as a rap or an advertising jingle) about a topical issue or current event and share with others the statement's purpose and development	1, 6, 5
2.3	**adapt** excerpts/motifs/themes from an existing piece of music by changing its feel, style, or underlying harmony	3, 5, 6
	Participating and music-making	
	Students should be able to:	
2.4	**rehearse** and **present** a song or brief instrumental piece; **identify** and **discuss** the performance skills and techniques that were necessary to **interpret** the music effectively	4, 5, 8
2.5	prepare and **rehearse** a musical work for an ensemble focusing on co-operation and listening for balance and intonation; **refine** the interpretation by considering elements such as clarity, fluency, musical effect and style	4, 7, 8
2.6	**design** a rhythmic or melodic ostinato and add layers of sound over the pattern as it repeats, varying the texture to **create** a mood piece to accompany a film clip or sequence of images	2, 6, 8
2.7	**create** and **present** some musical ideas using instruments and/or found sounds to **illustrate** moods or feelings expressed in a poem, story or newspaper article	2, 3, 5
	Appraising and responding	
	Students should be able to:	
2.8	**analyse** the chordal structure of excerpts from a range of songs and compile a list of songs with similar chord structures and progressions	6, 8
2.9	**distinguish** between the sonorities, ranges and timbres of selections of instruments and voices; **identify** how these sounds are produced and **propose** their strengths and limitations in performance	4
2.10	**develop** a set of criteria for **evaluating** a live or recorded performance; **use** these criteria to complete an in-depth review of a performance	7, 8
2.11	**evaluate** the impact that technology is having on how we access music; **propose** ways that their music, and that of their fellow students, can be shared to reach a global audience	1

LO	Learning Outcome	UNIT
	Strand Three: Culture and context	
	ELEMENT: Creating and exploring	
	Students should be able to:	
3.1	collaborate with fellow students and peers to produce a playlist and a set of recordings to accompany a local historical event or community celebration	1, 3
3.2	**examine** and **interpret** the impact of music on the depiction of characters, their relationships and their emotions, as explored in instrumental music of different genres	1, 3, 4
3.3	make a study of a particular contemporary or historical musical style; **analyse** its structures and use of musical devices, and **describe** the influence of other styles on it	3, 4
	ELEMENT: Participating and music-making	
	Students should be able to:	
3.4	**compose** and perform an original jingle or brief piece of music for use in a new advertisement for a product, and record the composition	1, 5
3.5	**devise** and perform examples of incidental music that could be used in a variety of contexts or environments	8
	ELEMENT: Appraising and responding	
	Students should be able to:	
3.6	**associate**/match music excerpts to a variety of texts (words, film, language) and **justify** the reasons as to why this piece of music was chosen to match the text	1, 3
3.7	**compare** compositions by two or more Irish composers or songwriters; use listening, background reading, and scores (where appropriate) to **explain** and **describe** differences and similarities in the compositions	4
3.8	select a particular advertisement and **analyse** the role music plays in supporting the message and promoting the product	1, 2
3.9	**investigate** the influence of processing effects (e.g. distortion, reverb, compression) on the recording process; select some recordings and **evaluate** the use and effectiveness of such effects within them	6, 7, 8
3.10	**discuss** the principles of music property rights and **explain** how this can impact on the sharing and publishing of music	2, 3, 4, 8
3.11	**explore** the time allocated to Irish artists and performers on a variety of local or national Irish media and **present** these findings to their class	4

Your *Sounds Good 2* CDs

Track	CD 1	Page no.	Track	CD 2	Page no.
1	Variation 14 from Trio Sonata Op. 1 no. 12 'La Follia' by Vivaldi	14	1	Triplet rhythm pattern	86
2	Ticking clock	26	2	'All Blues' by Miles Davis	90
3	United States Air Force Band, Airmen of Note, DV8	26	3	'I've Got a Heart Full of Rhythm' by Louis Armstrong	95
4	'The Circus' from Piano Concerto by Robert Wells	26	4	Listening exercise 1	98
5	Excerpt from the Finale of Symphony No. 4 by Bruckner	30	5	Listening exercise 2	99
6	Low and high pitches	31	6	Listening exercise 3	100
7	Seven octaves	32	7	Melody of Tallis's Canon on organ	106
8	One octave, twelve pitches	32	8	Trio Sonata for recorder in C major II Alla Breve by J.J. Quantz	111
9	*Chromatic Fantasy Sonata*, movement 1 by Dave Brubeck	32	9	Two octave scale	118
10	Identify the instruments	33	10	Star Spangled Banner	119
11	'The Spanish Lady' by The Dubliners	34	11	'The Elephant' from *Carnival of the Animals* by Saint-Saëns	120
12	'The Spanish Lady' by Ailish Tynan and Ian Burnside	34	12	Gigue from Cello Suite No 1 in G major by J.S. Bach	126
13	'The Spanish Lady' accompaniment	35	13	Examples of 3/4 and 6/8	129
14	'Wiegenlied' lullaby by Brahms	42	14	Clapping back 6/8 pattern	130
15	Door-knock pattern	42	15	'Humpty Dumpty'	130
16	Clap-it-back patterns	43	16	'La ci darem la mano' from *Don Giovanni* by Mozart	132
17	Minuet from *Water Music* by Handel	44	17	*Spem in allium* by Thomas Tallis	138
18	'The Best is Yet to Come' introduction played on clarinet	45	18	'Gretchen am Spinnrade' by Schubert	140
19	'The Best is Yet to Come' introduction with metronome	45	19	'Sleep Song' by Ina Boyle	145
20	Toccata and Fugue in D minor by J.S. Bach	51	20	Nocturne No. 1 in E♭ major by John Field	146

Track	CD 1	Page no.	Track	CD 3	Page no.
21	Symphony no. 5 movement 1 by Ludwig van Beethoven	51	1	'Eleanor Plunkett' by Turlough O'Carolan performed by William Dowdall and Anne-Marie O'Farrell	149
22	'Bridal Chorus' from *Lohengrin* by Richard Wagner	52	2	'Eleanor Plunkett' by Turlough O'Carolan performed by Patrick Ball	149
23	'The Flight of the Bumblebee' by Rimsky-Korsakov	57	3	Rhythm clap back 1	157
24	'Happy' by Michel Legrand	58	4	Rhythm clap back 2	157
25	'Rejouissance' from Overture-Suite in D major by Telemann	62	5	Rhythm pattern 1	163
26	Keyboard Sonata in C major by Scarlatti	62	6	Rhythm pattern 2	163
27	*Galliard Battaglia* by Samuel Scheidt	64	7	Rhythm pattern 3	163
28	Nocturne Op. 9 No. 2 by Chopin	64	8	Rhythmic dictation 1	163
29	Opening melody Nocturne Op. 9 No. 2 by Chopin without sustain pedal	65	9	Rhythmic dictation 2	163
30	Opening melody Nocturne Op. 9 No. 2 by Chopin with sustain pedal	65	10	Rhythmic dictation 3	163
31	'The Blue Bird and Princess Florine' from *The Sleeping Beauty* by Tchaikovsky	70	11	Rhythmic dictation 4	163
32	Sunrise from *Also sprach Zarathustra* by Richard Strauss	71	12	Rhythmic dictation 5	163
33	Extract from 'Meditation' from Thais by Massenet	74	13	Rhythmic dictation 6	163
34	*Modern Times* extract one	79	14	Rhythmic dictation 7	164
35	*Modern Times* extract two	79	15	Rhythmic dictation 8	164
36	*Modern Times* extract three	79	16	Rhythmic dictation 9	164
37	*Rhapsody in Blue* by Gershwin	82	17	Rhythmic dictation 10	164
38	Opening to *Rhapsody in Blue* by Gershwin	85	18	Melodic dictation in C major 1	174
39	Glissando	85			

Track	CD 3	Page no.	Track	CD 3	Page no.
19	Melodic dictation in C major 2	174	56	Ukulele note C	258
20	Theme to 'Morning Prayer'	176	57	Ukulele note G	258
21	F major four-bar melody	177	58	'My Dog Has Fleas' on ukulele	259
22	Melodic dictation F major	177	59	Four open strings strummed together	259
23	Four-bar melody	178	60	The pitches G, C, E and A on open strings	259
24	Canon in D by Pachebel	179	61	Ukulele strumming	259
25	Ostinato	179	62	The C chord	261
26	'Midterm Break' read by Seamus Heaney	187	63	The F chord	262
27	Excerpt from Overture to *The Magic Flute* by Mozart	194	64	The G chord	264
28	Intervals in a C major scale	196	65	The D chord	266
29	Intervals 1	197	66	Piano accompaniment to 'You Are My Sunshine'	266
30	Intervals 2	197	67	Piano accompaniment to 'Little John'	271
31	Intervals 3	197	68	Piano accompaniment to 'Red River Valley'	271
32	Major, minor and diminished triads	202	69	The Am chord	272
33	Chord progression I-V-vi-IV in G major	204	70	Strumming pattern	272
34	Chord progression I-V-vi-IV in D major	204	71	Piano accompaniment to 'Amazing Grace'	274
35	Chord progression I-V-vi-IV in C major	205	72	The Em chord	275
36	Chord progression vi-IV-I-V in C major	205	73	The Dm chord	276
37	Excerpt from Sonata in C, K 545 by Mozart	206	74	Play along with 'Drunken Sailor'	276
38	Four cadences	212	75	Piano accompaniment to 'Waltzing Matilda'	277
39	'God Defend New Zealand'	214	76	Piano accompaniment to 'Whiskey in the Jar'	278
40	The Minstrel Boy	215	77	The G7 chord	280
41	Processing effects – clean notes	217	78	The C7 chord	280
42	Processing effects – panning	217	79	Play along with 'Somewhere Over the Rainbow'	281
43	Processing effects – reverb	217	80	The Fm chord	281
44	Processing effects – distortion	217	81	The A7 chord	281
45	Processing effects – compression	217	82	The D7 chord	281
46	Clap it back pattern 1	225	83	Four bar rhythm pattern 1	294
47	Clap it back pattern 2	225	84	Four bar rhythm pattern 2	294
48	'Bring me Little Water, Sylvie'	235	85	Four bar rhythm pattern 3	294
49	'Adeste Fideles'	237	86	Two bar melodic pattern 1	294
50	Three Easter Allelujahs	237	87	Two bar melodic pattern 2	294
51	'Swing Low, Sweet chariot'	238	88	Two bar melodic pattern 3	295
52	'Wild Mountainside' accompaniment	242	89	Two bar melodic pattern 4	295
53	'The Moon' accompaniment	244	90	Musical excerpt 1	317
54	Ukulele note A	258	91	Musical excerpt 2	317
55	Ukulele note E	258	92	Musical excerpt 3	317

Acknowledgements

All music in this book has been reproduced with the kind permission of the publishers, agents, composers or their estates as follows:

Variation 14 from Trio Sonata Op. 1 no 12 'La Follia' by Vivaldi permission Naxos and Jeannette Sorrel; Unites States Air Force Band, Airmen of Note, DV8 permission Naxos; 'The Circus' from Piano Concerto by Robert Wells permission Naxos and MCPSI; excerpt from the Finale of Symphony No. 4 by Bruckner permission Naxos; Chromatic Fantasy Sonata, movement 1 by Dave Brubeck permission Naxos/MCPSI; 'The Spanish Lady' by the Dubliners permission Baycourt Ltd/MCPSI; 'The Spanish Lady' by Ailish Tynan and Ian Burnside permission Naxos/MCPSI; 'Weigenleid' lullaby by Brahms permission Naxos; Minute from Water Music by Handel permission Naxos; 'The Best is Yet to Come' introduction played by Lucy Taylor/MCPSI, sheet music permission Hal Leonard; Toccata and Fugue in D minor by J.S. Bach permission Naxos, Symphony no. 5 movement 1 by Ludwig van Beethoven permission Naxos; 'Bridal Chorus' from Lohengrin by Richard Wagner permission Naxos; 'The Flight of the Bumblebee' by Rimsky-Korakov permission Naxos; 'Happy' by Michel Legrand/MCPSI; 'Rejouissance' from Overture-Suite in D major by Telemann permission Naxos; Keyboard Sonata in C major by Scarlatti permission Naxos; Galliard Battaglia by Samuel Scheidt permission Naxos; Nocturne Op. 9 No. 2 by Chopin permission Naxos; opening to Nocturne Op. 9 No. 2 by Chopin with and without sustain pedal performed by Kevin Donnelly; 'The Blue Bird and Princess Florine' from The Sleeping Beauty by Tchaikovsky permission Naxos; Sunrise from Also sprach Zarathustra by Richard Strauss permission Naxos; excerpt from 'Meditation' from Thais by Massenet permission Naxos; Modern Times three extracts permission Naxos/MCPSI; Rhapsody in Blue by Gershwin permission Naxos/MCPSI; 'All Blues' by Miles Davis permission Naxos/MCPSI; 'I've got a heart full of rhythm' by Louis Armstrong permission Naxos/MCPSI; three musical excerpts pp98–100 permission Naxos/one MCPSI; Trio Sonata for recorder in C major Il Alla Breve by J.J. Quantz permission Naxos; Star Spangled Banner permission Naxos; 'The Elephant' from Carnival of the Animals by Saint-Saens permission Naxos; Gigue from Cello Suite No. 1 in G major by J.S Bach permission Naxos; 'La ci darem la mano' from Don Giovanni by Mozart permission Naxos; Spem in allium by Thomas Tallis permission Naxos; 'Gretchen am Spinnrade' by Schubert permission Naxos/lyrics translation from German by Lynn Thompson; 'Sleep Song' by Ina Boyle permission Naxos/MCPSI; Nocturne No. 1 in Eb major by John Field permission Naxos; 'Eleanor Plunkett' by Turlough O'Carolan performed by William Dowdall and Anne-Marie Farrell permission Naxos; 'Eleanor Plunkett' by Turlough O'Carolan performed by Patrick Ball permission Naxos; Classical Gas by Mason Williams permission Alfred Music; Midterm Break poem by Seamus Heaney permission Faber & Faber, read by the poet permission Poetry Archive; excerpt from Overture to The Magic Flute by Mozart permission Naxos; excerpt from Sonata in C, K545 by Mozart recorded by Kevin Donnelly; 'God Defend New Zealand' recorded by Kevin Donnelly, 'The Minstrel Boy' recorded by Kevin Donnelly; 'Bring Me Little Water, Sylvie' recording and sheet music courtesy of and permission Moira Smiley; 'Adeste Fideles' permission Naxos; Three Easter Allelujahs permission Naxos; 'Swing low, sweet chariot' permission Naxos/MCPSI; 'Wild Mountainside' by John Douglas recorded by Kevin Donnelly/MCPSI, sheet music permission Hal Leonard; 'The Moon' by Andy Beck recorded by Kevin Donnelly/MCPSI, sheet music permission Alfred Music; all ukulele chords and strums recorded by Rosa Downey; 'Kookaburra' lyrics and chords permission Hal Leonard; 'You Are My Sunshine' by Jimmie Davis and Charles Mitchell piano accompaniment recorded by Kevin Donnelly, lyrics and chords permission Hal Leonard; 'Blue Suede Shoes' by Carl Perkins lyrics and chords permission Hal Leonard; 'Three Little Birds' by Bob Markey lyrics and chords permission Hal Leonard; 'Singin in the rain' by Arthur Freed and Nacio Herb Brown lyrics and chords permission Hal Leonard; 'The Lion Sleeps Tonight' by Solomon Linda lyrics and chords permission Hal Leonard; 'Little John' and 'Red River Valley' piano accompaniments by Kevin Donnelly; 'Still Haven't Found What I'm Looking For' by U2 lyrics and chords permission Hal Leonard; 'Amazing Grace' accompaniment Kevin Donnelly; 'Drunken Sailor' audio recorded by Kevin Donnelly and Rosa Downey; 'Waltzing Matilda' recorded by Kevin Donnelly; Whiskey in the Jar' recorded by Kevin Donnelly; 'Dirty Old Town' by Ewan MacColl lyrics and chords permission Hal Leonard; 'Somewhere Over The Rainbow' by EY Harburg and Harold Arlen recorded by Kevin Donnelly and Rosa Downey/MCPSI, lyrics and chords permission Hal Leonard. All rhythm and melodic patterns, cadences, intervals, triads, chord progressions Kevin Donnelly.

Acknowledgements

The author and publishers would like to thanks the following permission to reproduce photos and other material: P1 LightField Studios/shutterstock; p2 Andrekart Photography/shutterstock; p3 Rohappy/shutterstock; p4 Melting Spot/shutterstock; p5 Rawpixel.com/shutterstock, Mitch Gunn/shutterstock; p6 Bibadash/shutterstock; p7 guruXOX/shutterstock, F.jarabica/shutterstock; p9 Featureflash Photo Agency/shutterstock; p11 YadvigaGr/shutterstock; p14 Sentavio/shutterstock, A_Lesik/shutterstock, Stocksnapper/shutterstock, neftali/shutterstock; p16 photos courtesy of Comhaltas; p17 photo courtesy of Sing Ireland; p19 photo courtesy of Pieta House; p20 artapartment/shutterstock, Manop/shutterstock; p24 madpixblue/shutterstock; p26 Miceking/shutterstock, pkana Design Image/shutterstock; p29 Labutin.Art/shutterstock; p31 Ching Design/shutterstock, Malgorzata Surawska/shutterstock; p33 Vecton/shutterstock; p34 Ollie Millington/Redferns/Getty, shutterstock, shutterstock, Cookie Studio/shutterstock; p39 magensphotos/shutterstock; p43 Mike Flippo/shutterstock; p45 Barandash Karandashich/shutterstock, Stamptastic/shutterstock; p46 wow.subtropica/shutterstock, Suzanne Tucker/shutterstock; p47 Chainfoto24/shutterstock, debasige/shutterstock, Mandy Godbehear/shutterstock; p49 RedlineVector/shutterstock; p60 pikselstock/shutterstock; p61 Antonio Guillem/shutterstock, Universal History Archive/UIG via Getty; p63 Voyagerix/shutterstock; p64 iQoncept/shutterstock; p65 davorana/shutterstock; p67 Hiroyuki Ito/Getty, dslaven/shutterstock; p68 Everett Historical/shutterstock; p69 NaxosUSA/shutterstock, pr2is/shutterstock; p75 Universal History Archive/Getty; p77 Martin Good/shutterstock, Anna Jurkovska/shutterstock; p78 Dan Porges/Getty, fulya atalay/shutterstock; p79 Ihnatovich Maryia/shutterstock; p80 Everett Historical/shutterstock; p81 Bokic Bojan/shutterstock, FPG/Archive Photos/Getty; p82 Movie Poster Image Art/Getty; p83 Roy Exports SAS; 84 phoelixDE/shutterstock; 85 AF archive/Alamy; p86 Everett Historical/shutterstock; p92 William P Gottlieb/Alamy; p93 David Redfern/Redferns/Getty; p95 Tom Hanley/Alamy; p97 Ye Choh Wah/shutterstock; p101 wavebreakmedia/shutterstock; 103 magic pictures/shutterstock; p103 Yasser Al-Zayyat/AFP/Getty, Daniel Mihailescu/AFP/Getty, Mairo Cinquetti/NurPhoto/Getty, Nacer Talel/Anadolu Agency/Getty, 104 Kudryashka/shutterstock; 105 Dm_Cherry/shutterstock, 3D renderings/shutterstock, Artem Avetisyan/shutterstock, Venus Angel/shutterstock; p110 Ben Martin/Getty; p111 Hiroyuki Ito/Getty; p119 shutterstock; p120 Boyd Ivey/Icon Sportswire/Getty; p124 Simone Joyner/Getty; p125 Painting by E. G. Hausmann/Getty; p126 stockfour/shutterstock; p128 Amy T. Zielinski/Redferns/Getty; p130 Richard Cummins/Getty; p131 sumire8/shutterstock, Boris Medvedev/shutterstock, DEA/A. Dagli Orti/De Agostini/Getty, Kiev.Victor/shutterstock; p132 George Lipman/Fairfax Media/Getty; p136 Sylvain Grandadam/Getty; p136 AFP/Getty, Nacer Talel/Anadolu Agency/Getty, Gerti Deutsch/Picture Post/Hulton Archive/Getty, Ivica Drusany/shutterstock, Robbie Jack/Corbis via Getty, Ron Scherl/Redferns/Getty; p137 Sahacha Nilkumhang/shutterstock, Pressmaster/shutterstock; p138 Karl Gehring/The Denver Post/Getty; p140 DEA/A. Dagli Orti/De Agostini/Getty, Pixeljoy/shutterstock; p145 Everett-Art/shutterstock; p146 DEA/A. Dagli Orti/De Agostini/Getty, DeAgostini/Getty, Library of Congress/Corbis/VCG/Getty; p146 Fine Art Images/Heritage Images/Getty; p147 James Fraher/Redferns; p148 RDImages/Epics/Getty; p150 X Fabio Diena/shutterstock, haak78/shutterstock, Rihardzz/shutterstock, JStone/shutterstock, JStone/shutterstock, DFP Photographic/shutterstock; p55 Stephen Barnes/Music/Alamy; P155 everything possible/shutterstock; p156 PrinceOfLove/shutterstock; p157 eggeegg/shutterstock; p159 fulya atalay/shutterstock, p160 Kong Vector/shutterstock; p166 hurricanehank/shutterstock; p167 stoatphoto/shutterstock; p168 TypoArt BS/shutterstock, artdig/shutterstock; p171 chrisdorney/shutterstock, Northfoto/shutterstock; Melanie Lemahieu/shutterstock, wpap_colies/shutterstock; p182 Valua Vitaly/shutterstock, Yuriy Kulik/shutterstock; p184 Richard E. Aaron/Redferns/Getty, Anwar Hussein/Getty; p187 Johnny Eggitt/AFP/Getty; p188 Onchira Wongsiri/shutterstock, shutterstock; p193 angkrit/shutterstock; Mazur Travel/shutterstock; p195 Oscar C. Williams/shutterstock, Ollyy/shutterstock; p209 PrinceOfLove/shutterstock; p212 Creativa Images/shutterstock; p214 Paolo Bona/shutterstock; p217 Cigdem Simsek/Alamy; p218 Pressmaster/shutterstock; P220 Golubovy/shutterstock; p221 Brian Goodman/shutterstock; p222 Nejron Photo/shutterstock; p223 Yakobchuk Viacheslav/shutterstock, Kent Sievers/shutterstock; p225 Alfa Photostudio/shutterstock; p226 Lim Yong Hian/shutterstock; p229 Sergey Nivens/shutterstock, Steve Mann/shutterstock; p230 Global Blended Learning, Liron Peer/shutterstock, drvector/shutterstock; p231 Zsschreiner/shutterstock; p233 Monkey Business Images/shutterstock; p237 bango/shutterstock; p238 Aleutie/shutterstock; p239 Graham Tucker/Redferns/Getty; p240 chrisdorney/shutterstock; p254 Art Photo/shutterstock; p255 FatCamera/Getty, shutterstock,

Marusya Chaika/shutterstock; p256 Karin Hildebrand Lau/shutterstock; p257 Compuscript;
p258 Compuscript; p259 PeterPike/shutterstock; pp261, 262, 264, 266, 267, 275, 276, 280, 281
Lucy Taylor and Rosa Downey; p263 ThongPooN/shutterstock; p272 Fabio Diena/shutterstock;
p290 FamVeld/shutterstock; p317 Anton_Ivanov/shutterstock, Annches/shutterstock

My Music Passport

Unit

1

In this unit

An opportunity to explore music you are presented with in your own context. Take time to reflect on our individual musical experiences and unique musical tastes. Unit 1 explores music in film, advertising, sport and our community but also the role music plays in our everyday life. We will have opportunities to collaborate and create music with others and reflect on the impact music can have on our wellbeing.

Checklist	LO	Intended learning
☐	1.10	**Discuss** the characteristics and defining features of contrasting styles of music represented in the local school or community.
☐	2.2	**Create** a musical statement (such as a rap or advertising jingle) about a topical issue or current event and share with others the statement's purpose and development.
☐	2.11	**Evaluate** the impact that technology is having on how we access music; propose ways that their music, and that of their fellow students, can be shared to reach a global audience.
☐	3.1	Collaborate with fellow students and peers to produce a playlist and a set of recordings to accompany a local historical event or community celebration.
☐	3.2	**Examine** and **interpret** the impact of music on the depiction of characters, their relationships and their emotions, as explored in instrumental music of different genres.
☐	3.4	**Compose** and **perform** an original jingle or brief piece of music for use in a new advertisement for a product, and record the composition.
☐	3.6	**Associate**/match music excerpts to a variety of texts (words, film, language) and **justify** the reasons as to why this piece of music was chosen to match the text.
☐	3.8	Select a particular advertisement and **analyse** the role music plays in supporting the message and promoting the product.

In *Sounds Good 1* we explored the important role music plays in our day-to-day life, in our community and in our wellbeing. We can possibly now all agree that, despite our varied tastes in musical **genres**, music is an essential part of living and living well.

As we grow up, our tastes in music can change. New experiences and even new friends can encourage an interest in different sorts of music. There will be some genres, bands or songs that will always be among our favourites, but it is good to explore new types of music too.

Music genre: a type or style of music, e.g. jazz, folk, pop and some styles can be combined, e.g. punk rock, folk blues, pop rock.

1

Me and My Music

Reflect on how your musical tastes have developed and changed since you started secondary school.

1 I listen to music

more than I used to [ ]   less than I used to [ ]

2 I listen to music

everyday [ ]   sometimes [ ]

rarely [ ] ·   never [ ]

3 I listen to music when I'm

getting ready in the morning [ ]   travelling to school [ ]

exercising [ ]   studying [ ]

going to sleep [ ]   other [ ]

4 The last piece of music I listened to was _____

5 My favourite band at the moment is _____

6 A song that makes me feel good is _____

7 I listen to music most when I feel

happy [ ]   calm [ ]

sad [ ]   energetic [ ]

tired [ ]

8 A piece of music that makes me feel calm is _____

9 In the first year, I enjoyed listening to **genres** such as _____

_____

10 Since starting to study music, I have enjoyed listening to new **genres** like _____

_____

11 I am a member of

a music group in my community [ ]

a music group in my school community [ ]

Can you name two radio stations you listen to?

1 _____

2 _____

Define the term **genre**:

_____

_____

_____

_____

12 I access music through

radio ☐

iPod ☐

phone ☐

other ☐

13 I download music using

_____

_____

_____

14 My favourite instrument is _____

15 In *Sounds Good 1* I enjoyed learning how to

listen to music ☐   describe music ☐

compose music ☐   perform music ☐

16 I enjoyed researching these three topics: _____

_____

17 I worked with my classmates to create these three things: _____

_____

_____

18 Three things I learnt about music were _____

_____

_____

19 Things I learnt about myself during music class were _____

_____

_____

20 One goal for music class this year is

_____

Name two apps you use to stream or download music from:

1 _____

2 _____

Define this symbol: ©

_____

_____

_____

Don't forget to look back at your *Sounds Good 1* Me and My Music questionnaire. You may not have noticed how much of an impact studying music in school has had on your life. Looking back and comparing your answers may give you a better picture.

Music for my wellbeing

Listening to music and making music can help us to feel better. Singing with others is scientifically proven to relieve stress and boost your mood by releasing happy hormones.

Singing on your own will work, too, but coming together with others to perform is much more fun, and it helps us to feel a part of our school community.

When choosing music for wellbeing, the choice of song is important. Ensuring the music and lyrics have happy qualities makes singing the song more beneficial.

Think–Pair–Share

◆ *Investigate* what makes a good song.

◆ *Identify* three **musical features** a happy song should have.

◆ *Suggest* two songs you could sing with your classmates to boost your mood.

> **Wellbeing**: the state we are in when we realise our abilities, take care of our physical health, can cope with the stress of everyday life, feel part of our community and have a sense of purpose.

Questions	What I think	What my partner thinks	What we will share
A good song has			
Musical features we hear 1 2 3	1 2 3	1 2 3	1 2 3
Suggested songs for listening to 1 2	1 2	1 2	1 2

Let's experiment

 Choose one song to sing with your classmates; find the lyrics and a track and sing it together! Report how you felt afterwards.

_____

_____

Music for staying well

A positive wellbeing allows us to flourish. To stay well we must be aware of our individual abilities and talents and manage the normal stresses we face in our everyday lives. We must take care of our physical and mental wellbeing and make sure that we maintain our sense of purpose and belonging in our community.

You are at a very important stage in your life, learning about yourself and taking responsibility for yourself too. You are also learning to cope with new experiences, influences and pressures. **Discuss how music can support your wellbeing**.

We have already looked at how music can psychologically affect us. We have explored how music has the power to impact our mood or our emotions. Music experts have done a lot of research into how music can impact our physical health too. Staying well requires that we are active and physically healthy. Music can help us with this!

Music and sports

Sport coaches know that music can improve the physical performance of their athletes and often add it to their coaching toolkit. Listening to the right music can encourage endurance and delay fatigue when training. It also helps athletes to keep their focus and prevent distractions from things going on around them. This is why we see swimmers still wearing headphones on the pool deck before an important race. Do you ever wonder what they are listening to?

Michael Phelps is the most decorated Olympian of all time with 28 medals for swimming. He has spent his entire career walking out to races with his headphones still on. Phelps is very aware of how music can boost his mind and focus. He told reporters he found listening to his favourite songs helped him to relax before big races during the Olympics. His choice of **genre** is often hip-hop. He even has a pre-race playlist on Spotify.

Music for being active should have

◆ a strong energising **rhythm pattern** suited to motion;

◆ positive **lyrics** which motivate athletes;

◆ uplifting **melodies**;

◆ tempo which suits the activity it is chosen for:

　fast for sprinting or steady for rowers or marathon runners.

　Synchronising movement to the tempo is important.

Once we are aware of how music can help us to be active and stay well, we can intentionally choose music to make staying active more enjoyable. Music is very personal and your music tastes are tied into your identity. Listening to music that brings out the best of you is an important part of self-care and promoting our wellbeing.

Propose a **playlist** for physical activity and test it out! Think about the **tempo**, **mood** and **genres** that will work best for your chosen activity. Choose five songs and consider the best order for them to go in, as skipping and shuffling playlists can be distracting. Insert your list of songs below.

Chosen activity for this playlist:	
Song title	**Reason for choosing this song**
1	
2	
3	
4	
5	

Then grab you headphones and get active!

Chances are there were one or two songs that didn't work as well as you'd hoped. Reflect on why this was. Was the **tempo** too slow or were the **lyrics** distracting? You may need to refine your playlist by making some changes to it.

1 *Identify* an Olympic sport and suggest **three** songs which would be suitable for use in a training session for these athletes.

2 *Outline* the purpose and benefits of creating personalised playlists.

_____

_____

Olympic Sport:	
Music suggestions	
1	
2	
3	

3 Reflect and *comment* on other learning experiences in music class that have supported your wellbeing.

_____

_____

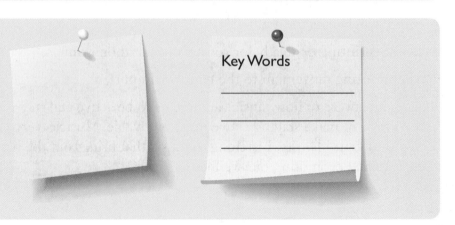

What stuck with you?

Evaluate your learning in this chapter. List what stuck with you and new key words.

Key Words

_____

_____

_____

Look back!

Briefly explain the following terms, explored in *Sounds Good 1*.

Film score	
Illustrative music	
Soundtrack	
Diegetic music	
Silent movie	

In *Sounds Good 1* we explored film music. We discovered the important role **film scores** play in illustrating the story being played out on the screen. We celebrated the creative flare needed to be a film composer. We researched and critiqued the film scores used in our favourite movies.

Think back: can you recall the movie you chose?

Who composed the music?_____

Explain the term '**illustrative music**':

_____

_____

List two composers of **film scores**:

1 _____

2 _____

Have you been to see a movie since?

Have you noticed the music in films more than you did before?

In *Sounds Good 1* we explored the impact film scores can have on the storyline in a film. We noticed the music had been cleverly composed to create a **mood** or evoke a particular emotion.

Movie 1: *Planet of the Apes*

Planet of the Apes was directed by Tim Burton in 2001. The **film score** for this science-fiction movie was written by Danny Elfman.

Set in 2029, the film documents the adventures of astronaut Leo Davidson (played by Mark Walberg). He crash-lands on a planet which is inhibited by fierce and intelligent apes. The apes speak English and use humans as slaves. The film is action-packed with a fast-paced plot, giving Elfman lots of material to illustrate with his music.

Search online for 'Planet of the Apes Soundtrack Suite – YouTube' to hear music from this film.

Describe how this film score illustrates the fierce and intelligent apes. What does the music tell us about them?

mood
fearful

large range, rhythmic, jarring clashing sounds,
tension, horn sound-visceral, unexpected

7

Active listening 1

Listen to a piece of music from the film and complete the grid below as you listen.

Watch the official trailer for this movie by searching online for 'Planet of the Apes (2001) – official trailer'. This will help you get a better sense of the plot and characters, which will help you to complete the listening activity.

Trailer music: music composed to accompany a movie's official trailer. Not always part of the soundtrack, this music has a marketing purpose of encouraging a response from viewers, enticing them to go and see the movie.

Film: _____

Director: _____

Year of release: _____

Film score composer: _____

Describe the **mood**: _____

_____

_____

Comment on the **instrumentation**:

_____

_____

Propose a suitable tempo marking for this piece:

_____

_____

Analyse the role of the dynamics:

_____

_____

_____

Comment on how the composer **illustrates** the plot in the music:

_____

_____

_____

Suggest one point of interest to listen out for in this piece:

_____

_____

Instrumentation refers to the particular choice or combination of instruments used in a composition.

Movie 2: *Jurassic Park III*

Research the film music *for Jurassic Park III*, also released in 2001 but composed by John Williams.

This is another piece of cinema with a fast-paced and exciting **film score**.

Watch the trailer by searching online for 'Jurassic Park 3 Official Trailer #1 (2001) – Sam Neill Movie HD'.

 Search online for 'Jurassic Park 3 2001 Soundtrack Suite OST Don Davis & John Williams – YouTube' to hear music from this film and complete the listening grid below.

Composer John Williams with film director Steven Spielberg

Film: _____

Director: _____

Year of release: _____

Film score composer: _____

Describe the **mood**: _____

_____

_____

Comment on the **instrumentation**:

_____

_____

Identify the **texture** of the music:

_____

_____

Describe the role of the **dynamics** in creating the mood:

_____

_____

Critique the composer's ability to illustrate the plot of this film in the music:

_____

_____

Suggest one point of interest to listen out for in this piece:

_____

_____

List the three types of texture used in music we have explored:

1 _____

2 _____

3 _____

Explain the term 'mood':

_____

_____

_____

Appraise the music in these film scores. Both are written for films released in 2001 and both are instrumental pieces.

Examine and *critique* the impact each of the film scores has on the depiction of the characters, their relationships and their emotions. Use the movie trailers to help you identify these qualities.

_____

_____

_____

_____

_____

_____

_____

Compare both film scores, written the same year by two American composers. Identify two similarities and two differences between them.

	Similarities	Differences
1		
2		

What stuck with you?

Evaluate your learning in this chapter. List what stuck with you and new key words.

Key Words

_____

_____

_____

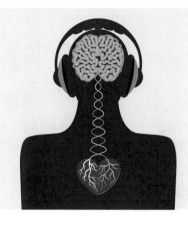

Film scores and **advertising** music have very similar characteristics. Evoking emotion is a crucial part of composing film scores. The main reason that music is added to advertisements is to create an emotional connection between the consumer and the **brand** being advertised. Music is therefore a very important part of creating a successful advertising campaign.

Selecting the right piece to represent a **brand** takes a lot of consideration. The music must affect the consumer as much as possible through their emotions, by making them feel happy, calm, scared, angry etc.

Advertising: a means of communicating with consumers to promote a product or service.

Brand: a name, design or symbol to identify a product or group of products, e.g. Apple, Google, Nike or Sony.

In groups consider what you already know!

◆ *Examine* **two** advertisements and research the music used.

◆ *Appraise* the **advertising message** the advertisement suggests.

◆ *Analyse* the role music plays in supporting the advertising message.

	Advert/brand	Music used	Message	Role of music
1				
2				

Advertising message: the point or message being made by the advertising campaign to the consumer.

How important is selecting the right piece of music for your advertisements? Would alternative pieces of music be just as effective? How easy is it to identify the right piece of music?

Use **one** advertisement from those you have identified above and *experiment* with adding alternative music choices. *Present* your findings in the grid below.

Advert/brand	Original music used	Suggested alternatives

1 Briefly *analyse* the **advertising message** in the advert you have chosen above. What is the message to the consumer? Discuss how it is shared.

_____

_____

_____

_____

2 Justify the reasons why the original piece of music was chosen to match the text. Is it successful in supporting the brand's message?

_____

_____

_____

_____

3 Report on your experiment. How did you go about identifying a suitable alternative? What did you have to consider during your search?

_____

_____

_____

_____

4 *Evaluate* the effectiveness of the alternative you have chosen. Was it more effective in supporting the brand's advertising message than the original music?

_____

_____

_____

5 Justify reasons why your piece of music was chosen to match the advertising clip.

_____

_____

6 *Peer Assessment Task*

Using iMovie, combine your chosen alternative piece of music with a clip from the advert you are working with. Allow your classmates to review it and give you feedback. Refine your choice of music if necessary.

Write a reflection on this task in your copy book.

Are there similarities between the original music and the music you have chosen as an alternative?

 Listen to both pieces of music and *identify* the similarities and differences between them. Use the Venn diagram below to help you.

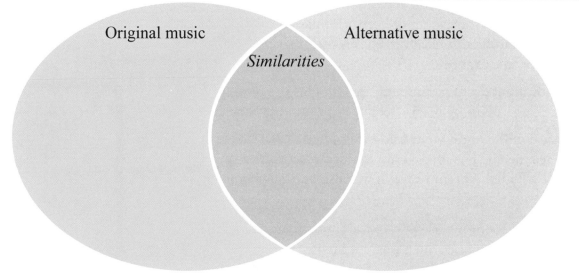

Original music

Alternative music

Similarities

For people who work in marketing, getting consumers to connect with a brand is very important. Studying a particular marketplace, finding out what customers want and need and then finding a way of delivering that to the consumer is very important. To do this, the marketing team must be motivated by the brand's message.

Every advertising campaign begins with a message or focus. The music which is selected for the advertisement must help to communicate this message.

Elements of music such as **tempo**, **rhythm** and **texture** are among the aspects considered when choosing the perfect piece of music for the campaign. The scenes or shots in the advertisement for example, must be in sync with the beat of the music used alongside it; tempo and rhythm are important considerations here.

Popular music can be used for advertising, but, more often than not, marketing teams decide to use fresh new music. Using something new to the listener helps them to connect the music only to their brand and their advertising campaign. This option also reduces difficulties around **copyright** licences too.

Identify a brand which has used popular music to endorse their products.

Classical music in advertising

Classical music is often favoured by advertising companies to promote the idea of opulence or luxury. Car companies will use classical music in their ads to reflect the luxury status they want to portray. The fact that so many car companies have used this formula tells us that it has been successful in selling cars to people who are, or wish to be considered, wealthy and successful.

Audi is one of the most expensive car brands in the market. In 2018 Audi used music by the Italian composer Guiseppe Verdi in the TV advert they designed to introduce consumers to their SUV, the Q8.

The Odessa Philharmonic Orchestra are filmed in the advert alongside a forty-person choir. The second movement of Verdi's Requiem, 'Dies Irae 1', is performed as the Q8 is unveiled. The advert makes use of a very clever **slogan**: 'It makes a bit of an entrance'.

Search 'Audi Q8-Big Entrance' online to watch this ad. Has the presence of the orchestra and the classical music been effective in promoting this luxury product?

Another use of classical music in car advertising is in Jaguar's 2018 advert to introduce their E-Pace model. The music used in this advert is from Vivaldi's Trio Sonata Op.1 no. 12 'La Follia'. Antonio Vivaldi was also an Italian composer, born in Venice in 1678.

> Advertising slogan: short phrase used to reinforce the brand or advertising message.

Guiseppe Verdi

1 *Discuss* what you think about the use of classical music to advertise commercial products. Is it right to use music which was originally created for a different purpose in this way?

2 Some composers and performers refuse to allow their music to be used in advertising, despite financial enticements. Suggest reasons why they take this position?

3 Suggest reasons why these pieces of music were chosen to match the TV advert above.

Active listening: Variation 14 from Trio Sonata 'La Follia' by Vivaldi

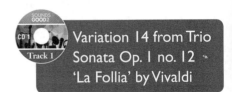

Variation 14 from Trio Sonata Op. 1 no. 12 'La Follia' by Vivaldi

 Listen carefully to how the notes the instruments played go up and down. Sometimes they move **stepwise** in **ascending** or **descending scales**, and sometimes there are **leaps**. Follow the upward and downward movement with your arm to show the shape of the music. Can you use both arms to show the patterns in two different instruments?

An anonymous portrait of Vivaldi painted in 1723

Listen again and complete the grid below.

Title	
Composer	
Era (period)	
Instrumentation	
Texture	
Tempo	
Dynamics	
Rhythmic features	
Melodic features	
Suggest other points of interest	

 Choose a short clip from the Audi or Jaguar advert or find another luxury car brand to work with. Work with another member of your class to *create* and *present* a short piece of music, using instruments and/or other sounds in response to the film clip.

Take time to consider what you are trying to illustrate and how you can go about it. Use your whiteboards for drafting ideas.

Compose an eight-bar melody to accompany the advert.

Use software such as Bandlab or Audacity to import your melody. Also import your recorded found sounds; remember these will have to match the moments of action in your clip. Work together on the timing of your melody and found sounds to create a musical clip which accurately accompanies the film sequence. GarageBand is an alternative to Audacity if you are using iPads. iMovie is another useful app to work with on this task.

Record the details of your experiment below.

Car brand: Car model:	**Found sounds** recorded and why:
What factors did you consider when writing your melody?	What difficulties did you face completing this task?

What stuck with you?

Evaluate your learning in this chapter. List what stuck with you and new key words.

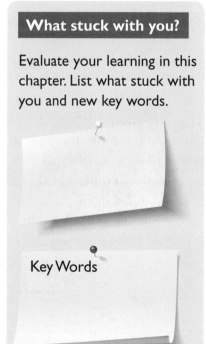

Key Words

Music and Community

In *Sounds Good 1* we considered the important relationships between musicians in the community. We recognised that feeling part of our community is very important for our own wellbeing and the wellbeing of others. Involvement with music groups in our community gives us an opportunity to make friends and share our love of music-making.

Many schools have music groups that come together to sing or play music at lunchtime or after school. You may have a **school choir** or band that rehearses together for performances during the school year.

In *Sounds Good 1* we explored the work **Comhaltas Ceoltóirí Éireann** have done in the community since 1951. One of the largest music communities in Ireland, Comhaltas promotes Irish music, song and dance throughout Ireland and across the world.

◉ COMHALTAS

What can you remember about Comhaltas?

1 *Explain* the organisation's name, 'Comhaltas Ceoltóirí Éireann', what does this mean?

_____

2 In what year was it founded? _____

3 Where is your closest Comhaltas Branch based? _____

4 What important yearly festival is Comhaltas responsible for?

_____

5 *Identify* the location of this year's festival.

_____

6 Briefly *describe* the work Comhaltas volunteers are involved in.

_____

7 *Outline* **one** fund-raising initiative Comhaltas is involved in.

_____

_____

In class we have sung together for fun, for learning and for our wellbeing. In most communities there are groups of people who love to sing and come together to do so as often as they can. Being part of a **choir** or **vocal ensemble** gives members a sense of belonging, a place to share their love of music with others and, most of all, an opportunity to make music! *List* the music groups members of your school community participate in, and suggest the benefits that participating in music-making with others has on their wellbeing.

> **Choir**: a group of people who sing together in public or at events such as church celebrations.

_____
_____
_____

Sing Ireland

Sing Ireland was set up in 1980 by Dr Geoffrey Spratt and Aiveen Kearney with a vision of enhancing life through singing. Since the beginning, their mission has been to promote singing in the community. Sing Ireland have developed education courses, established and continue to run a youth choir, and have developed a community of choral teachers across Ireland.

Sing Ireland in addition to this work have been keenly involved in community work. The association have lived out their mission of enhancing life through singing in many ways including:

1 National Choral Singing Week. This initiative is aimed at promoting positive mental health in communities. It began with a National Choral Singing Day on World Mental Health Day back in 2008. It was so successful that the association moved to celebrating singing for the entire week instead. Each year the event coincides with World Mental Health Day on 10 October.

2 Another important initiative Sing Ireland has developed in the community is the Dawn Chorus, in partnership with Bealtaine. The Dawn Chorus brings community choirs and active retirement groups together to sing, inspiring greater participation in community music. Typically these choirs meet at dawn, close to the waterfront to perform together. The Bealtaine Festival celebrates creativity as we age, what better way to be creative than to sing together? The first Dawn Chorus took place on Culdaff Beach in Donegal in 2009.

 Discuss the importance of involving the older generation in community music initiatives like the Dawn Chorus?

◆ *List* the benefits. _____

◆ *Verify* the positive impact this has on their lives and their wellbeing.

_____

Interpret this evidence to draw some conclusions about these benefits.

_____

_____

1 Reflect on your discussion and consider the possible benefits participating in a music activity with your school community would have on your own wellbeing.

2 Brainstorm with your classmates. What are the main characteristics and defining features of the styles of music represented in your community?

Compile your ideas in the thought bubble.

Compose a short article for your school newspaper detailing the varied styles of music that are enjoyed in your school community. *Compare* the defining features of these different styles of music and include information about where readers can access more information about them, e.g. compare school choir and senior rock band, recorder ensemble and chamber choir.

Today's blog title

Time

Darkness Into Light

Darkness Into Light is Pieta House's flagship annual fundraising and awareness event. It started with approximately 400 people in the now iconic yellow Darkness into Light T-shirts walking the 5 km course in Dublin's Phoenix Park in 2009. Over 215,000

people took part in Darkness into Light last year at 160 venues across the globe before dawn on 12 May 2018, crossing the finish line as the sun began to rise.

Every year people take part to share the light and help to tackle the stigma around mental ill health. The event is a symbol of hope and a celebration of life.

If you are experiencing a time of crisis please call 1800 247 247 or text HELP to 51444, all services are private and confidential.

For more information, or to sign up for Darkness into Light please visit www.pieta.ie.

Work together to produce a **playlist** for this year's Darkness Into Light event in your community.

1 *Explore* and *discuss* the important message Pieta House wants to share with us.

2 *Identify* types of music that would help to create an atmosphere suitable for this very special community event.

Playlist title:			
	Song	**Artist**	**Reasons this song is suitable for this playlist**
1			
2			
3			
4			
5			
6			
7			
8			

Technology is important when it comes to sharing music with others. Discuss with your classmates the developments which have led to this.

Explore ways you could make your Darkness Into Light playlist available to participants across the globe.

List the steps you would take to successfully share your music with others in the flowchart below.

Step 1

Step 2

Step 3

Step 4

Step 5

Promotion of an event through advertising

Promotion of community and national events such as Darkness Into Light is essential. The event is currently sponsored by Electric Ireland. Each year Pieta House will raise awareness of their important message using radio and TV adverts. Advertising slogans and **jingles** are an important element of advertising campaigns.

Slogans are short, memorable phrases used in advertising. Charities such as Pieta House can use these to remind us of their central message or vision rather than to promote a brand. Raising awareness of the work they do and the support they offer to those in crisis is vital in their advertising campaigns.

As we learnt in *Sounds Good 1*, a **jingle** is a short song or tune used in advertising. It is a form of sound branding typically for use in commercials. Let's create a slogan and a jingle that could be used in an advert to promote this year's walk. Pieta House's message of hope should be central to your thinking. Words are important, but there shouldn't be too many of them, so choose them carefully.

Consider the two examples of slogans below and *design* a **rhythm pattern** to match the words on the rhythm lines provided.

'A brighter future'

'Let the light in'

good support for jingle in SG 1, pgs 126 + 127

Create your own **slogan** and then compose a **jingle** to go with it. Apply rhythm and/or melody to the slogan to help make it more memorable.

Thinking, drafting, creating … record your ideas here

Eg.
- Washing machines live longer with Calgon
- McDonalds I'm lovin' it
- 123.ie
- Band aids 1997

earworms

Jingle: jingles contain ideas which explicitly promote products or services in advertising campaigns.

Final slogan:_____

Write your **jingle** on the stave below.

Design an image or logo to go with your slogan and jingle. Draw it on the screen below.

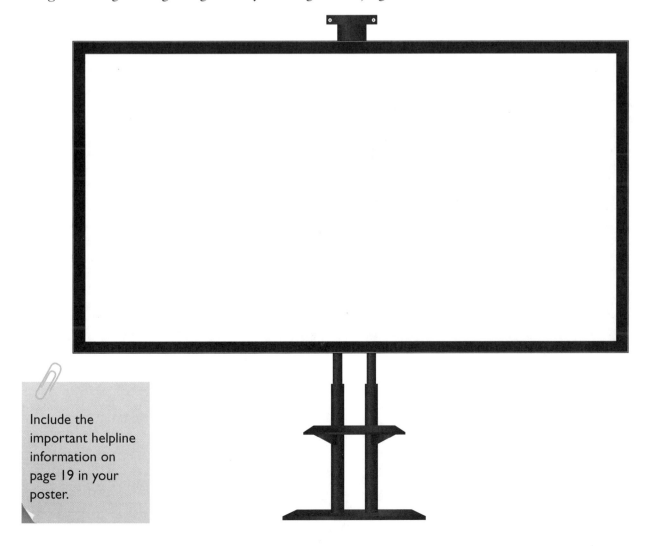

Include the important helpline information on page 19 in your poster.

Think–Pair–Share activity

Investigate what makes a good advertising campaign for Darkness Into Light.

◆ *Discuss* how you developed your slogan and jingle. *Evaluate* the purpose and strengths of what you have come up with.

◆ Listen to your classmate's ideas and *discuss* the purpose and strengths of these jingle.

◆ Fill in the table below, offering positive feedback to your classmate.

◆ *Present* your ideas to your class.

My slogan and jingle	
Purpose of my statement	Strengths
How I developed my idea	

My partner's slogan and jingle	
Purpose of his/her statement	Strengths
How he/she developed their idea	

What we feel would make a good advertising campaign for this event, which supports the topical issue of Mental Health in Ireland

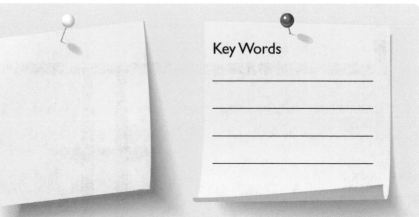

What stuck with you?

Evaluate your learning in this chapter. List what stuck with you and new key words.

Key Words

Reflection and Evaluation Sheet

Unit title:

Learning Outcomes (LOs) I worked with:

Music I listened to:

_____

Learning and exploring

I really enjoyed…

_____

Something interesting I learnt…

_____

My biggest challenge was…

_____

I overcame this by…

_____

One improvement I have made is…

_____

Traffic-light your learning

Learning Outcomes	😟	😐	🙂	✔
1.10				
2.2				
2.11				
3.1				
3.2				
3.4				
3.6				
3.8				

Rate your learning ⭐⭐⭐⭐⭐

Learning

Key words	Action verbs
_____	_____
_____	_____

Key skills

_____

I got better at x skill by _____

_____

This unit reminded me of learning about… _____

_____

What still puzzles me is…

_____

_____

Feedback and goal setting…

_____

_____

_____

Unit 2

Elements of Music

In this unit

You will explore the expressive qualities of pieces of music and be creative with your knowledge. Through understanding, experimenting and appreciating the role the elements play in musical works we acquire and develop the necessary skills for creating and analysing music. You will have a chance to imagine the composers' intentions in their works and the elements of music in their creative endeavours. This knowledge helps us to be innovative and creative in our own creating of music.

Checklist	LO	Intended learning
☐	1.1	**Compose** and perform or playback a short musical phrase and support these phrases by **creating** rhythmic/melodic/harmonic ostinato to accompany them.
☐	1.3	**Design** a harmonic or rhythmic accompaniment, record this accompaniment and **improvise** over it.
☐	1.6	Listen to and **transcribe** rhythmic phrases of up to four bars and melodic phrases of up to two bars.
☐	1.13	**Compare** different interpretations or arrangements of a piece of Irish traditional folk music, paying attention to musical elements and other features.
☐	2.1	**Experiment** and **improvise** with making different types of sounds on a sound source and notate a brief piece that incorporates the sounds by **devising** symbolic representations of these sounds.
☐	2.6	**Design** a rhythmic or melodic ostinato and add layers of sound over the pattern as it repeats, varying the texture to **create** a mood piece to accompany a film clip or sequence of images.
☐	2.7	**Create** and **present** some musical ideas using instruments and/or found sounds to **illustrate** moods or feelings expressed in a poem, story or newspaper article.
☐	3.8	Select a particular advertisement and **analyse** the role music plays in supporting the message and promoting the product.
☐	3.10	**Discuss** the principles of music property rights and **explain** how this can impact on the sharing and publishing of music.

We began developing our knowledge of the language of music in Unit 2 of *Sounds Good 1*. At the start of our learning journey, we may have experienced some difficulties in describing what was happening in a piece of music.

Together we explored the fundamental **elements** of music and had some fun experimenting with these. As your musical language developed, so did your awareness of how the elements of music all work together when a piece of music is created.

The **pulse** is influenced by the **tempo** and the **rhythm** is organised to fit between the pulses. In the same way, the **melody** leans on the **rhythmic patterns** but is also connected to **pitch**, **timbre** and **dynamics**, which combine to produce the **mood** and **expressive qualities** the composer sets out to create.

The elements of music play an important role in any composition, as they underpin the character of all pieces of music. They are central across all **genres** or styles of music, including pop, classical, rock, jazz, soul and even nursery rhymes!

To illustrate how the elements of music are interlinked, in *Sounds Good 1* they were placed on a wheel diagram. To help you recall your learning, complete the unlabelled version of this diagram below, giving a brief definition for each element.

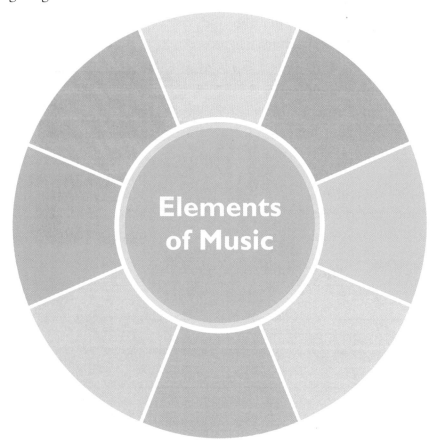

Collaborate with another student and *discuss* the elements you have added to the illustration. Can you remember the role each element plays in a piece of music?

Work in pairs to complete the summary grid below. Include **texture** and **form**.

The elements of music summary		
Element	**Definition**	**Key Words**

Pulse

Let's recap!

Our study of the elements began with pulse, also referred to as beat. Sometimes when we listen to music, we have an impulse to tap our pen along to the music. We may even find ourselves doing it without realising. This is because pulse makes us react kinaesthetically; in other words, it encourages motion or movement. For this reason, we dance, march, tap our feet or clap to the pulse rather than to the rhythm pattern.

The steady tick-tock of a clock is an example of a pulse. Each tick of the clock separates the pulses into one beat. Each pulse or beat is identical in time or length – in this case, one second. In music **genres** such as pop or rock, the pulse is heard on the bass drum or bass guitar. When the orchestra or another musical **ensemble** perform, who helps musicians to identify the pulse of the music they are playing?

Listen to two pieces of music from different **genres** and identify the pulse. Make a visual representation of the pulse using a form of movement: tap your foot, clap your hands or click your fingers.

Ticking clock

United States Air Force Band, Airmen of Note, DV8

Activity 1

Listen again to the two pieces. *Identify* the **genre** and *examine* the similarities or differences between pulse and **two** other elements of music of your choice. *Indicate* your findings in the grid below.

'The Circus' from Piano Concerto by Robert Wells

Elements	Airmen of Note	The Circus
Genre		
Pulse		

Tempo

Tempo is the speed of a piece of music. It is the speed of the **pulse** we have just explored above. There are many words used to describe tempo.

The word **tempo** goes all the way back to the Latin word *tempus*, meaning time. It was originally used by Italian composers to describe the timing of music or the speed at which a piece of music is played. For example, a soothing lullaby can be described as a slow **tempo** song.

Briefly explain the term '**lullaby**' and its purpose.

_____

_____

List two features of a lullaby: 1 _____

2 _____

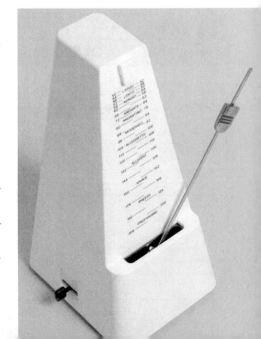

Compile the tempo markings you learnt about in *Sounds Good 1* by inserting them on the mind map, include their approximate BPM. The first one is done for you.

A tempo

It is important to note that composers can change the tempo markings during a piece; just because a piece of music begins in one tempo, doesn't mean it has to remain at that tempo throughout. When composers change tempo during a piece, they may write '*a tempo*' later in the score to tell the musician to resume the normal speed or return to the original tempo.

Accelerando

Accelerando means to gradually increase tempo. It is indicated on the score as *accel.*----. The dashed horizontal lines indicate the duration of the accelerando.

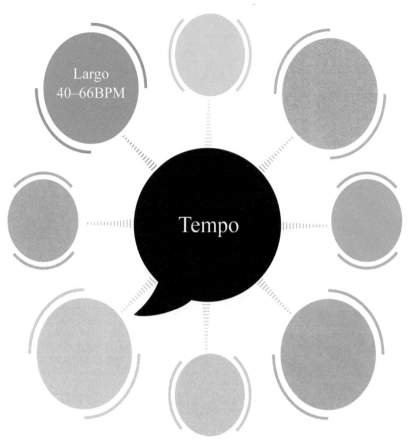

Rallentando and Ritardando

These Italian terms quite often feature towards the end of a piece of music and sometimes in the middle of a piece. They tell the musician to slow down.

Can you guess what composers will write on the score afterwards to indicate musicians should return the original tempo?

Look at this music and complete the grid on page 28.

Bloch

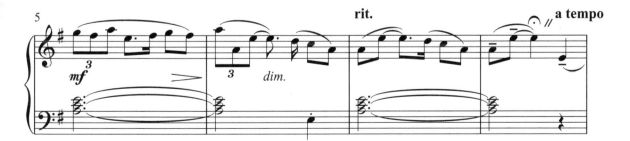

Work together to research and *define* the words and symbols relating to tempo in the grid below. They all appear in the score printed on page 27.

Tempo Key word	Definition
Poco rit.	
Andante	
Caesura //	
Fermata ⌢	

In popular and traditional groups musicians indicate the tempo by counting one or two bars out low or play a solo introduction before the vocalists enter.

Activity

Italian terms or **metronome marks** are printed on music scores to indicate to musicians the recommended speed at which a piece of music should be performed.

Complete the four-bar melody below in C major. *Indicate* the piece is to be played 'Largo', ensuring you add the tempo marking in the correct place.

 Rehearse and perform your melody for your classmates using your recorder or the rhythm using percussion instruments available to you. Then try it performed '**vivace**' and '**presto**'.

What stuck with you?

Evaluate your learning in this chapter. List what stuck with you and new key words.

Key Words

Dynamics

Dynamics are used by composers to indicate the loudness or softness of any piece of music. Dynamic markings are indicated **beneath the stave,** and in nearly all cases the dynamics will change during the piece.

In *Sounds Good 1* we investigated the interesting changes of dynamics in Stravinsky's *The Firebird*. Listen to this piece again and remind yourself of the range of dynamic changes used by Stravinsky.

The table below outlines the most common dynamic markings. Can you briefly explain these?

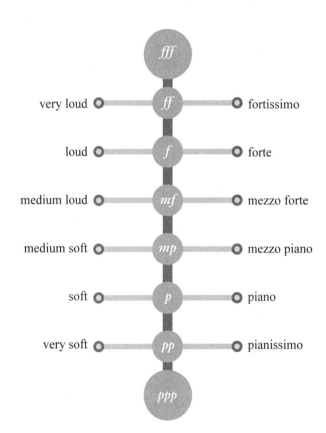

Dynamic marking	Meaning
pp	
p	
mp	
mf	
f	
ff	

Crescendo and diminuendo

Other important terms when we are talking about dynamics are ***crescendo*** or *cresc.*, which means to gradually get louder, and ***diminuendo*** or *dim.*, which means to gradually get softer. They are often indicated on the score using hairpin shapes.

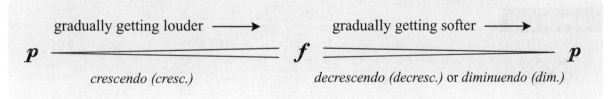

Listening activity

Listen to the first three minutes of the fourth movement of Symphony No. 4 by Anton Bruckner. You will hear many sections with contrasting dynamics, often with crescendos and diminuendos between them. As you listen, make a note of the instruments you can hear prominently, the dynamic and anything else that strikes you as interesting, for example, the texture, a change in tempo or a particular motif. The first column has been filled in for you. You may listen to the extract several times.

Excerpt from the Finale of Symphony No. 4 by Bruckner

Music timeline for the opening of the Finale from Bruckner Symphony No. 4

Time	0.00	0.04	0.34	0.48
Instruments	cellos double basses	woodwind violins		
Dynamics	pp	⟨cresc./dim.⟩		⟨cresc.⟩
Other observations	repeated notes			

Time	1.18	1.37	1.44
Instruments	timpani	polyphonic!	
Dynamics		ff	⟨dim.⟩
Other observations			stepwise violins.

Time	1.53	2.17	2.35	2.49	3.00
Instruments	full orchestra			Brass + strings	
Dynamics				⟨dim.⟩	
Other observations	Stepwise movement				

You can watch a video of a performance of the same work by searching on YouTube for 'Bruckner: Symphony No 4, movement 4 – François-Xavier Roth and London Symphony Orchestra'.

What stuck with you?

Evaluate your learning in this chapter. List what stuck with you and new key words.

Key Words
_____
_____
_____
_____

Pitch

In a nutshell, **pitch** is how high or low a specific note sounds when registered by the human ear. We discovered in *Sounds Good 1* that pitch is determined by the frequency of vibration of the **soundwave** – in other words, how quickly the soundwave is making the air vibrate.

Faster vibrations will be heard as higher pitches and slower vibrations will register as low-pitched sounds. The vibrations are measured in Hertz (Hz).

Listen to the **arpeggio** figure played at a low, then higher pitch.

Identify two high- and two low-pitched instruments used in the orchestra.

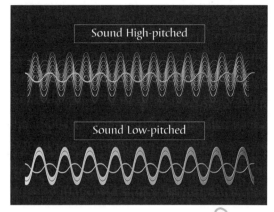

Sound High-pitched

Sound Low-pitched

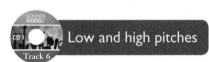

Low and high pitches

CD 1 Track 6

> Can you remember how many vibrations per second middle C has?
>
> _____

	High-pitched instrument	Low-pitched instrument
1		
2		

In pairs, *experiment* with **found sounds** that could be used to illustrate a mood or feeling. Record a high- and a low-pitched found sound. *Present* them to your classmates and explain how you might use them in a piece of **illustrative music**. Can they identify the found sound you have recorded?

> **Found sounds**: sounds created by everyday objects, e.g. birds chirping or car engine noise.

	List your two found sounds here	Mood or feeling it illustrates
1		
2		

Twelve pitches

In Western music there are twelve definite pitches. All instruments that play Western music can play these twelve pitches.

Most pianos have eighty-eight keys. Each of these keys plays a different sound, pitch or note. We know that the keys on a piano are not arranged at random; the lowest notes are at the left-hand end, and, as we move to the right, the notes gradually get higher until we reach the highest notes at the right-hand end of the keyboard.

> **Arpeggio**: the notes of a chord played one after another, either ascending or descending.

A piano keyboard is made up of white and black keys. These keys can be separated into seven **octaves**. Three octaves have been illustrated for you on the image below. Count how many piano keys there are within the octave C to C?

Seven octaves

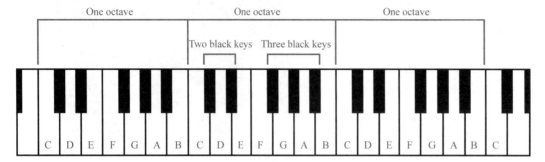

The piano keyboard above has labels on the the white keys. There are seven different white notes in each **octave** before the pattern is repeated. The five black keys also have their own **pitch** which is between that of the white key above it and the white key below it. 'Twelve pitches' refers to each available note within each octave (7+5).

Activity: Circle the pitches which belong to the scale of **C major**.

When all twelve pitches are played in a scale, we call it a **chromatic scale**. Each pitch is a semitone apart. Some composers really enjoy exploring the twelve pitches and compose music with lots of **chromaticism** in it.

Chromaticism: when melodies move in semitones, using notes outside of the chosen key signature.

One octave, twelve pitches

Listen to all twelve pitches within the octave being played and move your finger along with the notes on the keyboard below. There are two ways of naming the black keys, but both labels represent the same pitch. D♭ and C# have the exact same pitch and frequency.

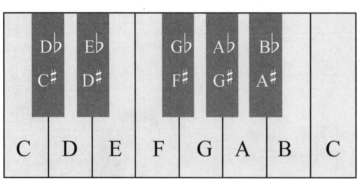

Chromatic Fantasy Sonata, movement 1 by Dave Brubeck

Listen to the opening of **jazz** pianist and composer Dave Brubeck's *Chromatic Fantasy Sonata*. This piece was inspired by J.S. Bach's *Chromatic Fantasy and Fugue*. Complete a listening grid for this piece with your teacher.

Jazz is a music **genre** that originated in New Orleans in the late nineteenth century.

Timbre

Timbre is understood as the distinctive sound qualities that different instruments make. It is what makes two instruments sound different when they are both playing the same note at the same volume.

The material an instrument is made of, its shape, the type of sound it produces and how it is played all have an impact on its timbre.

If a musician plays the note E on a guitar and then the same E pitch on the trumpet, will we be able to distinguish them easily?

These two instruments are made from different materials. They have very different shapes. They are not played in the same way: strumming the guitar strings is very different to pushing air through the trumpet by blowing into it. The sound quality these two instruments produce is therefore not at all alike. Can you give a similar example of two instruments with very different **timbres**?

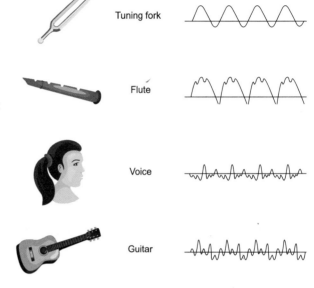

1	2

Activity

Listen to the short motif being played and *identify* the instrument playing it each time. Each instrument plays the motif twice.

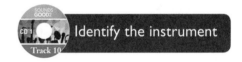

Motif	Instrument
1	Piano
2	Clarinet
3	Guitar
4	Violin
5	~~Cello~~ Double Bass

Activity

Write a brief statement explaining the importance of **timbre** when composing a piece of music for orchestra. *Identify* a **mood** and *suggest* instruments a composer could choose to help establish this mood.

_____

_____

_____

_____

33

Folk Music

So far, we have revisited six elements of music. Complete the listening task below by comparing the role the elements of music play in two interpretations of the same **folk song**.

A folk song is a song that originates from a specific country or culture and is passed on and preserved in the **oral tradition**. For this reason, many versions of the same songs exist. In Ireland, it wasn't until the 18th century that **collectors** such as Edward Bunting began to notate and preserve our folk songs. They are an important part of our heritage as they record everyday events from our past and tell us much about our ancestry.

Song types include **love songs**, **laments** and **working songs**. We explored some of these in Unit 6 of *Sounds Good 1*.

Explain the following terms:

◆ Oral tradition _____

◆ Collector _____

◆ Lament _____

◆ *Sea nós* _____

Well-known Irish folk songs include 'Molly Malone', 'Wild Rover' and 'Raglan Road'. Name two more:

1 _____

_____

2 _____

_____

The Dubliners

'The Spanish Lady'

 This **folk song** has been performed by many Irish performers including The Dubliners, Celtic Woman, Ronnie Drew. Christy Moore refers to his childhood memories of this song in his book *One Voice: My Life in Song*.

 'The Spanish Lady' by the Dubliners   Track 11

 'The Spanish Lady' by Ailish Tynan and Ian Burnside   Track 12

You will hear two very different performances of this song. *Investigate* how the **elements** of music we have explored so far contribute to the same folk song sounding so different. Include a brief description of the performance referring to the **vocalists** and the **instrumentation** of the individual performances.

Revisit pages 132–7 of *Sounds Good 1* and identify the common features used in traditional singing. Can you hear these too?

Features	The Dubliners	Ailish Tynan and Ian Burnside
Pulse		
Tempo		
Texture		
Melodic features		
Rhythmic features		
Voices		
Instrumentation		
Traditional features of the performance		

Performing Together!

The score for this well-known Irish **folk song** as performed by The Dubliners is printed below. In groups, *rehearse* it for performance. An accompaniment has been recorded for your performance. Sing it together or play it on your **recorder**.

You might decide to perform this for the practical component of your Junior Cycle exam.

'The Spanish Lady' accompaniment

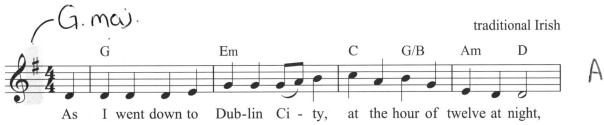

As I went down to Dub-lin Ci - ty, at the hour of twelve at night,

Who should I see but a Spa-nish la - dy wash-ing her feet by can-dle-light.

First she washed them, then she dried them o - ver a fire of am-ber coal, In

all my life I ne'er did see a___ maid so sweet a - bout the sole.

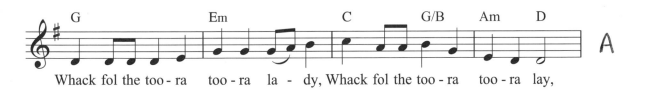

Whack fol the too - ra too - ra la - dy, Whack fol the too - ra too - ra lay,

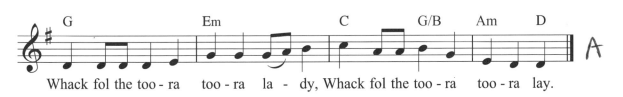

Whack fol the too - ra too - ra la - dy, Whack fol the too - ra too - ra lay.

Identify and insert the **form** plan for this song using the letters A and B on the score.

Programme note

Compose a programme note for this song.

_____
_____
_____
_____
_____
_____
_____

At this point in your learning journey, I am pretty certain you won't need me to convince you of the importance of **mood** and **expression** in how we experience a piece of music.

Suggest why composers give thought to the mood and expressive quality of the music they are composing. *Provide* examples.

_____
_____
_____
_____
_____

What stuck with you?

Evaluate your learning in this chapter. List what stuck with you and new key words.

Key Words

_____
_____
_____
_____
_____

Music in Advertising

In *Sounds Good 1* we explored the music used in marketing and advertising campaigns. We identified and discussed the role music plays in supporting the messages contained in an advertisement.

The background music chosen for adverts has been proven to influence consumers. Specific songs or musical **genres** are considered to support certain brands or product types.

Marketing teams choose music for their advertising campaigns very carefully, hoping it will give the consumer a gentle nudge towards buying their product. The emotional response we have to music is key to supporting the message being shared in an advertisement.

Cover song: in popular music a cover song is a new performance or recording of an already recorded song by a new artist. Covers can sometimes be more successful than the original. Under copyright law, a licence must be sought and royalties paid to the **original** artist.

John Lewis is a British department store acclaimed for its spectacular Christmas adverts. The first of these was released in 2007, and they have since become an eagerly awaited tradition at Christmas time. These adverts attract a lot of media attention when they are aired. The London-based marketing agency which has worked on these campaigns since 2009 is called adam&eveDDB.

The adverts typically use **covers** of existing songs by popular artists. In 2013 Lily Allen performed a **cover** of Keane's 2004 hit song 'Somewhere Only We Know'. Ellie Goulding and Tom Odell are two other artists who have featured in the John Lewis Christmas campaigns.

In 2018, Sir Elton John became the first artist to star in the advert, performing his own song, 'Your Song'. The first campaign in 2007 stands apart from the more recent ones, it uses Prokofiev's 'Morning Serenade' from *Romeo and Juliet*, rather than a cover version of a popular song.

There is no doubt that the more recent adverts place much importance on the emotive message of each advertisement. In 2009 the message was 'Remember how Christmas used to feel'; in 2015 it was 'Show someone they are loved this Christmas'.

Discuss the principles of **music property rights** and consider how these laws impact on the creation of John Lewis adverts.

◆ Select one of John Lewis's Christmas adverts.

◆ Identify the piece of music chosen for the advert.

◆ Research its origins and the performer who covers for the campaign.

◆ *Analyse* the role this piece of music plays in supporting the John Lewis message in the campaign for that year.

Write a blog post detailing your findings in the space below.

Blog Name   Home   Search

Info   Photos   Blog   Archives   +

Today's blog title

List six **moods** that can be recognised in pieces of music and choose a suitable piece of music to reflect each mood.

Mood	Piece of music
1	
2	
3	
4	
5	
6	

Music for Wellbeing

Music has the power to influence our own emotions. Music can affect us deeply when we listen to it. Choose a piece of music which makes you feel happy or calm or both. Name the song and the composer or performer and *identify* the reasons you have chosen this song to support your wellbeing.

Other than listening to music, *discuss* ways we can support and promote wellbeing in our school community.

Song	
Composer/performer	
Reasons for choice	

Creating moods to illustrate atmosphere or feeling

In music composed for film or television, **mood** counts for a great deal. It helps to generate the atmosphere and emotion of a scene for viewers. It supports and enhances the theme. Mood in composition plays an important role in illustrating the storyline of films but also in bringing poetry to life, representing an image or illuminating the key theme of a story. Setting poetry to music was popular with composers.

Bright, cheerful, angry, dramatic, happy, hopeful, humorous, lonely, optimistic, romantic, sad and scary are moods which composers have worked with when creating illustrative music. Below is an excerpt taken from a poem written by Irish poet James Joyce. The poem describes the calming and continuous to-and-fro motion of the sea.

Poems set to music by known composers are called **art songs**. Name a poem by an Irish poet which has been set to music.

'All Day I Hear the Noise of Waters' by James Joyce

Verse 2

The grey winds, the cold winds are blowing
Where I go.
I hear the noise of many waters
Far below.
All day, all night, I hear them flowing
To and fro.

Compose a piece of music inspired by Joyce's poem. Using instruments or **found sounds** available to you, *devise* a short rhythm or melody which you feel **illustrates** the **mood** of the poem.

Your creation should be designed to accompany the words of this verse, helping to illustrate the mood of the poem as it is read to listeners. Record and play back your composition as you read the verse aloud.

Looking back!
Revisit Chapter 22 of *Sounds Good 1* for tips on inventing rhythms to match with lyrics.

Before you begin, create a success criteria together and indicate this information on the rubric for assessment below.

Success Criteria

Unit:			Date:			
Learning goals:			**Learning Outcomes:**			
Success criteria I can…						
Feedback: Strengths: Areas for improvement: Goals:						

Use your whiteboard to draft and *refine* your ideas. *Synthesise* your ideas/drafts to create your final composition. *Transcribe* it in the space below.

Compositional portfolio

Your composition has been inspired by Joyce's poem. The music you have composed in response to this piece of poetry can be included in your compositional portfolio.

Remember you must include **draft material** relating to this Classroom Based Assessment. You can *present* this creation in **written, digital, visual or audio formats**.

An important element of composing is **reflecting on and evaluating the creative process** and the end result. *Use* the space below to evaluate and reflect on this creative project.

Reflect and evaluate!

◆ Include information about where you got your ideas for this composition.

◆ *Outline* the skills required to complete this project.

◆ What have you learnt from this experience and what would you do differently next time?

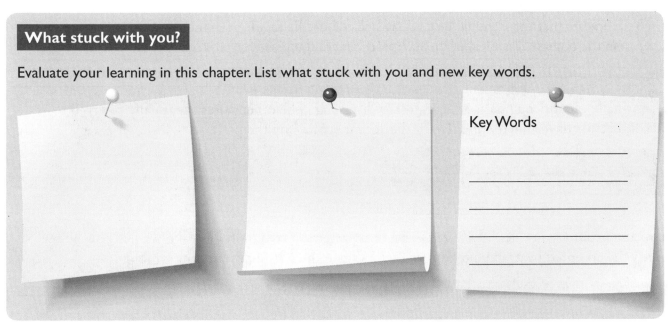

What stuck with you?

Evaluate your learning in this chapter. List what stuck with you and new key words.

Key Words

Rhythm is the pattern of long and short sounds and moments of silence within a piece of music. Rhythm is written onto sheet music using note values which represent how long or short the sounds should be. It is important not to confuse rhythm with pulse or beat. Rhythm patterns are built on the pulse of a piece of music and slot across and in between the pulses.

Listen to this short musical excerpt. Tap your foot to the pulse of the music and clap the rhythm pattern.

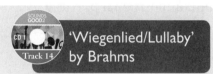 'Wiegenlied/Lullaby' by Brahms

We often think of rhythm as only appearing on a music stave, but rhythm really is all around us: the ocean tide, our phone ringtones or your own style of knocking on a door! I bet if you tap this out on the table, you won't all share the same knocking pattern.

Identify different door-knock patterns and share them with your classmates.

To notate these patterns, we will need to write them onto a rhythm stave as a short **motif**. Refresh your knowledge of **note values** by completing the grid below.

Motif: a short rhythmic or melodic idea.

Note value	Symbol	Duration
Semibreve		
	𝅗𝅥	
		One and a half beats
Quaver		

Here is a rhythm pattern. Try it out on your desk. Do you use this knock pattern too?

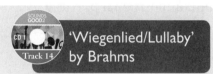 Door-knock pattern

Listen to how this sounds. You will notice there is an **accent** symbol on the first crotchet. This symbol is used to indicate that there should be emphasis placed on the first beat of the pattern, making it a little louder than the others. This is called an **accented beat** and typically occurs on the first beat of the bar.

In music, an **accent** is an emphasis, stress or stronger attack placed on a note, and you can normally identify emphasised beats just by listening. The other notes are usually referred to as **offbeats** or unaccented notes. Insert the accent symbol on the patterns below.

Experiment and listen to each other's door-knock patterns.

Share and explore your ideas. *Indicate* the rhythm pattern of **two** more door-knock patterns below. *Identify* the accented beats in your pattern and indicate them using the accent symbol.

Syncopation

We are used to hearing rhythm organised in a steady way, where the first beat in every bar is emphasised, indicating the metre. **Syncopation** is a form of rhythm which disturbs or changes this order.

In music, some parts of the bars are naturally accented. Naturally accented beats are called strong beats. In 4/4 time, beats 1 and 3 are strong beats. Beats 2 and 4 are called weak beats. *Look* at the bar of rhythm indicating these beats and clap it out.

Sometimes music plays around with this rule and places the **accents** on the notes which are normally unaccented. Tricky right? When this occurs, we hear a **syncopated rhythm pattern**. Below are three examples of syncopated rhythms. Each is played twice.

Listen to the rhythm pattern and clap it back. Each pattern will be played twice.

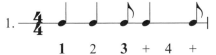

Identifying syncopation

Examine the three examples below and *identify* which of these patterns are **syncopated**. Circle the syncopated beats in each case.

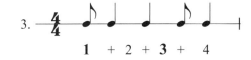

In pairs rehearse and perform the two part rhythm patterns below

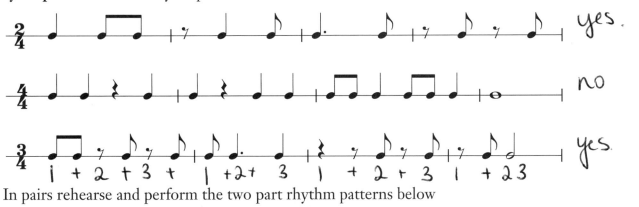

Syncopation in music

Syncopation is used in virtually all contemporary music and forms an important part of dance music. However, it is not just a contemporary phenomenon. Renaissance composer Giovanni Gabrielli used it in madrigals as well as in his **sacred works**. A good example of early usage of syncopation is in G.F. Handel's 'Minuet' from *Water Music*.

This minuet has an interesting time signature!

How many beats are there per bar? _____

Circle three examples of syncopation in the first four bars below.

Label each of the pitches in this tune to revise notation. The key is D major, the notes F♯ and C♯ are used here. Use your whiteboard to write out the D major scale.

> Handel is a Baroque composer. Identify the dates for this period.
>
> _____ – _____

Minuet from *Water Music* by Handel

Handel

Jazz and syncopation

Jazz has been called the most American form of music. This **genre** emerged in New Orleans at the beginning of the twentieth century and is characterised by **improvisation**, heavily **syncopated** rhythms and **polyphonic** ensemble playing.

Define the key words:

Polyphonic _____

_____

Improvisation _____

_____

Search online for the 1959 hit song 'The Best is Yet to Come' performed by Frank Sinatra. This song was originally made famous by jazz-great Tony Bennett. It was the last song sung by Sinatra in public before his death in 1995, and the song title is etched onto his tombstone.

This song is an example of **syncopated** music common in **jazz**.

As you listen to the intro, count 1 2 3 4 and you will notice that on beats 2 and 4 the music is clearly more emphasised than it is on beats 1 and 3.

Frank Sinatra

| 1 | **2** | 3 | **4** |

Listen to the clip of this short melodic **motif** taken from 'The Best is Yet to Come'. The arrows indicate the syncopation occurring in the melody.

 'The Best is Yet to Come' introduction played on Clarinet

 Sing this lyric together and notice how you emphasise the offbeats identified by the arrows below.

 'The Best is Yet to Come' introduction with metronome

music: Cy Coleman
words: Carolyn Leigh

You think you've seen the sun,— but you ain't seen it shine.———

 Now listen again with a metronome playing on the strong beats. This contrasts with the melody, revealing the way the rhythm falls on the weak beats or between the beats.

Ostinato: a repeated rhythmic or melodic pattern used in accompaniments.

Composing syncopated rhythm patterns

Compose a two-bar syncopated **ostinato** which repeats, with a metre of 4.

$\frac{4}{4}$ | | | |

Improvisation

"CREATIVITY IS INTELLIGENCE HAVING FUN"
ALBERT EINSTEIN

Improvisation is also an important element of jazz. Improvisation involves the spontaneous creation of music, without any previous preparation.

 Jazz or blues musicians rely on their **improvisation** skills when performing solos.

Improvisation seems like a tricky concept to understand but, remember, most of the time when we speak we are improvising; what we say and how we say it is spontaneously decided and not pre-prepared.

Improvising with rhythm is a fun way of being creative!

Activity

Record the **ostinato** you have created using GarageBand (or similar software) and set it to repeat or **loop**. *Use* this rhythmic ostinato as an accompaniment and *improvise* over it in two ways.

1 Clap patterns that do not use syncopated rhythms over it.

2 Experiment by singing or playing (using an instrument available to you) a short melodic motif that you feel fits over your ostinato.

> A **loop** is a recorded clip of music which repeats to create an ostinato.

More creative feel good fun!

Pen tapping

Search online for 'pen beats'. Watch Shane Bang and Kevin Key improvise in a **metre** of four using their pens! You will notice they tap the **pulse** of four to set the **tempo** before they begin to improvise.

This fun video shows how creative we can be with rhythm and pitch! The ruler used in this video is playing **pitches** based on the vibrations of the ruler at different lengths.

 Experiment and collaborate in pairs using the contents of your own pencil cases, explore your creative side! *Compose* a short piece and perform it together.

Record short video clips of your improvised patterns and share them with your classmates.

Composing Using Rhythmic Features

We explored **repeated rhythmic patterns** and rhythmic **ostinatos** in *Sounds Good 1*. This composing activity requires us to work with rhythm to create a **mood piece** to accompany a video clip or set of images. If you decide to use a film clip, keep it short – maybe 20–30 seconds.

Alternatively, use the image sequence below or select your own images to create your own personal mood board. The most important thing is that you are clear on what **mood** you wish to illustrate.

Compose a **two-bar syncopated ostinato** using a **repeated rhythmic pattern** with your mood in mind. *Transcribe* it on the rhythm line below, repeating it twice to complete four bars.

To create a fuller **texture**, *compose* a four-bar melodic motif and a four-bar rhythmic line to create a three-part piece to accompany your chosen mood board or film sequence. Your ostinato can repeat as the underlying rhythmic part.

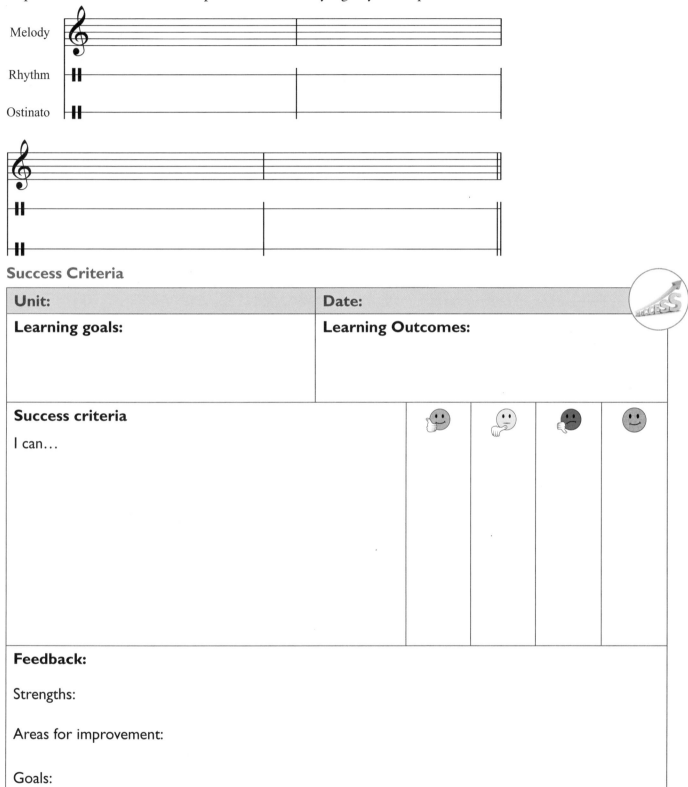

Success Criteria

Unit:	Date:				
Learning goals:	**Learning Outcomes:**				
Success criteria I can…					
Feedback: Strengths: Areas for improvement: Goals:					

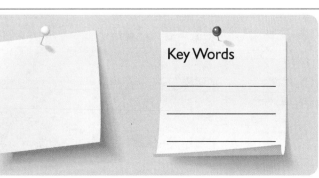

What stuck with you?

Evaluate your learning in this chapter. List what stuck with you and new key words.

Key Words

_____

_____

_____

Melody is the result of combining rhythms with pitch. Other words used for melody are 'tune', 'air' or 'theme'. In simple terms, when we take some pitches and organise them into rhythmic patterns, we have a melody. This combination also takes into account the beat or **pulse** by way of the **metre** or **time signature** we decide to use.

From a very young age, we experience melodies through soft lullabies or nursery rhymes. Think of some of the nursery rhymes you know well; can you recall the melody? Similarly, in most cases, when we hear our favourite song in our heads, it is the melody we hear, isn't it?

 In pairs work together to recognise the missing pitches of the well-known nursery rhyme 'Twinkle, Twinkle, Little Star'. The rhythm has been given above the stave to help you. Insert the lyrics and align them correctly with the rhythm pattern.

The reason the melodies of nursery rhymes are so easy for us to recall is that typically they have a very clear tune that is easy to remember. Also, the melody is the clearest and most recognisable element of the music, and our attention is most likely drawn to this element before the others.

Melody plays a central role in all music cultures. It is difficult to find music around the world that doesn't place importance on melody. Maybe this is because as humans we are musical beings. Our voice and how we can use it make us a melody-based life force, no? We all have a voice inside us which is perfectly capable of combining **pitch** and **rhythm** to sing a **melody**.

It is important that we can use words to describe how melodies move. Look back at the commonly used words for describing melody listed on page 39 of *Sounds Good 1*. Complete the grid below.

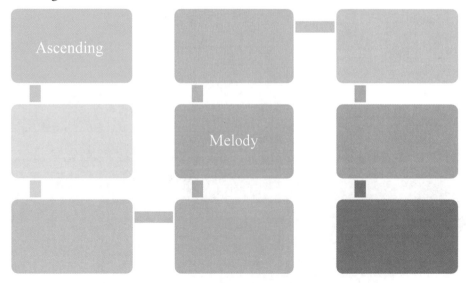

Melodic line

All composers understand the importance of creating a memorable melody. When pulse, rhythm and pitch are brought together, they create a melodic line or theme.

Early composers often sketched how their melodies should flow by drawing a line to represent the movement of the melody. This is often referred to as the melodic shape or **contour**. But what makes a melody memorable?

When trying to identify what makes melodies memorable and expressive, musicians talk about the melodic contour. This is the motion or movement of a melody indicated by a continuous line.

Look back at your melody Key words. How many of these describe movement? Ascending, descending, moving by step etc.

Activity: *Compose* one bar of melody which moves by step or leap in the space below.

Indicate two notes moving by step and two notes moving by leap below.

Can these concepts be represented visually?
Here is a visual representation of 'Twinkle, Twinkle, Little Star' using coloured circular symbols.

Sing it together and *discuss* how the image is a clever symbolic representation of the melody or tune. Can you guess what the different colours are used to illustrate?

Sketching the contour of a melody was a skill that many famous composers shared. Mozart was gifted in his ability to recall the shape of melodies he had heard, and he often notated them correctly onto a stave afterwards. This skill is known as **dictation**.

Here is an example of 'Twinkle, Twinkle' laid out for you on the stave. Compare the sheet music to the symbolic representation above and the version on page 48.

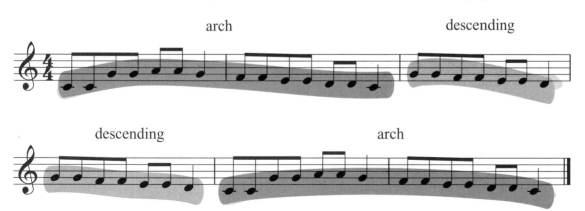

Find another well-known tune or nursery rhyme and *transcribe* the melody on to the stave provided.

Tune/Nursery Rhyme: _____

Composer: _____

Create a **symbolic representation** of these melodies in the space provided.

Describing melody

This table lays out the common words used to describe the shape of melodies. An example of the symbols used in symbolic or **graphic notation** to represent the contour of each melodic line is also shown for each one.

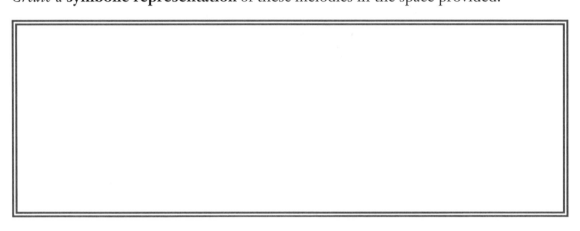

Description of melodic contour	Melodic contour		Possible shape used for graphic notation
	Traditional notation		
Ascending			
Descending			
Disjunct			
Conjunct			
Arch			
Wave			

'**Ascending**' and '**descending**' are clear descriptors of how a melody moves. '**Stepwise** movement' and 'leaps' are terms that we often use to describe melody. These types of movement are correctly identified as 'conjunct' or 'disjunct'.

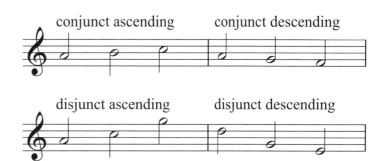

Conjunct melodic motion is stepwise, moving from one note to the next.

Disjunct melodic motion is when the melody moves by leaps or distances wider than one tone. Most melodies will make use of both types of melodic motion.

Other melodic features we can hear are **octave leaps** and **scales**. On the stave below, transcribe an octave leap followed by a descending scale. Work in the key of **C major**.

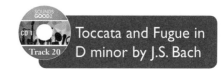

Listening activity

Listen to three short melodic excerpts, which were all written by well-known composers. Draw a melodic contour line in each box to *illustrate* the overall shape of the main theme or melody according to how it moves.

J.S. Bach's Toccata and Fugue in D minor

You may not know its name, but you will certainly have heard this dark melody before. You may recognise it from *The Phantom of the Opera*. The melody often features in the horror film **genre** and regularly appeared in **silent movies** to illustrate a spooky **mood**.

Toccata and Fugue in D minor by J.S. Bach
Track 20

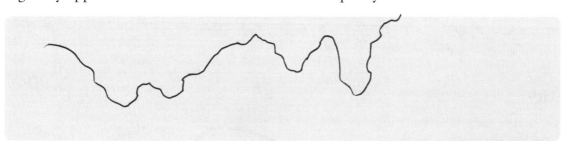

Ludwig van Beethoven's Symphony No. 5

There are many interesting stories around how this melody came to Beethoven. It's a short but very recognisable theme and remains the most-performed melody in all of Classical music's history. We find examples of it used in every twentieth-century **genre:** rap, blues, disco, heavy metal, rock and roll etc.

Symphony No. 5, movement I by Ludwig van Beethoven
Track 21

Richard Wagner's 'Bridal Chorus' from *Lohengrin*

If you have ever been a guest at a wedding, you have probably heard this melody. It is important to note it is not actually called 'Here Comes the Bride' although it does feature in Wagner's opera *Lohengrin* as the character Elsa makes her way to the chapel to be wed.

'Bridal Chorus' from *Lohengrin* by Richard Wagner

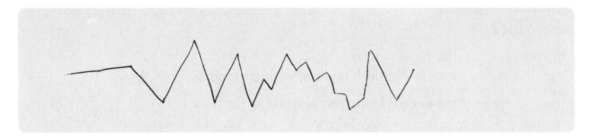

The **themes** from these melodies are set out for you below. Using your sketches above, try to **match** each melody to its title by drawing a line to connect them.

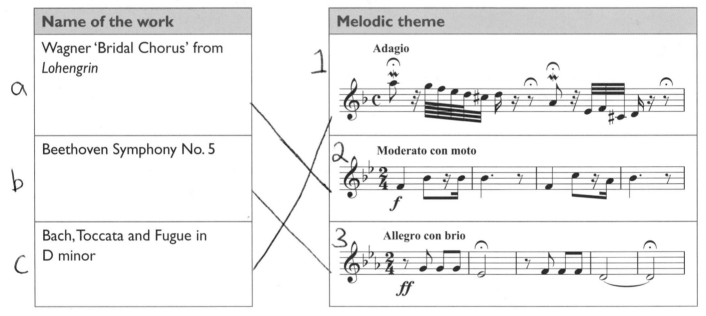

Name of the work	Melodic theme
a Wagner 'Bridal Chorus' from *Lohengrin*	1 Adagio
b Beethoven Symphony No. 5	2 Moderato con moto
c Bach, Toccata and Fugue in D minor	3 Allegro con brio

Composing activity

Work independently to *compose* a four-bar melody which replicates the melodic shape or contour drawn for you here. Work in the key of C major and end on the tonic note, also known as **doh**. *Transcribe* your melody on the stave provided.

On the rhythm line below *design* a **rhythmic ostinato** to accompany your melody. Remember to consider the emphasised beats in the bar and avoid using **syncopated** rhythm patterns.

Define the term **ostinato**:

_____

_____

_____

Once you have completed your melody and rhythmic accompaniment, complete the two-part score below to combine the parts together for performance.

Using the technology software available to you, **input** your creation and **play it back**. Choose suitable melodic and rhythmic instruments.

Look back at the advice on improving your melody writing in *Sounds Good 1* on page 111.

Evaluate the quality of the melody and how the ostinato you have created fits with it. Reflect on the **composition skills** you have developed that helped you with this task and make a short note about them in the box below.

Have you written the melody clearly? Does it have a melodic shape with suitable dynamics and **articulation** added? Does your **ostinato** align correctly with the melody line?

Recap on learning

Revise the music elements we have been working with and *list* them on the memory wall below. Include the two further features we learned about in *Sounds Good 1*: texture and form.

Musical Element Wall

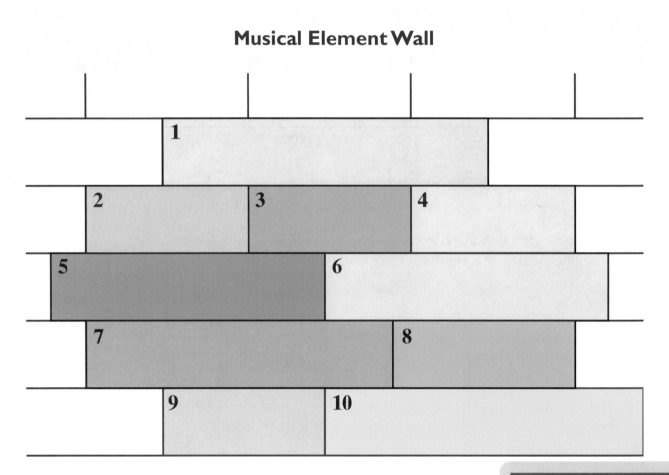

Briefly explain the term 'form' _____.

List three forms you have studied and briefly describe each of them.

Form	Brief description
1	
2	
3	

Define the tem 'texture' _____.

List the three common terms used to describe texture and briefly explain them.

Texture	Description
1	
2	
3	

Reflection and Evaluation Sheet

Unit title:

Learning Outcomes (LOs) I worked with:
e.g. 1.2, 3.4, etc.

Music I listened to:
_____
_____

Learning and exploring

I really enjoyed…
_____
_____

Something interesting I learnt…
_____
_____

My biggest challenge was…
_____
_____

I overcame this by…
_____
_____

One improvement I have made is…
_____
_____

Traffic-light your learning

Learning Outcomes	😞	😐	🙂	✓
1.1				
1.3				
1.6				
1.13				
2.1				
2.6				
2.7				
3.8				
3.10				

Learning

Key words	Action verbs
_____	_____
_____	_____

Key skills
_____

I got better at x skill by _____
_____

This unit reminded me of learning
about… _____
_____

What still puzzles me is…
_____
_____

Feedback and goal setting…
_____
_____
_____

Rate your learning

Unit 3

Listening Lab

In this unit

We will explore music as a way/means of understanding who we are and our historical story. Listening and responding to music from different eras and genres allows us to discover more about the period in which the music was composed. Developing our active listening skills improves our ability to analyse, compare and evaluate music. These learning experiences develop our music vocabulary and understanding of the elements of music. A study of the historical eras builds on Sounds Good 1, while chapters on the silent movie genre and jazz offer us an insight into more recent styles.

Checklist	LO	Intended learning
☐	1.11	**Illustrate** the structure of a piece of music through a physical or visual representation.
☐	1.14	**Compare** pieces of music that are similar in period and style by different composers from different countries.
☐	2.3	Adapt excerpts/motifs/themes from an existing piece of music by changing its feel, style, or underlying harmony
☐	2.7	Create and present some musical ideas using instruments and/or found sounds to illustrate moods or feelings expressed in a poem, story or newspaper article
☐	3.1	Collaborate with fellow students and peers to produce a playlist and a set of recordings to accompany a local historical event or community celebration.
☐	3.2	**Examine** and **interpret** the impact of music on the depiction of characters, their relationships and their emotions, as explored in instrumental music of different genres.
☐	3.3	Make a study of a particular contemporary or historical musical style; **analyse** its structures and use of musical devices, and **describe** the influence of other styles on it.
☐	3.6	**Associate**/match music excerpts to a variety of texts (words, film, language) and **justify** the reasons as to why this piece of music was chosen to match the text.
☐	3.10	**Discuss** the principles of music property rights and **explain** how this can impact on the sharing and publishing of music.

Active Listening

Before you began to study music as a subject in school, you may have only used music as a background for other activities and rarely focused your full attention on listening to the music itself.

For many people, listening to music is a passive activity; whilst they may be enjoying the music as they busy themselves with other tasks, they are not actively listening to the music. We learnt about this in *Sounds Good 1* and explored how hearing and listening are not quite the same thing.

Active listening requires that we focus on what is happening in the music. We need to concentrate on the sounds we hear and process these sounds into knowledge. We have developed our awareness of the elements of music and practised ways of describing and articulating this information during our learning in *Sounds Good 1*. To focus our attention whilst we listened, we experimented by listening to Debussy's *La Mer* whilst we drew images or visual representations inspired by the music. This is a great way to focus the mind on the music itself.

Listen to this fun piece by Rimsky-Korsakov and use washes of colour, draw shapes or any images that come to mind as you listen. Share your creation with your classmates. You may be surprised by each other's interpretations of the music.

'The Flight of the Bumblebee' by Rimsky-Korsakov

Nikolai Rimsky-Korsakov (1844–1908) composed 'The Flight of the Bumblebee' in 1899. This piece of **programme music** was intended for use as an orchestral interlude in his opera *The Tale of Tsar Saltan*. This motif musically suggests to the listener the picture of a bumble bee in chaotic flight through the air.

Programme music: instrumental music which suggests a mood or emotion, or suggests visual images.

57

Active Listening 1: 'Happy' by Michel Legrand

Work in pairs to recognise the key musical elements and how they are mixed together in this piece of music.

'Happy' by Michel Legrand

Discuss what you have heard with your partner and complete the think–pair–share grid below to report your findings.

Elements of music	What I think	My partner's thoughts	What we agreed
Style/Genre			
Tempo			
Dynamics			
Mood			
Texture			
Instrumentation			
Rhythm			
Melody			

Active listening: Teacher's choice

Your teacher will choose another piece for you to listen to. Complete the grid below as you listen to describe how the musical elements are used.

Texture ☐	
Tempo ☐	
Dynamics ☐	
Rhythm ☐	
Melody ☐	
Any other points of interest included:	

Active listening: Your choice

Now make your own choice of music and complete the grid as before.

Activity: create a listening map or checklist for use during listening activities.

Title	
Composer or singer	
Genre	
Expression	☐
Tempo	☐
Dynamics	☐
Rhythm	☐
Melody	☐
Other points of interest included:	

_____

_____

_____

_____

In today's world it is very difficult to avoid the many distractions around us. External distractions affect our concentration and prevent us from **actively listening** to music.

Active listening is a very important communication skill which helps us to develop our relationships with others by listening to our friends and expressing ourselves.

If we consciously try to relax and give our full concentration to a piece of music, we might be surprised by just how many interesting things are unfolding. In *Sounds Good 1* we learnt how to deconstruct what we were listening to and categorise this information using the **elements of music**, which we have just revisited in Unit 2 of this book. Listening in this way is like listening in layers.

It is important to remember to enjoy music as you listen to it. Analysing music will never replace how music makes us feel or the importance of listening to music for enjoyment, but you will now also understand what is happening in the music. The more you understand **how** composers and musicians have created their masterpiece, the more you will appreciate it.

Explain the term categorise: _____

_____

_____

As a music student you may listen to your favourite songs now and question the **tempo**. Does it move quickly or slowly? What is the **time signature**? You may notice little musical **motifs** are repeated or return played on a different instrument. **Leaps** and moments of silence created using **rests** won't escape your notice either. Remember the composer has put these there for you to enjoy and appreciate!

Song questionnaire

Select **one** of your favourite songs and find a quiet space to listen to it.

Listen carefully to the song from start to finish and complete the questions below.

1 Name the artist/composer. _____

2 Give the title of the song or piece. _____

3 Name the album it is taken from. _____

4 *Briefly explain* why you have chosen it. _____

_____

_____

5 *Analyse* what is happening in the opening section. _____

_____

_____

6 *Identify* an **instrument** which plays the **melody** and describe how the melody is constructed.

_____

_____

_____

7 *Identify* the type of voice that sings the lead **vocals**? _____

8 *Suggest* what the **mood** of the song is. _____

9 *Describe* the **texture** of the song. _____

_____

10 *Identify and describe* the **rhythmic features** in this song. _____

_____

_____

Reflect on why you like this song so much. Is it the **melody**, the **rhythm** or the story being told in the **lyrics** that you like most? Give a brief reason for choosing this song in the space below. Make reference to the music itself.

_____

_____

_____

_____

Music History Timeline

In the rest of this unit, we will explore different styles and periods of music and investigate how the different **elements** of music feature in the creative efforts of well-known composers.

We will discover some new elements of music as we go along, and you will have an opportunity to develop your research and analysis skills. Exploring pieces of music and comparing the work of **composers** is very important in helping us understand our history.

Reflecting on the social and cultural context of eras in which pieces of music were composed and the traditions and individuals who lived during these historical periods makes the music more meaningful to listen to. It will also help us learn much about our own culture, traditions and identities.

In *Sounds Good 1* we used a timeline to help us to trace the key periods in the history of music. Refer back to this timeline and complete the blank timeline set out below including the dates.

◆ For each period, list **two** composers who lived in different countries.

The first period has been completed for you.

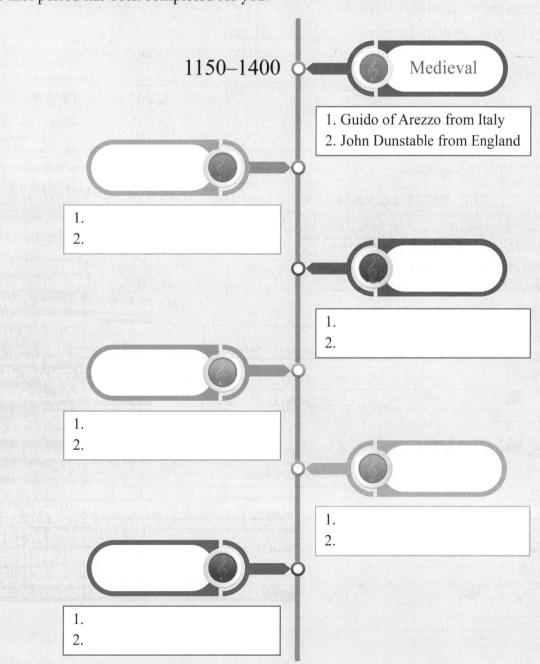

1150–1400 — Medieval
1. Guido of Arezzo from Italy
2. John Dunstable from England

1.
2.

1.
2.

1.
2.

1.
2.

1.
2.

The Baroque Era

The Baroque era spanned from **1600 to 1750** and is recognised for its ornate and extravagant style of architecture, sculpture, painting and music. Some of the general characteristics of the music of this time were composers' use of **ornamentation** within the melodic line, the use of **polyphonic textures** and the sound of a **small orchestra** with particular interest in the **strings** and the **harpsichord**.

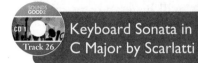

'Réjouissance' from Overture-Suite in D major by Telemann

Keyboard Sonata in C Major by Scarlatti

Two pieces of Baroque music will be played for you. The first piece is from George Philip Telemann's Overture-Suite, Movement 8, called 'Réjouissance'. The second piece is Domenico Scarlatti's Sonata in C major for Keyboard.

Listen to and *compare* these pieces of music and report your findings in the grid below.

	Overture-Suite 'Réjouissance'	**Keyboard Sonata**
Composer	Telemann	Scarlatti
Composer's homeland	Germany	Italy
Instrumentation	Harpsichord, flute, strings recorder	Harpsichord
Melodic features	Conjunct, stepwise repetitive	Lots of ornamentation, stepwise movement
Rythmic features	Fast, Allegro	Allegro, Vivace (lively)
Ornamentation	Yes	Yes
Texture	Polyphonic	Homophonic

Once you have completed your listening activity, reflect on the information you have gathered. Write a blog post for a school website in which you *distinguish* between these two pieces of music by *discussing* their similarities and differences. Include information on the **composers**, and the **features** of performances common in the Baroque era.

Today's blog title

_____

_____

_____

_____

_____

_____

_____

Ornamentation: ornaments are notes which have been added to decorate or embellish the melodic line; they are also known as musical flourishes.

The Baroque orchestra

Here is an image of a typical Baroque **ensemble**. Research the instruments common to ensemble playing during this era, in particular the strings, and write a note on the Baroque orchestra. Report your findings below.

_____

_____

_____

_____

_____

Baroque key words

Define the following key terms associated with Baroque music and identify a piece of music associated with these terms.

Term	Brief definition	Musical example
Canon		Pachelbel's Canon
Suite		
Polyphonic		
Patronage		
Ornamentation		
Keyboard		
Fugue		

In *Sounds Good 1* we listened to Samuel Scheidt's *Galliard Battaglia*, which illustrates two sides participating in a gallant battle. Do you remember it? Listen to this piece again and using the Venn diagram below compare it with Scarlatti's keyboard piece you have just listened to. Aim to make comparisons using your knowledge of the elements of music. Use them as key headings for analysis and also comment on texture and instrumentation.

Galliard Battaglia by Samuel Scheidt

Composer	Country
Scheidt	German
Scarlatti	Italian

Scarlatti keyboard Sonata

Galliard Battaglia

Absolute music is unlike programme music. It is music which is not intended to illustrate something and is not inspired by something or someone.

The Romantic Period

In the early 1800s a new music was beginning to emerge across the Western world. Reportedly jumpstarted by the wonderful Beethoven, this new form of music was freer and focused on the listener. Works were longer, composers based their creations more on themes; the orchestra was growing in size and the piano was established as a solo instrument, popular with composers.

Before the **Romantic period** most composers wrote **absolute music.** They didn't tap into the emotions of listeners and instead focused on the sound or **form** of the music they were composing, keeping it organised and balanced. Then Beethoven changed this with his intensely expressive compositions. He and the other romantic composers worked tirelessly to create music which would stir up all sorts of emotions. This was a new freedom which allowed composers to focus on the story or emotions they wanted to share with their audience.

Ludwig Van Beethoven

Tempo rubato

Listen to Frederic Chopin's Nocturne Op. 9 No. 2 in E flat major for piano. Did you notice anything interesting about it?

Nocturne Op. 9 No. 2 by Chopin

Before the Romantic era, structure and balance were very important for composers and musicians. As you listen to this excerpt, you will notice there is a freeness in the **tempo**. This freedom allows for a performance full of tenderness and expression. Never gaining or losing time, the performer sometimes rushes ahead and then in turn pulls back. This changing of tempo is known as ***rubato*** and allows a performer to speed up or slow down in order to achieve an **expressive** performance. If you listen to other performances of this piece you will notice each performance varies in terms of the tempo.

Tempo and **dynamics** are central expressive qualities of any piece of music. Give **three** reasons to argue why this statement is true.

1 _____

2 _____

3 _____

Comment on one other **element** of music which adds to the expressive quality of a piece of music.

_____
_____

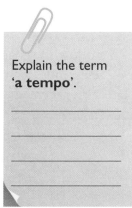

Explain the term 'a tempo'.

_____
_____
_____
_____

Frédéric Chopin

Frédéric Chopin was a Polish composer and piano player from the Romantic period, and most of his compositions were for **solo** piano including his twenty-one nocturnes. A **nocturne** is a musical composition which illustrates feelings and moods associated with the night time. Interestingly, Chopin was influenced by Irish composer John Field.

Like Field, Chopin wrote songlike melodies for the right hand and a rhythmic or chordal part for the left hand. Some describe this as the vocal part being played by the right hand while the **broken chords** in the left hand have been added to accompany the vocalist.

Frédéric Chopin

Chopin also used the piano's **sustain pedal** frequently across his twenty-one nocturnes, as did Field. Most modern pianos have three pedals, although some have only two. Piano pedals are operated by the feet and each have the ability to change the sound or tone of the piano. The sustain pedal (the one on the right) 'sustains' the pitches played on the piano by releasing the dampeners on the strings inside the piano, allowing the sound to ring out freely.

Broken chord: when the individual notes of a chord are played successively

Two short clips of the same melody will be played on the CD for you. The first without the sustain pedal and the second with it. Can you hear the difference?

 Track 29 Opening melody of Nocturne Op. 9 No. 2 by Chopin without sustain pedal

 Track 30 Opening melody of Nocturne Op. 9 No. 2 by Chopin with sustain pedal

Suggest reasons why the Romantic composers like Chopin favoured the sustain pedal so much.

_____
_____

Pedal note

A sustained note which sustains over several bars.

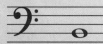

This Nocturne was composed by Chopin between 1830 and 1832. The music has featured in many films and TV programmes, even an episode of *The Simpsons*! The **mood** of the piece is reflective and gentle. The **form** is based on two repeating themes – A and B – and closes with a coda section. The main themes become more elaborate and **ornamented** each time we hear them and gradually build towards a climax, only to return to the gentle mood at the end.

Follow the score as you listen and trace the development of theme A and theme B. Consider the techniques used by Chopin to create the climax section.

Nocturne Op. 9
No. 2 by Chopin

Nocturne Opus 9 No. 2

by Frédéric Chopin

Compile a bank of words and symbols found on this score. In pairs, research and record a brief definition explaining each of them.

Symbol / Word	Definition
Ped.	

Below is a list of features common to Chopin's nocturnes. Listen to Nocturne Op. 9 No. 2 again and try to identify these features in this piece. *Briefly describe* how they are presented. Refer to the music in your answer.

Nocturne Op. 9 No. 2 by Chopin
Track 28

Nocturne features	Description of feature in Op. 9 No. 2 in E flat major
Solo instrument	
Emotional mood	
Illustrates night time	
Rubato	
Songlike melody in the right hand	
Rhythmic left hand	
Use of the sustain pedal	
Expressive dynamics	
Less restricted tempo	

Whilst there is no doubt Chopin was heavily influenced by John Field, it is important to recognise the impact Chopin's work had on other composers like Claude Debussy and Franz Liszt. These short piano pieces played a significant role in the development of composition in the Romantic period.

Compose a programme note for 'Nocturne' and present it in poster format.

Looking Back

In *Sounds Good 1* we listened to Romantic composer Tchaikovsky's 'The Blue Bird and Princess Florine' from the **ballet** *Sleeping Beauty*. Listen again to this piece of **illustrative music**. It opens with a songlike melody on flute, illustrating the blue bird's song to the character Florine.

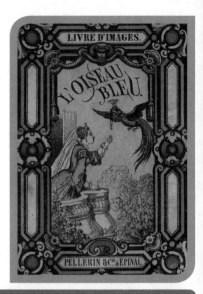

> Compare and contrast 'The Blue Bird and Princess Florine' and Chopin's Nocturne Op. 9 No. 2 in E flat major.

Both were written in the Romantic period but by two composers who resided in different countries. Tchaikovsky was born in Russia, and Chopin in Poland. Can you find these countries on the map?

Comparing pieces of music can be tricky, so plan ahead. In the grid below *identify* and *list* the specific elements you aim to listen out for. Listen attentively to each piece as you *analyse* and *describe* the music.

'The Blue Bird and Princess Florine' from *The Sleeping Beauty* by Tchaikovsky

Element	Tchaikovsky's 'Blue Bird'	Chopin's Nocturne Op. 9 No. 2
Interesting signpost		

When you have collated the information on each piece individually, set about making comparisons and identifying the differences between them.

Record your findings in the Venn Diagram below.

'The Blue Bird and Princess Florine'   Nocturne Op. 9 No. 2

Similarities

What stuck with you?

Evaluate your learning in this chapter. List what stuck with you and new key words.

Key Words

Illustrative Music

Music which expresses ideas, emotions or moods and can illustrate a story or the characters in a story is known as **illustrative music**. Illustrative music brings out our own emotions and triggers our imaginations as we listen to it. Illustrative music is also known as **programme music**.

Reflecting emotions in their music was very important to the Romantic composers but so too was imaginative imagery. Using music to set a scene or create colourful imaginative images was essential in telling a story and setting a **mood**. Composers often composed music to illustrate scenes from nature. There are many pieces of music which illustrate a sunrise for example.

Richard Strauss

German composer Richard Strauss wrote *Also sprach Zarathustra* in 1896. This symphonic poem was inspired by the Romantic philosopher Fredrich Nietzsche's novel of the same title. This work has nine sections, each named after the chapters in Nietzsche's novel.

Sunrise from *Also sprach Zarathustra* by Richard Strauss

> **Philosopher**: a person who studies or writes about the meaning of life. The word means lover of wisdom.

Research and define the term **symphonic poem**. Write a definition for it below.

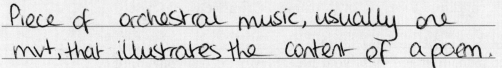

Piece of orchestral music, usually one mvt, that illustrates the content of a poem.

The first movement is called 'Sunrise'. The opening music begins in the lowest **ranges** of the **orchestra**, played by the double basses, contra bassoon, organ and timpani. The music develops from this eerie darkness and slowly builds to illustrate the majestic dawn of the sun rising, finally announced by four trumpets. Strauss uses the trumpets to play a dramatic **fanfare** based on a three-note **motif**, known as the 'dawn motif'.

Dawn motif

doh soh doh
5   4

> **Intervals**: the distance between two notes.

Strauss uses three ascending notes to create his imagery of the sunrise. He develops these **intervals** slowly, building up to the highpoint in the melody. Count the intervals between the three notes, which are presented above on the stave for you.

The timpani play dramatic rhythm patterns which help build suspense, and the clash of the cymbals announces the sun's light breaking through. The final notes of this movement are long and sustained, with the organ holding on after the rest of the **orchestra** as if to illustrate the enduring power of the sun.

> **Fanfare**: a short elaborate flourish on trumpet announcing an event or the arrival of royalty.

Strauss's dawn **motif** is steady and **ascending**, which is often the case with music which illustrates the sun rising. Historically composers used descending motifs to illustrate death, erratic motifs for panic or uncertainty, whilst love themes were depicted as long flowing melodies.

Watch the Vienna Philharmonic Orchestra's performance of Also sprach Zarathustra conducted by Gustavo Dudamel. You will find it by searching online for 'Strauss – Also sprach Zarathustra – Dudamel – YouTube'. The Sunrise movement is 1 minute 30 seconds long.

Make three suggestions of ways we can use music to illustrate types of movement.

Take Strauss's dawn motif and adapt it by changing its rhythm or melody to create a new sunrise motif based on Strauss's ideas. Decide which instrument will play it and insert your motif on the stave below.

Can you think of other emotions or images that can be created by large **ensembles** like the **orchestra**? Discuss some of the orchestral instruments a composer may use to illustrate your ideas.

_____

_____

Choose one idea that you could illustrate from the suggestions below. Work in pairs to compose a **melodic motif** which illustrates your chosen idea.

- ◆ Jumping
- ◆ Climbing the stairs
- ◆ Raindrops
- ◆ A clock

Consider the **pitch** of the notes, how the movement of notes would illustrate your idea and, most importantly, **rhythm**. Discuss what instruments' **timbre** would best suit your motif.

Use your whiteboard to plan, draft and *refine* your idea. Play or record your motif so you can *evaluate* how effective it sounds. *Transcribe* your final draft in the space below and draw an image or simple sketch of what your melodic motif has been designed to illustrate.

Melodic Motif (a short musical idea)

Title:

Reflect on and *evaluate* this learning experience together. What worked well? What challenges did you face and how did you overcome them?

Comment on how you felt about this task in the space provided.

_____

_____

_____

_____

List the percussion instruments used by Strauss:

_____

_____

_____

_____

Strauss also depicts the sunrise in *An Alpine Symphony* Op. 64. This illustrative work also uses **brass** to evoke images of the sun rising in the mountains and ends with the sun setting. *An Alpine Symphony* is scored for one of the largest orchestras ever assembled at this time.

The Romantic **orchestra** was growing in size. In *Also sprach Zarathustra* Strauss included instruments such as piccolo, cor anglais, tuba, contrabassoon and harp. These instruments were new to the Romantic orchestra and traditionally would not have been written into works during the Classical era.

Research the Romantic orchestra and give details of your findings in the space below.

_____

_____

_____

_____

Incidental Music

Incidental music is music which is used in a play, film, computer game or a radio programme.

Unlike **programme music**, incidental music is used more as background music, intended to add atmosphere. This type of composition dates back to Greek drama and was popular with composers such as Mozart, Schubert and Mendelssohn.

Overtures are played before a play to announce the **mood** of the play, and **intermezzi** are pieces of music which were played during scene changes or at the end of an act.

Jules Massenet composed 'Méditation' for use in his opera *Thais* in 1894. It is a symphonic intermezzo, which is a piece of music composed for performance between acts of a play or large orchestral work. 'Médiation' was skilfully composed to continue Massenet's telling of the story of Thais, even though it would only be performed between scenes in Act II.

The character Thais has been invited by a monk called Athanaël to leave her life of riches and comfort, to follow God. This piece of incidental music was composed to illustrate her pensive moments of reflection before the opening of the next scene, in which she decides to leave with Athanaël.

Listen to an excerpt from this piece and consider how Massenet illustrates Thais's moment of reflection.

Excerpt from 'Méditation' from *Thais* by Massenet

Name a piece of gaming music:

_____

_____

_____

Analyse the music to *identify* **three elements** which help to create this image for us as we listen and give a *brief description* of their role in the excerpt you hear.

	Element	Description
1		
2		
3		

Other famous performers to have recorded this song include Yo-Yo Ma and Irish-born James Galway. Galway is a world-renowned flautist, nicknamed 'the man with the golden flute'. He recorded Massenet's 'Méditation', accompanied by the National Philharmonic Orchestra.

You can watch a performance of this much-loved piece of music by searching online for 'Katica Illényí – Thais Meditation – YouTube'. Make some notes on the performance below.

James Galway

Yo-Yo Ma

Earlier in this unit we listened to Rimsky-Korsakov's 'The Flight of the Bumblebee' and drew a picture inspired by the music itself. This piece of music is an example of incidental music, heard between the acts of his opera *The Tale of Tsar Saltan*.

 'The Flight of the Bumblebee' by Rimsky-Korsakov

Listen to this piece of music again. Examine and interpret the impact of the music in its depiction of the bumble bee and the images created for us by Rimsky-Korsakov. Briefly describe the images he creates of the bumble bee for the listener in the box below.

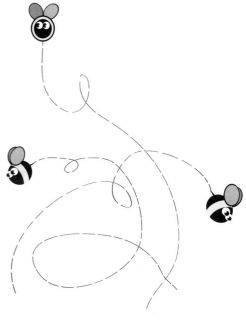

What stuck with you?

Evaluate your learning in this chapter. List what stuck with you and new key words.

Key Words

It is important to recognise the significant impact that the pieces of music we have just listened to have had on later genres. For example, **illustrative** and **incidental music** have influenced how music came to be created for film, in particular **silent movies**.

In *Sounds Good 1*, silent movies were mentioned as the earliest form of films, spanning from the early 1880s to the 1920s. Silent movies are exactly that – silent! Music was added to provide drama to the sequence of images, typically performed live by a pianist in the cinema.

Thomas Edison

The creation of silent films was the beginning of cinema as we know it today and began with a man called Thomas Edison. Edison, an American inventor, developed a device which could capture a sequence of images and the art of creating motion pictures had begun.

From the beginning, music was seen as central to the success of these movies. Musical **accompaniment** made an essential contribution not only to the story telling itself but also in setting the right atmosphere, giving the audience important emotional nudges as the film progressed. In Unit 2 we listened to the opening **motif** of Bach's Toccata and Fugue in D minor; this was a go-to melody with directors of silent movies who wanted to create a spooky atmosphere. Listen to it again.

Edison failed to patent his invention and, without copyright, other inventors were quick to 'borrow' his ideas!

Excerpt from Toccata and Fugue in D minor by J.S. Bach

Until the 1920s, there was no practical way of adding sound to movies. Directors could not synchronise dialogue or important **sound effects** with the film sequence. Some historical accounts suggest the music was also important for drowning out the very noisy projectors of that time and possibly noise from the audience too.

How does copyright law protect composers and musicians?

_____

_____

_____

A pianist, theatre organist or small orchestral **ensemble** performed live alongside the films. **Scores** were available, but often musicians had to **improvise**, frequently adding exciting flourishes during action shots. Some clues were given to the audience by the use of cards with written messages for viewers giving some information about the plot or the characters on screen. These are known as **intertitles** and were later replaced with a running commentary recorded by famous silent film actor Charlie Chaplin.

Synchronise: to make things happen at the same time.

Intertitles activity

Create and present a short sound clip, using instruments and/or other sounds to illustrate the text in the intertitles below.

THE SOLDIERS ARE COMING!

LATER THAT NIGHT

Matching music to scenes

Listen to these three short excerpts from the film and analyse the images below. Match the excerpts to the scene you think they feature in and discuss why you have chosen them. These images are stills taken from the scenes they feature in. You can watch these three scenes on YouTube.

The Factory Scene

Search online for 'YouTube – Charlie Chaplin – Factory Scene – Modern Times (1936)'

Dance Scene

Search online for 'YouTube – Charlie Chaplin Sings Nonsense Song (Titine) – Modern Times'

The Workers Protest

Search online for 'YouTube – Charlie Chaplin – Protest Scene – Modern Times (1936)'

Extract	Scene
1	
2	
3	

Choose one of the clips from *Modern Times* and analyse why you think this music was used to match this scene in the film.

_____

_____

_____

_____

_____

CBA Activity: Creating a silent film

> Organise yourselves into groups of three or four, depending on the size of your class. Together you are going to *create* your own **silent movie**. Using a school device, tablet or phone, film a short clip.

Try to capture an action shot like a busy corridor, a locker door opening and closing, students going up and down the stairs or use a time lapse that you can speed up for dramatic effect. You might decide to act something out as a group with one person filming it.

Once you have your short clip, examine it for opportunities for illustration using music. Work together to identify a suitable piece of music to match your clip or, better still, compose an original piece together in class and record it. If you want to add **sound effects** to a piece of music that already exists or your own composition, you can use GarageBand to add layers to your track.

Use iMovie or similar software to combine your clip with the music you have chosen.

If you enjoyed doing this activity you might consider adding it to your compositional portfolio. If you decide to do this, remember that it is important to include draft work relating to your composition. Your final draft can be presented in a visual, digital or audio format.

Once you have completed this project, *present* your work to your classmates and *explain* the creative thinking behind what you did and how you did it.

Compile evidence of your initial draft work; list ideas and music clips you considered.

_____

_____

_____

_____

Evaluating and reflecting

What software/apps did you use to complete this project? How did they assist your learning?

_____

_____

_____

Reflecting on your work is central to any CBA assignment. *Compose* a short evaluation and reflection for this task in the space below.

What did you learn from this creative project and what would you do differently next time?

_____
_____
_____
_____
_____
_____
_____

It is important to recognise how these types of compositions have had an impact on the music of today. We have already mentioned the importance of Beethoven's work as a Romantic composer earlier in this unit.

You may not have listened to much of Beethoven's music intentionally, but if you enjoy watching movies there is a good chance you have heard his music many times before: *Mission Impossible* uses his Symphony No. 3; *Dead Poets Society* and *The King's Speech* feature his Piano Concerto No. 5, and *Star Trek* and *Jurassic Park* movies share excerpts from his Piano Sonata No. 8.

The King's Speech

Investigate **illustrative music** which has been written by well-known composers and which has appeared in movies. List **two** examples below.

Composer	Piece	Movie
1		
2		

What stuck with you?

Evaluate your learning in this chapter. List what stuck with you and new key words.

Key Words
_____
_____
_____
_____

Rhapsody in Blue by George Gershwin

Sometimes it is better to listen focusing only on **one** element at a time before moving on to another one, especially when there is a lot happening in a piece of music. Analysing too much at once is very distracting.

Listen to George Gershwin's *Rhapsody in Blue*. It was composed by this American composer in 1924 for **solo piano** and jazz band. This piece is a **fusion** of classical and jazz features.

George Gershwin

Define the term 'fusion'. ~~musical styles are combined to make something new~~

Describe one other example of fusion. _____

As you listen to the segment of *Rhapsody in Blue* on your CD, try to focus on the music and avoid distractions around the room. This is a busy piece with interesting **themes** which are heard, developed and heard again and again. Each theme is heard played on the piano and in the orchestral section.

theme - melodic idea

Rhapsody in Blue by Gershwin

Track 37

> For the duration of the clip, keep your focus on two things:
>
> 1 identifying a **theme** and following the development of the theme. ~~five main themes~~
>
> 2 dynamic changes.

Rhapsody in Blue resembles a **concerto**. A concerto is a piece of music written for a solo instrument accompanied by an orchestra.
The performance we have just listened to is performed on

~~a piano.~~ _____, accompanied by ~~trumpets, timpani, violins, French horns, saxophones, glockenspiel~~

As you listened, I hope you noticed that there are many contrasts in the tempo, dynamics and even texture of the music.

Listen again and *comment* on these elements.

Tempo	energetic, Andante 97BPM
Dynamics	forte.
Texture	begins monophonic, moves to homophonic frequently changes

> Gershwin played the piano for the premier performance of this piece in New York in 1924, watched by important composers of our time Sergei Rachmaninoff and Igor Stravinsky. As a jazz musician, Gershwin was a master of **improvisation**, and his performance of this piece at the premiere was different to that of the written score, which wasn't transcribed until after the performance. Also, legend has it that on the band's score it tells them to 'wait for nod' to join in the performance rather than to start playing in a specific bar!

Did you count how many themes there were? They are contrasting, and, due to their repetition, they can be difficult to hear at first. Listen again, focusing only on the form and the presentation of each new motif or melody.

Graphic Score – Love + Conflict Themes.

UAE Symphone
March 2018 ✓
R+J by T
Listen for change @ 2:02

In the grid below, *illustrate* each **theme** you have identified using a coloured shape and *comment* on the features of this theme next to your visual representation.

Visual representation	Details of the theme
Beginning	

Creating a visual representation of a piece of music is a good way to *analyse* what is happening in the piece. Composers of **graphic scores** often use shapes or lines of varied thickness to represent themes or ideas instead of relying on standard notation.

 Listen to the excerpt again and use your whiteboard to help you identify how many times you hear each theme and whether there are any developments made to it. Is it longer or shorter? Are the dynamics louder or softer? Is it heard on another instrument?

Name a graphic score composer:

_____

Use the images or shapes you have drawn illustrating the themes in Gershwin's *Rhapsody in Blue* to create a visual representation of this excerpt. The entire piece is sixteen minutes long, but your visual representation need only cover the three-minute excerpt we have been listening to.

Decide whether you will use a **cell notation** or a **spiral score**. Look back to the activity in *Sounds Good 1* 'Creating your own graphic score' on page 122.

Insert your visual representation of the excerpt from George Gershwin's *Rhapsody in Blue* below.

Reflect and evaluate

Summarise your learning activity
Something interesting I learnt
Skills I developed whilst completing this task
Challenges I faced
How I overcame these
One thing I would do differently if I were to complete this task again

Glissando

The opening moments of this piece are iconic in twentieth-century music. The clarinet performs a really fun opening to this piece, known as a glissando.

Glissandos are a common feature in **jazz** and are typically notated on a score using a squiggly line between one note and the next.

Take a look at the sheet music below and listen again to follow the clarinet as it introduces itself with a trill and then sweeps up through the glissando that spans more than two octaves.

CD 1 Track 38 — Opening to *Rhapsody in Blue* by Gershwin

CD 1 Track 39 — Glissando

Glissando: a glissando is a performing technique where a musician glides from one pitch to another.

George Gershwin

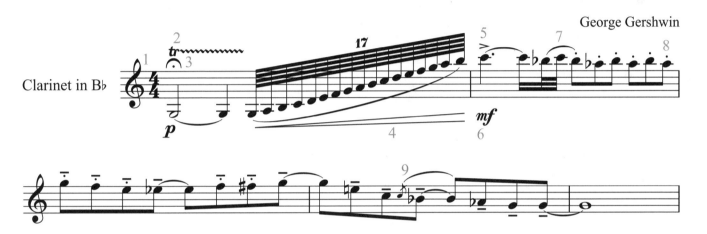

Clarinet in B♭

Important musical symbols have been marked on the opening bars of *Rhapsody in Blue* above. Work in pairs to match the number to the name of the symbol in the grid below and briefly explain what it means.

Symbol	Number	Definition
Time signature	1	
Crescendo	4	
Slur	7	
Pause mark	3	
Mezzo forte	6	
Acciaccatura		
Staccato marking	8	
Trill	2	
Accent		

Triplet

A triplet is a group of three notes played in the time of two notes of the same value.

A triplet's total duration is therefore the same as it would be for two notes of the value indicated.

Listen to the rhythm pattern below on your CD.

 Triplet rhythm pattern

Clap and tap activity

The motif below is from 'March of Wooden Soldiers' from *The Nutcracker Suite* by Tchaikovsky. In pairs, try clapping this pattern.

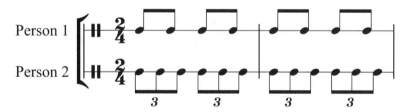

Work in pairs to clap this pattern. One person claps the quavers and the other claps the triplets. Listen to how they fit together. Can you hear the rhythm of the pharse 'Nice cup of tea' comming through?

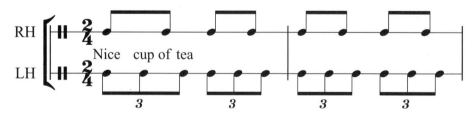

Now both try tapping the quavers with your right hand and the triplets with your left. Try saying the words 'Nice cup of tea' until you get the hang of it.

When you can do this easily, try stomping the quavers with your feet and clapping the triplets, fitting the three claps into every two stomps. It's harder than it looks!

The airline carrier American Airlines uses *Rhapsody in Blue* in their advertising campaigns. Comment on the how companies like American Airlines can do this in terms of copyright permission. Refer to the principles of music property rights.

_____

_____

_____

Writing a programme note

Write a programme note on Gershwin's *Rhapsody in Blue* or another of his famous pieces.

A brief introduction to the composer
The circumstances surrounding the composition, and why the composer chose to write this music
What was happening in the composer's country at the time of the composition
The voices or instruments involved
Interesting musical sign–posts to listen out for
Your favourite section of the piece, and why

What stuck with you?

Evaluate your learning in this chapter. List what stuck with you and new key words.

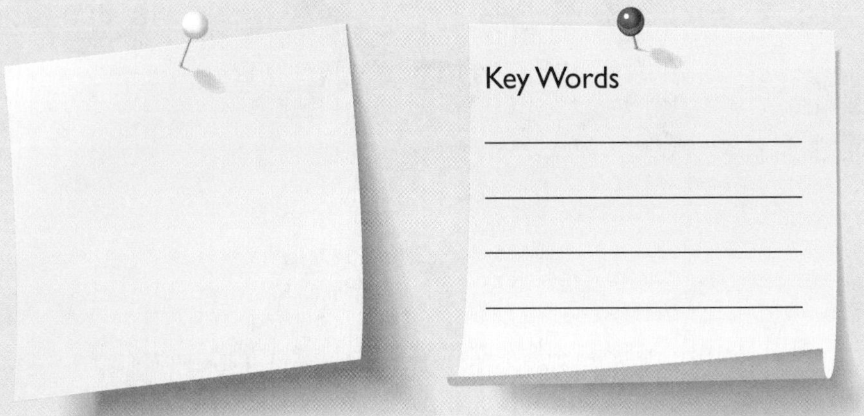

Key Words

_____

_____

_____

_____

Rhapsody in Blue is a **fusion** of jazz and classical music. What do you already know about the jazz genre?

In Unit 2, we were introduced to three very important elements of jazz music: **chromaticism**, **syncopation** and **improvisation**. Look back and remind yourself of these important elements.

Name two jazz composers/performers.

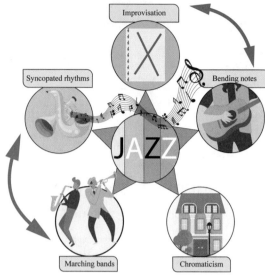

1
2

Jazz is a style of music which emerged in America around the beginning of the twentieth century. Jazz is easily recognisable for its use of improvisation, syncopation and swing rhythms. In fact, Louis Armstrong once said, 'If you have to ask what it is, you will never know!' Researching and gathering information are skills you developed whilst using *Sounds Good 1*. What can you find out about jazz?

 Using your whiteboard, write down any words or ideas about jazz that come to mind. Collate the information as a class group and, with your teacher's help, record the key ideas in the concept box below.

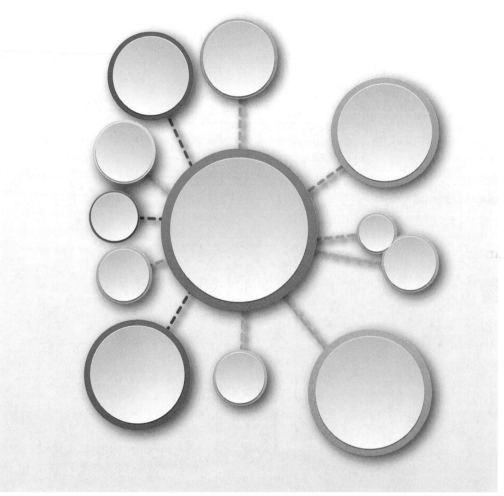

Researching Jazz

Research this genre and find out what you can about the roots of jazz.

What influenced performers of this time to develop this style of playing? Important performers to research include Scott Joplin, Louis Armstrong, Ella Fitzgerald and Miles Davis. Explore the instruments, musical features and elements central to this genre. The importance of improvisation, syncopation and blues notes are also important to mention.

Comment briefly on the **roots of jazz**.

Louis Armstrong

_____

_____

_____

_____

Key terms:
African music, fusion, blues, ragtime, syncopated rhythms, New Orleans, marching bands

Research the **instruments** connected with jazz. What instruments give this genre its unmistakable sound?

_____

_____

_____

_____

_____

Key terms:
virtuoso playing, improvisation, instruments, jazz orchestras

Syncopation is a defining rhythmic feature of jazz music. We explored syncopation in Unit 2. Explain syncopation in the space provided below, include an example of a bar of syncopated rhythm.

_____

_____

_____

_____

Compile a list of well-known jazz musicians and famous pieces of jazz music.

Listen to some musical examples of jazz pieces to identify the instruments and how the musicians play them. Miles Davis was a jazz trumpet player, composer and band leader. He was one of the most important figures on the American jazz scene. *Kind of Blue* is one of his most acclaimed albums, released in 1959.

Six musicians feature on this album:

◆ Miles Davis on trumpet

◆ Julian 'Cannonball' Adderley on alto saxophone

◆ John Coltrane on tenor saxophone

◆ Bill Evans on piano

◆ Paul Chambers on double bass

◆ Jimmy Cobb on drums

Listen to 'All Blues' from this album.

Miles Davis

'All Blues' by Miles Davis

This piece is based fully on **improvisation**. Explain this term.

There were very few rehearsals before the recording was made. Miles gave the other musicians an idea of the **scales** they would work with. The musicians had no sheet music in front of them during the recording. The sheet music was transcribed later using the recording.

The time signature is 6/4. Using your knowledge of metres compose a rhythm pattern in 6/4.

The players memorised a twelve-bar **chord progression**, and each soloist took their turn to improvise over this progression of chords. The twelve-bar chord progression is called a **chorus** and it is repeated many times. Each chorus is introduced by a **riff** on solo instruments.

Explain the term **riff**.

_____

The piece opens with an **intro** and ends with an **outro**. The intro is heard on piano, bass and drums and is followed by the first riff played by the saxophones.

Choose another well-known jazz piece and compile some details about the performance with some background information on the composer or performer.

Apply your new knowledge by writing an article entitled 'What's the Jazz?' for your school website. *Transcribe* your final draft of this article into the space below.

'What's the Jazz?'

Test your knowledge!

1 Which American City is recognised as the birth place of jazz?

   a New York

   b New Orleans

   c Chicago

2 Jazz is a fusion of different **genres**, *explain* what this means.

_____

_____

Ella Fitzgerald

3 *Explain* the term **improvisation**.

_____

_____

4 *Identify* a **rhythmic feature** of jazz.

_____

5 Miles Davis plays

   a alto saxophone   b trumpet   c bass

6 Explain the term **riff**.

_____

_____

7 List two female jazz musicians.

   a) _____

   b) _____

8 Name a jazz piece for piano.

_____

9 Name an Irish jazz composer.

_____

10 What **genres** have been influenced by jazz?

_____

_____

Irish jazz composers

Described as the Godfather of the Irish contemporary jazz scene, Ronan Guilfoyle is one of Ireland's greatest composers, jazz musicians and educators. Guilfoyle began playing bass guitar at a young age and soon became a master of creativity and imagination. He has composed works for symphony orchestra, toured the globe as a musician, recorded over fifty albums and founded Ireland's first non-classical performance degree. He is currently director of Dublin City University's BA in Jazz and Contemporary Performance degree.

Ronan Guilfoyle

In January 2012, the RTÉ National Symphony Orchestra performed Guilfoyle's work *Hands*, a **concerto** for electric guitar and orchestra for the first time, with Rick Peckham as soloist. It is a three-movement work with an improvised **cadenza** section.

Define the term 'concerto'. _____

Define the term 'cadenza'. _____

Explain the term 'improvisation'. _____

A six-day documentary style video diary detailing the compositional process for this piece is worth watching! Search online for 'YouTube – Composition Diary 1 Concerto for Electric Guitar and Orchestra' and look for Days 1 to 6 to watch each part in sequence. This series of videos provides a real window into the creative life of composers and the musicians and conductors that work on these projects.

In March 2018, Guilfoyle released his latest work called 'Life Cycle Suite' and brought together an ensemble of jazz musicians to perform it. Each performance of this work is unique. Sections of the work are composed and sections are **improvised** leaving opportunity for 'chance'. The work reflects the reality of everyday life and our need to improvise as we navigate the spontaneous events which occur from day to day. Ronan reminds us of an important fact of life in this work: we cannot control everything that happens to us.

"My, and our life cycle is a combination of planned and unplanned events, with many surprises along the way – this piece will reflect that aspect of all our life cycles," Ronan Guilfoyle

Reflect on this idea and discuss the importance of being able to improvise and navigate the surprises we face during our lives. What skills help us to do this and how can developing these skills contribute to our sense of wellbeing?

_____

_____

_____

_____

Jazz festivals

Jazz music is a genre that is still going strong, and there are jazz musicians throughout Ireland making and creating jazz music. One place we can go to find these talented musicians is the Cork Jazz Festival, held each October Bank Holiday weekend since 1978. The festival was set up by hotelier Jim Mountjoy, who originally hoped it would fill his hotel rooms for the night!

Jazz greats Ella Fitzgerald and Dave Brubeck have come to Cork for the festival. Research an Irish jazz composer and musician. Write a short note on him/her below, including details of their compositions.

Cork Jazz Festival

List two other international jazz festivals.

1 _____

2 _____

Collaborate with your fellow students to produce a playlist and a set of recordings to accompany a local jazz festival being held in your community this summer.

Song title	Reason for choosing this song
1	
2	
3	
4	
5	

We mentioned Louis Armstrong earlier. You may have found out about him in your jazz research. Listen to him singing 'I've Got a Heart Full of Rhythm'.

'I've Got a Heart Full of Rhythm' by Louis Armstrong

There is lots of wisdom in the **lyrics** of this song. Pick one statement or sentence which stands out to you and write it in the space provided below. Compose a rhythmic pattern to match the lyrics and write it on the rhythm line below. Remember to align the lyrics underneath.

Lyrics:

_____

_____

‖——————————————————————————————‖

Complete the jazz keyword grid below by giving a definition for each term.

Riff	
Chord progression	
Chorus	
Improvisation	
Syncopation	
Soloist	
Ragtime	

What stuck with you?

Evaluate your learning in this chapter. List what stuck with you and new key words.

Key Words

_____
_____
_____
_____
_____

Listening Project

Across our learning in *Sounds Good 1* and the units covered so far in this book, we have looked at several historical and contemporary periods along with various music styles and genres. Choose one of these and make a study of this period or genre, *analysing* its structures and use of musical devices, and *describe* the influence of other styles on it.

Use the mind map below to think about your project.

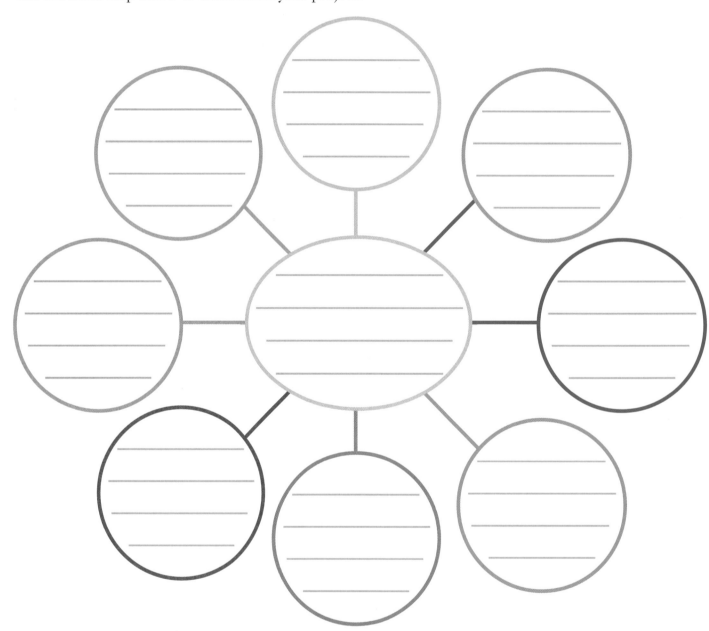

A page has been provided for you to insert a written summary of your study. As you work on your project, try to summarise and compile other important information in the grid provided on page 97. Include the name of artists and pieces of music to listen to.

 Present your project to your classmates. Use Google Slides or PowerPoint to present your information. Imbed video or music clips in your slides and allow your audience to experience the music you have chosen to discuss with them.

Reflection and evaluation

Other genres I considered	Opportunities to work with others
_____ _____ _____	_____ _____ _____
Key skills I relied on	Ways I researched and gathered information
_____ _____ _____	_____ _____
Pieces of music I listened to	Apps and software used
_____ _____ _____	_____ _____ _____
Helpful websites I used	Reflecting on and evaluating my learning
_____ _____ _____	_____ _____ _____

Listening Exercises

Each excerpt will be played three times for you. Listen carefully and answer the questions below.

 Excerpt 1

1 *Identify* the instrument which plays the melody.

_____

2 *Describe* the accompaniment.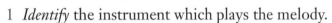

_____

3 The melody in this excerpt features

   a   step-wise movement   b   leaps   c   broken chords

4 *Identify* one other feature of the melody line.

_____

5 *Explain* the term **trill**.

_____

6 The **style** of the music played is

    a   Renaissance   b   Romantic   c   Jazz

7 Justify your answer.

_____

_____

8 The **texture** of the music you hear is

    a   polyphonic   b   homophonic   c   monophonic

9 *Justify* your answer.

_____

_____

10 Name the era which followed this one.

_____

Excerpt 2 (CD 2 Track 5)

1 What family of instruments plays the opening fanfare?

_____

2 *Explain* the term **fanfare**. _____

3 *Describe* the accompaniment. _____

_____

4 The music is played

    a   pizzicato   b   with accents   c   legato

5 *Describe* the dynamics. _____

_____

6 *Distinguish* **two** ways in which the music heard in the later section contrasts with the music heard in the opening section.

    a) _____

    b) _____

7 *Suggest* a scenario or occasion where this music may be heard.

_____

Excerpt 3

1 *Identify* the brass instrument which plays the main **melody**:

   a   flute   b   trombone   c   saxophone

2 *Identify* the style of music heard in this excerpt.

   _____

3 List two features of this **genre**.

   a) _____

   b) _____

4 *Describe* two features of the soloist's performance.

   a) _____

   b) _____

5 *Identify* and *briefly describe* the **texture** of this piece.

   _____

   _____

6 *Explain* the term **glissando**.

   _____

7 *Explain* the term **improvisation**.

   _____

8 *Describe* the music heard at the end of this excerpt.

   _____

   _____

What stuck with you?

Evaluate your learning in this chapter. List what stuck with you and new key words.

Key Words

_____

_____

_____

_____

Reflection and Evaluation Sheet

Unit title:

Learning Outcomes (LOs) I worked with:
e.g. 1.2, 3.4, etc.

Music I listened to:

_____

_____

Learning and exploring

I really enjoyed…

_____

Something interesting I learnt…

_____

My biggest challenge was…

_____

I overcame this by…

_____

One improvement I have made is…

_____

Traffic-light your learning

Learning Outcomes	😞	😐	🙂	✓
1.11				
1.14				
2.3				
2.7				
3.1				
3.2				
3.3				
3.6				
3.10				

Learning

Key words	Action verbs
_____	_____
_____	_____

Key skills

_____

I got better at x skill by _____

_____

This unit reminded me of learning about… _____

_____

What still puzzles me is…

_____

_____

Feedback and goal setting…

_____

_____

_____

Rate your learning

Ensemble Lab

In this unit

Unit 4 provides us with an opportunity to explore a broad range of musical ensembles and performance styles. Through this study of ensembles you will build on your knowledge of the orchestra from Sounds Good 1. Unit 4 explores more instruments including those that perform from the bass clef. You can explore vocal music through opera, art songs and the work of Irish songwriters. The new knowledge in this unit aims to inspire your creativity and offer you opportunities to communicate your creative ideas with others.

Checklist	LO	Intended learning
☐	1.7	Perform music at sight through playing, singing or clapping melodic and rhythmic phrases.
☐	1.8	**Rehearse** and perform pieces of music that use common structural devices and textures.
☐	1.9	**Demonstrate** an understanding of a range of metres and pulses through the use of body percussion or other means of movement.
☐	1.13	**Compare** different interpretations or arrangements of a piece of Irish traditional or folk music, paying attention to musical elements and other influences.
☐	1.14	**Compare** pieces of music that are similar in period and style by different composers from different countries.
☐	2.4	**Rehearse** and **present** a song or brief instrumental piece; **identify** and **discuss** the performance skills and techniques that were necessary to **interpret** the music effectively.
☐	2.5	Prepare and **rehearse** a musical work for an ensemble focusing on co-operation and listening for balance and intonation; **refine** the interpretation by considering elements such as clarity, fluency, musical effect and style.
☐	2.9	**Distinguish** between the sonorities, ranges and timbres of selections of instruments and voices; **identify** how these sounds are produced and **propose** their strengths and limitations in performance.
☐	3.2	**Examine** and **interpret** the impact of music on the depiction of characters, their relationships and their emotions, as explored in instrumental music of different genres.
☐	3.3	Make a study of a particular contemporary or historical musical style; **analyse** its structures and use of musical devices, and **describe** the influence of other styles on it.
☐	3.7	**Compare** compositions by two or more Irish composers or songwriters; use listening, background reading, and scores (where appropriate) to **explain** and **describe** differences and similarities in the compositions.
☐	3.10	**Discuss** the principles of music property rights and **explain** how this can impact on the sharing and publishing of music.
☐	3.11	**Explore** the time allocated to Irish artists and performers on a variety of local or national Irish media and **present** these findings to the class.

In Units 4 and 6 of *Sounds Good 1* we explored many new musical concepts through movement, sound and symbol. The learning experiences in these units provided you with an opportunity to develop your musical knowledge and skills but also to gain some awareness of our own musical heritage.

In Unit 4 we became musical **conductors** and learned about the instruments of the orchestra. Through listening to and appraising pieces of music, we gained an understanding of the complexities of composing and **ensemble** performing. We had fun creating our own creative compositions using **graphic scores** to communicate our creative ideas with others.

In Unit 6 we focused on the indigenous music of Ireland. We reflected on music as part of our own unique cultural identity and realised its importance as a source of knowledge which can help us to appreciate our own history. We demonstrated our understanding of the **musical elements** and instruments associated with the Irish tradition by rehearsing and performing together. In this unit we will revisit and build on what we learned in Units 4 and 6 of *Sounds Good 1*.

In Unit 3 we listened to many different performances. Each of these pieces of music was performed by a unique combination of instruments, decided by the composer during the creative process. Groupings of musicians which come together in various formats and styles are known as **ensembles**.

The more common combinations have their own distinct names, such as

◆ **wind trios**

◆ **string quartets** or

◆ **concert bands**.

Some ensembles are made up of groups of instruments. These include

◆ **Baroque recorder consorts**

◆ **jazz quartets** and

◆ **orchestras**.

String quartet

Choir

Irish artist Hozier

Orchestra

Others are solely for vocalists like **choirs** or **barbershop quartets**. Of course there are many types of ensemble which contain instrumentalists and vocalists, such as **chamber choirs, opera companies** and **rock bands**. The part of the world in which a piece of music has been composed can influence the type of **ensemble** the composer may choose to write for.

In Western culture, musical ensembles have looked and sounded different over time because of the different instruments and techniques that were favoured by composers in each of music's historical periods. Can you name the musical periods we have explored? Beginning with the Renaissance, complete the timeline below. Include the dates associated with each period. Name two composers from each era who were born in different countries.

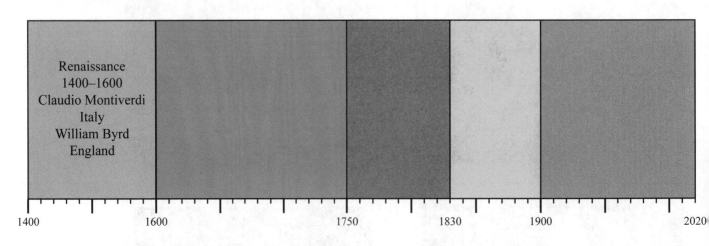

The Renaissance

The **Renaissance period** followed the Medieval period, and historians typically date its beginnings to around 1400. *Explore* the Arts during the Renaissance era and write a short note on the features which defined it.

Instruments played in Renaissance music

The invention of the printing press in 1439 had a significant impact on the music of this time. Music **scores** no longer had to be written or copied by hand, meaning **musicians** could access more music. Instruments were evolving and new additions like the bassoon and the trombone added to the sound and size of the Renaissance ensemble.

Renaissance composers often composed using **polyphony**.

Research and *define* the following popular **forms** favoured by Renaissance composers.

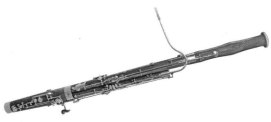

In Europe, the printing press was developed by Johannes Gutenberg in about 1440. Its invention allowed information to be distributed relatively easily, paving the way for not only the Renaissance but also the Reformation, the Enlightenment and the Industrial Revolution.

The Renaissance was a period of exploration. Can you name an important explorer from this era?

Renaissance forms	Brief definition
Madrigal	unaccompanied song for several voices
Rondeau	4 stanza sung poem in AB form
Ballade	narrative heroic poem → instrumental piece
German lied	setting poetry to classical music - polyphonic

Recorder consorts

In the Renaissance period, the phrase 'a consort of instruments' meant an instrumental ensemble. In *Sounds Good 1* we learned that the descant recorder is part of a family of recorders. All five members of the recorder family played together in a **consort**. Music composed for recorder consorts was elaborate, technically difficult and nearly always polyphonic.

Identify and *illustrate* the range of your descant recorder on the stave.

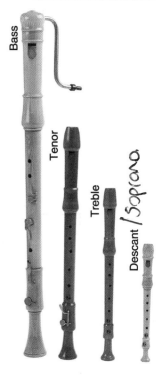

Bass

Tenor

Treble

Descant / Soprano

Explain the term **range**. distance from highest to lowest note

We performed **polyphonic** recorder pieces in *Sounds Good 1*. Look back at Unit 8 page 191 and rehearse and perform 'Summer is icumen in' as a **round**.

Identify and *discuss* the performance skills and techniques that are necessary for ensemble playing. How do these skills ensure we interpret the music as the composer intended? *Report* back to your classmates and make a note on what you have discussed in the space below.

Ensemble playing	'Summer is icumen in'
Performance skills	
Performing techniques	

Texture

When we sing or perform a **round** or **canon** the texture of our performance is <u>polyphonic</u>.

Briefly explain this term and draw a visual representation of it in the space provided below.

Definition	Visual representation

Identify and *define* two other **textures** we have learnt about.

1 monophonic
2 homophonic

Tallis's Canon

English composer Thomas Tallis was born in 1505 and is celebrated as one of England's greatest early composers of **sacred** and **secular music**. An organist and composer for the British monarchy in the Chapel Royal, he composed and performed for Henry VIII, Queen Mary and Queen Elizabeth I. In 1567, Tallis composed nine **psalm** chants in four parts for the Archbishop of Canterbury, one of which was a setting of **Psalm 67** which became known as Tallis's Canon.

Rehearse and *perform* the short tune below on recorder.

Sacred music: religious music composed or performed for religious celebrations

Secular music: non-religious music

A psalm: a sacred hymn or song of praise usually from the Book of Psalms in the Bible

The melody of Tallis's Canon on organ

Thomas Tallis

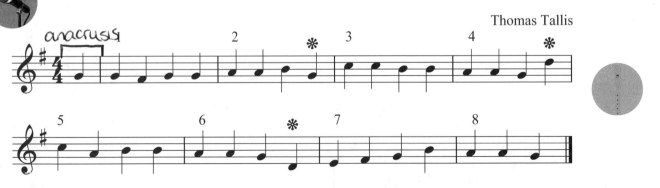

Tallis had not intended for his piece to be performed in **unison**, instead he used the **compositional technique** known as **canon** to create a polyphonic texture.

On the stave below create a score to illustrate this melody as a four-part canon. The distance between parts is eight crotchet beats, or two bars. The opening phrase is inserted for you below.

An anacrusis (also known as an upbeat) is a note (or series of notes) that occurs before the first beat (or downbeat) of a bar in a piece of music. The anacrusis leads into the next bar and is 'unstressed'. If you sing the first words of 'Happy Birthday' you will notice you emphasise 'birthday'. This is because the word 'Happy' occurs on an anacrusis leading into the stressed word 'birthday' which begins on the first beat of the next bar.

Rehearse and *perform* this **four-part canon** as a class on recorder. Focus on **listening** and **cooperating** with each other.

Large ensembles need a leader, known as a _____. One student should direct the ensemble to help communicate the points at which each group begins their part, which has been marked with a ❋ on the score.

Suggest reasons why listening and cooperation are important for ensemble performance.

In 1709, Thomas Ravenscroft added **text** to Tallis's Canon. Ravenscroft added an adaptation of English cleric Thomas Ken's **hymn** 'All praise to thee, my God, this night'.

This **arrangement** of Tallis's Canon and Ken's lyrics was heard regularly in English church services.

Hymn: a religious song of adoration

 Work in pairs to set the lyrics below to Tallis's melody. Identify the syllables in each of the words and carefully align them with the relevant notes. Use your whiteboard to draft your work.

Lyrics:

Glory to Thee my God this night, for all the blessings of the light.

Keep me, O keep me, King of Kings, beneath thine own almighty wings.

Thomas Tallis

This hymn is easy to learn due to its simple rhythmic pattern. Usually sung in four parts, you could challenge your vocal ensemble to singing it in eight! This will test your performance skills of listening, cooperating and communicating, and develop your ability to listen carefully to each other. You will hear how polyphony was used by the early composers to create beautiful harmonies.

Hava Nashira in Unit 7 of *Sounds Good 1* (page 160) is another **round** you could perform together. Standing in a circle formation whilst you perform will help you to listen and communicate with each other whilst you sing.

When we perform as part of an ensemble, rehearsing and cooperating is very important. Record your performance of Tallis's Canon and listen back. Work together to give feedback on how it sounds. Identify elements of the performance that you could refine. Record your considerations below.

To **arrange** a piece of music means to adapt or change it to make it suitable for performance on different instruments or voices.

Feedback!

What went well: _____

_____

Ways in which we could improve: _____

_____

_____

Early Baroque composers were influenced by the Renaissance composers. Bach and Handel included recorders in their orchestral scores, and composers like Henry Purcell composed **sonatas** for recorder. Polyphony was also here to stay, with many of the Baroque composers frequently choosing to compose music in this texture.

Sonata: a multi-movement instrumental work for soloists or ensemble

In *Sounds Good 1* we listened to John Cage's Piano **Sonata** No. 6 for **prepared piano**.

Explain what is meant by the term 'prepared piano'.

_____

_____

_____

To which musical period does Cage's work belong?_____

Explain the term **sonata**: _____

_____

John Cage

Make a study of Renaissance music;

Analyse its structures and use of musical devices and *describe* the influence other styles had on it.

Include information on composers, instruments and forms popular in this period and mention some Renaissance music you have listened to. Provide a short summary of your study below.

_____

_____

_____

_____

_____

What stuck with you?

Evaluate your learning in this chapter. List what stuck with you and new key words.

Key Words

_____

_____

_____

The Trio Sonata

The **trio sonata** is a genre in its own right. This form of **chamber music** emerged during the seventeenth century and proved very popular with the composers of the time. A trio sonata is a multi-movement instrumental work for three parts. It's important to note that a trio is written for **three parts** and not necessarily just three instruments. This is because the accompanying part (called the **continuo**) consisted of a harmonic accompaniment usually played on a **keyboard instrument** and a **bass line** that was often performed by cello or bassoon. In the Baroque period, the keyboard instruments were organ or harpsichord.

 Listen to the second movement of Johann Joachim Quantz's Trio Sonata for Recorder in C major – Alla Breve.

The sheet music is on pages 112–115 and has been composed for flauto dolce, flauto traverso and **basso continuo**. Do you recognise these instruments? Research these terms with your teacher and write a short note on basso continuo and figured bass in the grid below.

> **Chamber music**: music composed and performed by small groupings of musicians in a small space

Baroque instrument	Description
Basso continuo	
Figured bass	

> Basso continuo means continuous bass; the music provides a continuous flow of notes.

Quantz 1697–1773

German composer Johann Joachim Quantz was a master flautist. Quantz began teaching flute to Frederick the Great in 1728 and went to live with him in Berlin after he became King of Prussia, in 1740. It was here as a teacher, composer and flute master that Quantz remained for the rest of his life.

As well as composing hundreds of **concertos** and **sonatas** for flute he wrote a book called 'On Playing the Flute'. This was a valuable resource for musicians, filled with information and guidance on performing techniques.

CD 2 Track 8
Trio Sonata for recorder in C major II Alla Breve by J.J. Quantz

Turn over to listen to a Quantz sonata and follow the music of the stave.

Trio Sonata for recorder in C major II Alla Breve by J.J. Quantz

Trio Sonata in C Major

J.J. Quantz

No.	Name
1	
2	
3	
4	
5	
6	
7	
8	
9	
10	

Score Scavenger Hunt A

Score Scavenger Hunt B

Indicate another example of symbols 1–10 identified on page 112. Circle and number each symbol on pages 113–115.

1   Identify the instrument which plays the **melody** in bars 1–10. _____

2   Describe the change in instrumentation from bar 10 onwards and describe the

    music played. _____

3   Describe the **texture** of this piece. _____

4   Comment on what is happening in bars 37–43 (marked W on the score).

    _____

5   Explain the numbers found underneath the score.

    _____

6   Name and explain the symbols found in bars

    a) 61 marked X on the score _____

    b) 74 marked Y on the score _____

    c) 82 marked Z on the score _____

> **Figured bass**: numbers under the bass line were a form of shorthand in the seventeenth and eighteenth centuries, designed to indicate the chords a musician should play and at which interval you build up from the given note in the bass line.

7   List two melodic features of the continuo part heard in

    bars 85–88. _____

8   Describe one change in the music in bars 96–107. _____

9   Explain the term 'trill' and insert on the score the final trill heard on the CD.

    _____

    _____

10 Name and explain the symbol used above the music in the final bar.

    _____

    _____

The **basso continuo** is an interesting part which was commonly used by Baroque composers in their compositions. It has a specific role in providing a **bass line** and **harmony** for compositions. The term itself means 'continuous bass', and it was typically played by two instruments, a keyboard instrument and a low-pitched melody instrument such as a cello or bassoon.

Copy the opening four-bar section of Quantz's basso continuo line onto the stave below. Identify two melodic features of this melody.

In Unit 3 we explored jazz ensembles. We listened to *Rhapsody in Blue* to identify how the soloists **improvised** over the **chord progressions**. Explain the term improvisation.

_____

Jazz musicians were not the first to appreciate the creativity and freedom of improvisation. Baroque musicians were free to improvise over melodies too. In order to read a basso continuo line from which musicians improvised, we must first learn about the **bass clef**.

The Bass Clef

The low-pitched instrument and the keyboard instrument which perform the basso continuo parts read from the bass clef. Bass-clef instruments include cello, double bass, bassoon, trombone, tuba, bass guitar, timpani and instruments which read from the grand stave (harp and keyboard instruments).

The grand stave looks like this.

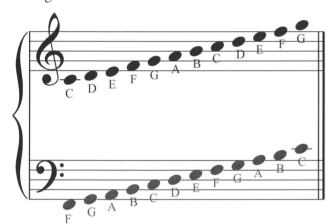

In *Sounds Good 1* Unit 4 we learned about the earliest forms of notation and the efforts of Guido of Arezzo.

Clefs are placed onto the stave to indicate pitches. In fact, the treble and bass clefs are actually based on the letters G and F. The treble clef is also known as the G clef because it is written on the G line.

This is an image of the G clef illustrating how it evolved over time.

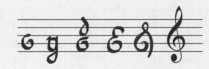

 The **bass clef** was no different. It is used to indicate pitches on a stave for lower-pitched instruments and is placed on the F line. When placed on the stave, this clef indicates where F is, the two dots sit above and below the F line. As with the treble clef, each line or space has its own name.

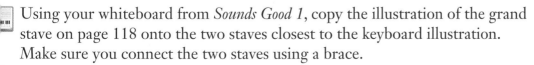 Using your whiteboard from *Sounds Good 1*, copy the illustration of the grand stave on page 118 onto the two staves closest to the keyboard illustration. Make sure you connect the two staves using a brace.

Grand stave

The image of the piano keyboard indicates what notes are played on the bass stave which are typically played by the left hand and the notes of the treble clef typically played by the right hand.

Listen to your CD and follow the notes of the piano and the grand stave to see where the parts separate from left hand to right hand, but also from bass clef to treble clef.

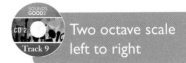

Two octave scale left to right

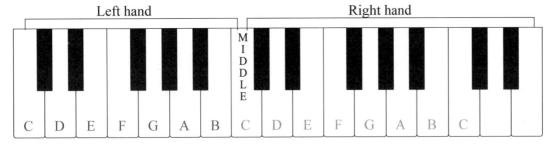

Label the keyboard on your whiteboard in the same way, under the grand stave of pitches you completed earlier. Use one colour to identify the bass-clef pitches and another colour for the treble-clef pitches.

Practise drawing the bass (F) clef below.

Using your whiteboard information as a guide, insert the scale of C major two octaves ascending on the **bass line** below. Start by writing the bass clef.

Do you remember the mnemonic that we used to remember the notes of the treble-clef pitches? Write it in the grid below and work together as a class to create a suitable mnemonic for the bass-clef pitches.

Treble clef	Bass clef
Lines: E G B D F	Lines: G B D F A
Spaces: F A C E	Spaces: A C E G
Mnemonic:	Mnemonic:

Use your mnemonic to help you identify the following bass-clef pitches.

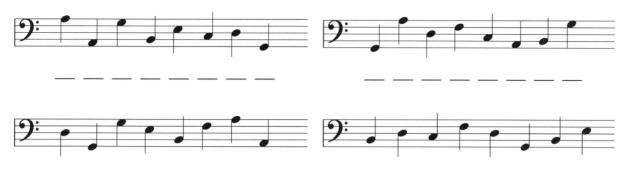

Using the letter names for notation, indicate five words which can be spelt using only these letters. Enter the pitches which spell these words on the staves below.

Example

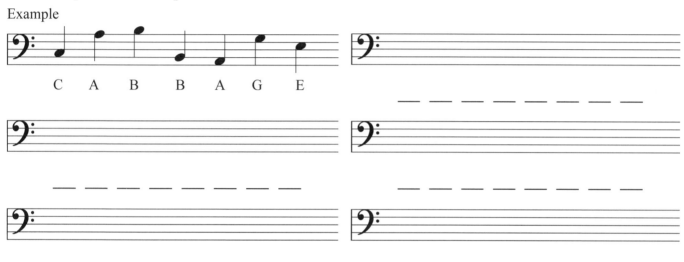

C   A   B   B   A   G   E

The bass and treble staves are separated by a **ledger line** used to pitch middle C. Ledger lines are used to extend single staves where an instrument's range stretches beyond the five lines and four spaces.

Identify the following pitches found on ledger lines

'Star Spangled Banner'

The 'Star Spangled Banner' is the American national anthem. The lyrics are from a poem written by Francis Scott Key, inspired by the fifteen stars and stripes of the American flag. The words were later set to the tune of 'To Anacreon in Heaven', a well-known British song composed by John Stafford Smith.

This is a difficult song to perform with a **wide range**. It became the official anthem on 3 March 1931.

Beyoncé performed this song at the official inauguration of President Obama in 2013 accompanied by the USA Marine Band. Composer John Williams wrote a new arrangement of the US anthem to be performed on the 200th anniversary of the **song**. Watch the performance by searching 'YouTube – John Williams – National Anthem'.

The tune for 'Star Spangled Banner' has been arranged for trombone on the stave below. Identify the pitches on the space provided.

melody: John Stafford Smith

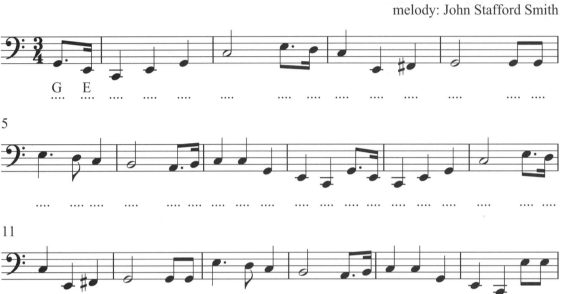

G E

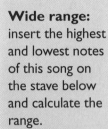

Wide range: insert the highest and lowest notes of this song on the stave below and calculate the range.

range:

Earlier in this unit, the term 'arrangement' was explained. Give a brief definition of the term.

The **double bass** is an interesting string instrument. Listen to 'The Elephant', from Camille Saint-Saëns's *Carnival of the Animals*. Discuss reasons why this instrument was a suitable choice for this movement. Comment on how the composer has illustrated images of the elephant for the listener. Search 'YouTube Carnival of the Animals-Elephants' to watch a performance of this piece.

'The Elephant' from *Carnival of the Animals* by Saint-Saëns

Transposition

Some composers use **transposition** when arranging a piece of music for an instrument which reads from a different clef to the instrument the original part was written for. For example, if a composer is arranging a violin piece for performance on the cello, the violin melody needs to be transposed from the treble clef to the bass clef in order for the cellist to play it.

Transposition means 'move to another space'. In music, this **compositional technique** is used to move a collection of notes up or down a certain distance or to rewrite the notes in a new key. The distance between the notes does not change. Transposing is a useful skill to develop as it allows you to lower the pitch of a song that is too high to sing or to take a melody written for one instrument and rewrite it to suit another.

Here is an example of a short melody in the treble clef which has been transposed **down an octave** so it is written in the bass clef.

Treble-clef melody	Transposed to bass clef

An **octave** is eight notes. Look at your whiteboard keyboard to see that from middle C to high C is an octave leap of eight notes.

High C   Middle C

If we need to transpose on to the bass clef, it will look a little different. The pitch will still be middle C, but it will be notated on the bass clef. Look at the example shown for you.

Middle C   Middle C

Transposition is a tricky but important **compositional skill** for composers and arrangers who write for large ensembles.

Transposing melodies

It is important you are clear on the **direction** and the **distance** you are transposing to prevent confusion. Remember when transposing an octave distance the note *names* stay the same, but you are working with them on the bass lines and spaces.

Transpose the well-known melody given below on the treble clef **down one octave for bass clef,** so it can be played by trombone, an instrument which reads from the bass clef.

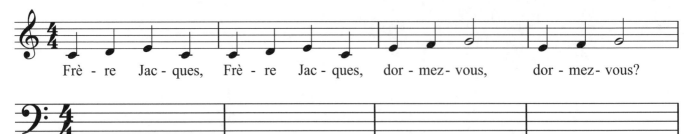

Frè - re   Jac - ques,   Frè - re   Jac - ques,   dor - mez - vous,   dor - mez - vous?

Transcribe the scale of C major descending on the bass stave below and label your scale using tonic solfa.

Using your scale as a guide, write the rhythm pattern of this first phrase of 'Frère Jacques', below and indicate the pitch using solfa.

doh

Baroque ensembles

Trio ensembles were common in the Baroque period, but there are other chamber ensemble groupings. A **soloist** cannot be considered an ensemble. Duets, trios and brass and string quartets are common forms of ensemble. **Chamber ensembles** used smaller groupings of instrumentalists. Research and record a brief description of these chamber ensembles.

Ensemble	Description
Duet	
Trio	
Quartet	
Quintet	
Sextet	
Septet	
Octet	
Nonet	
Dectet	

Camille Saint-Saëns's *Carnival of the Animals* used eleven instruments and was referred to as a 'hendectet'.

String ensembles

In *Sounds Good 1* we explored the use of the harpsichord in Baroque music. Strings were also a defining feature of Baroque ensembles and often represented the largest proportion of instruments in ensemble groupings. Can you name the four instruments in the string family in order of pitch, highest to lowest?

Highest Pitch   **String section**   Lowest Pitch

The string section covers a very wide **range** of pitch. This, and the fact that they are capable of producing so many sound colours or **timbres**, has made them popular with composers across most periods.

Examine the piano keyboard below. It indicates the range of the four string instruments; violin, viola, cello and double bass. Identify the range of the violin and the double bass and indicate it on the staves below.

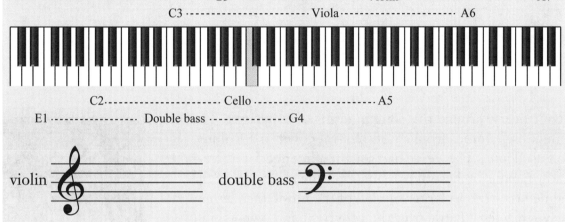

String instruments are versatile and can play in various interesting ways. Composers often indicate on the score for string players to use a particular **performance technique** whilst playing. We learnt about these in *Sounds Good 1*. Research and briefly explain the techniques associated with stringed instruments listed below.

Performance technique	Definition
Pizzicato	
Arco	
Tremolo	
Senza vibrato	
Col legno	

Present your work to your class using images, actions and musical examples to support your work.

Which string instrument reads from the bass clef? _____

Name an ensemble which features string instruments. _____

Where on stage would I find the string section within the orchestra? _____

Choose one other family of instruments from the orchestra and complete a detailed profile of the instruments which belong to this section. Propose the strengths and limitations of these instruments. Give details of their **range** and the common performing techniques used.

123

Search 'YouTube – The Verve – Bittersweet Symphony' (Extended Version) and answer the following questions.

1 This song is written in 4/4. Identify the number of bars heard before Violin 1 enters.

   _____

2 Identify two instruments that join in before vocals enter. _____

3 This four-bar motif continues to repeat. How many times do we hear it before vocals enter. _____

4 Describe the texture of the music. _____

5 The opening four-bar motif remains throughout the song. Therefore it can be

   identified as an _____.

> Use your 4/4 conducting pattern to help you with questions 1 and 2.

There was much controversy around this song in terms of **copyright**. The string accompaniment uses a motif from an **orchestral cover** of a Rolling Stones song, 'The Last Time'. The Verve had sought a **licence** for a five-note **sample** for their now famous orchestral riff, but, after the managers of the Rolling Stones claimed they used a larger section of the music than agreed, they found themselves in a legal battle over the copyright and ownership of the song itself.

Following an out-of-court settlement The Verve no longer own the rights to the music, and Rolling Stones members Mick Jagger and Keith Richards were added to the song-writing credits alongside the lead singer of The Verve, Richard Ashcroft. For more detailed information on this, search online for 'Did The Verve Steal Bitter Sweet Symphony – YouTube'.

Richard Ashcroft of The Verve

Despite the copyright mess they found themselves in, The Verve had released a massive hit. The music video recorded for this song was equally famous. The documentary-type filming shows Ashcroft walking through London streets seemingly oblivious to the work around him. He doesn't change his stride or direction until he walks in front of a car. Watch this music video and consider the message within this song. *Transcribe* some of the lyrics which resonate with you and explain why in the space below.

> **Pop Orchestras**: a pop orchestra performs classical covers of popular music or show tunes from musicals or film. They have grown in popularity in recent years.

> **Sample**: in music, sampling means to take a short clip from another piece of music and to use it as the basis or part of a new piece of music.

Stop press!

In 2019, Mick Jagger and Keith Richards returned all rights to this song to The Verve lead singer Richard Ashcroft, meaning all future royalties from this song will go to him.

Research and identify two other examples of popular music which have used string ensembles in their recordings. Give details of the performance below.

Song:	Performance
Composer/Performers:	
Genre:	
Song:	**Performance**
Composer/Performers:	
Genre:	

Baroque composers Bach and Handel often composed for dances, and these works became known as **suites**. A suite is a group of short dances. Bach has written many pieces for the string section, We often hear the violin and viola easily when listening to pieces of music but fail to notice the cello and double bass. Would you agree?

To help you develop your awareness of the tone and timbre of the cello, listen to music from Bach's Cello Suite No. 1 in G major – Gigue (see page 126).

Bach's cello suites were composed for **unaccompanied** cello and are possibly the best-known pieces of music composed for solo cello. It is hard to believe there is only one cello playing, don't you think? The melody almost sounds polyphonic.

Each movement of the work is based on a popular Baroque dance. Baroque suites include dances like allemandes, courantes, sarabandes, gavottes, minuets, bourrées and gigues. We have just listened to the sixth movement of one of the cello suites, which is a **gigue**. A gigue is a lively Baroque dance with a fast tempo and is usually written in the time signature 6/8. It developed in England in the sixteenth century and was typically placed as the last dance by all composers in their suites. It came to Ireland in the seventeenth century and, although we call it a 'jig' in the Irish tradition, this dance also uses a compound time signature: 6/8.

J.S. Bach

Define **minuet**:

Define **sarabande**:

The cello part for Bach's Gigue is printed below for you. Look at the music and follow it as you listen. The gigue is a fast-tempo dance so you may need to do this a few times to improve your score-reading skills. Try to follow the flow of the melody as it **ascends** or **descends** and watch out for the repeat sign in bar 13.

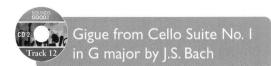

Gigue from Cello Suite No. 1 in G major by J.S. Bach

CD 2
Track 12

Research and listen to one of the following suites:

1 *The Music for the Royal Fireworks* by Handel
2 *The Nutcracker Suite* by Tchaikovsky

The symbols on the sheet music offer important information to the cellist. They are numbered for you. Work together in pairs to *identify* them and briefly *explain* what the symbols mean in the grid below.

Symbol	Definition	Symbol	Definition
1		5	
2		6	
3 *tr*		7 ♭	
4 ♯		8	

Identify the pitches of the notes heard in the final two bars of this piece.

_____

Transpose them **up one octave** to the treble clef and *transcribe* them on the stave below.

What stuck with you?

Evaluate your learning in this chapter. List what stuck with you and new key words.

Key Words

_____

_____

_____

_____

_____

Chapter 18

Conducting Lab

In Unit 4 of *Sounds Good 1* we learned about the time signatures 2/4, 3/4 and 4/4. Look back and remind yourself of the conducting patterns we used to illustrate the metre.

Name **three** well-known conductors and the countries they were born in.

1	
2	
3	

Well–known conductor Marin Alsop

Name **three** ensemble types which require a conductor.

1	
2	
3	

Looking back!

◆ Draw the composing gesture for each time signature in the grid below.

◆ Identify one piece of music composed in that metre which you have listened to.

◆ Compose a bar of rhythm in each metre.

Time signature	𝄞 2/4	𝄞 3/4	𝄞 4/4
Conducting pattern			
Musical example			
Bar of rhythm	2/4	3/4	4/4

A Compound Time Signature: 6/8

Bach's Gigue is written in 6/8. This is known as a **compound time signature**. 6/8 means there are six quavers per bar. These are divided into two beats each lasting three quavers.

The common time signatures 2/4, 3/4 and 4/4 are known as **simple time signatures**. This is mainly because each (crotchet) pulse or beat in these time signatures can be divided **equally** into a pair of quavers.

4 pulses in $\frac{4}{4}$

What does this mean? Take a look at the bar of 4/4 shown here. When we divide each pulse into two we get eight *equal* quavers.

Each bar of 6/8 is equal to **six quaver beats per bar**. Different combinations of note values can be used, but they always add up to six quavers. However, they are grouped in threes rather than twos.

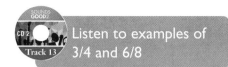

Listen to examples of 3/4 and 6/8

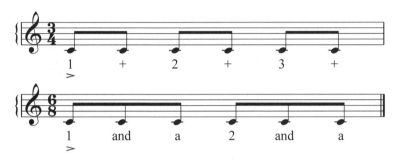

Listen to the examples on your CD. In this example the quavers are grouped in twos.

In this example the quavers are grouped in threes.

This makes the rhythm sound quite different, doesn't it?

Look at the difference between the bar of 3/4 and the bar of 6/8 above. Try saying the 3/4 pattern: '**one** and **two** and **three** and'. Now speak the 6/8 rhythm: '**one** and a **two** and a'. In the 6/8 example here we hear the pulse occur twice. When we divide six quavers into two, we get three quavers or a dotted crotchet. As the pulse breaks down (**subdivides**) into two dotted crotchets per bar, 6/8 is an example of a **compound time signature**.

Rehearse and clap the rhythmic patterns for both time signatures below. Accents have been placed on the emphasised beats to help you hear the different placement of the pulse in compound and simple time.

Accent

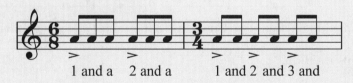

In pairs, test each other on identifying which pattern your partner claps.

Sight-clapping in 6/8

Below are four examples of 6/8 sight-reading. Before you attempt them, insert the accent symbol under the emphasised beats and the numbers 1–6 in each bar to help you.

Compose your own patterns in 6/8

Rhythms commonly used in 6/8

Listen and clap back the rhythm pattern below.

Listen and clap back this 6/8 pattern

1 2 3 4 5 6   1 2 3 4 5 6   1 2 3 4 5 6   1 2 3 4 5 6

Compose a C major melody in 6/8 for cello

Humpty Dumpty

'Humpty Dumpty' is an English nursery rhyme in 6/8. It is a one-verse rhyme with a rhythm pattern which uses a stressed syllable followed by an unstressed one, a common feature in nursery rhymes.

Can you think of another nursery rhythm which has this feature? _____

Listen to the melody of 'Humpty Dumpty' on your CD and sing along.

'Humpty Dumpty'
Track 15

Listen again and this time clap the rhythm with your hands whilst tapping the **pulse** with your foot. Then circle the notes on which you tapped your foot. What do you notice about the pulse?

Hump - ty Dump - ty   sat on a wall,   Hump - ty Dump - ty   had a great fall.

All the king's hor-ses and   all the king's men   Could-n't put Hump-ty to - ge-ther a-gain.

1 Identify the **key signature** of this melody. _____

2 Name and explain the **rest** which features in bar 2. _____

3 Identify one feature of the melody line. _____

4 Name one feature of the rhythm. _____

5 Identify the **range** of the melody. _____

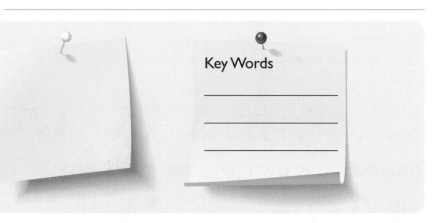

What stuck with you?

Evaluate your learning in this chapter. List what stuck with you and new key words.

Key Words

_____
_____
_____

Identify the dates of the Classical period. _____

Identify **three** Classical composers and list **three** works you have listened to from this era.

Composer	Work
1	1
2	2
3	3

Not only was the Classical period more balanced with a new focus on the **melodic line**, but **ensembles** also increased in size, sound and range. Larger ensembles known as symphony orchestras became more common. The harpsichord was replaced by the piano. Instrumental ensembles favoured by composers included trios and quartets, but many wrote symphonic works and concertos which were composed for virtuoso soloists accompanied by an orchestra.

Define the following terms

Term	Definition
Concerto	
Sonata	
Symphony	
Virtuoso	

Opera

Concertos for flute, violin and piano were common during this period but so too were pieces composed for vocalists, particularly opera. Opera is one of the most respected art forms in Western music. An **opera** is a theatrical production or dramatic play with music, in which the main characters sing, rather than speak their parts. The popularity of this genre led to the construction of opera houses throughout Europe, such as the famous La Scala in Milan, Italy, which was built in 1778.

In *Sounds Good 1* we explored one of the greatest composers that ever lived: Wolfgang Amadeus Mozart. Mozart was particularly famous for his operas. During his time, opera was show business; it was the Hollywood of Classical music. Operas had colourful and elaborate sets with expensive costumes and famous stars performing in them.

Big cultural and social changes were taking place during the Classical period, and composers used their operas as a platform for telling this story. Mozart's operas became known for their social

Wolfgang Amadeus Mozart

La Scala in Milan

commentaries and complex characters. The social divide between aristocratic and peasant classes was a prominent issue for society at the time, and the American and French Revolutions are a reflection of this tension.

Mozart's *Don Giovanni*

Mozart's opera *Don Giovanni* premiered in Prague in 1787. It is an **opera buffa**, an Italian term meaning comic opera. Whilst Don Giovanni is comical, it is also quite dark, the tension between social classes being an important theme in the storyline. Lorenzo de Ponte was the **librettist** for Mozart. The main character Don Giovanni is a Spanish nobleman and womaniser who has exploited his aristocratic power.

Mozart composed a score for **strings, woodwind, trumpets, horns and trombones alongside timpani and basso continuo**. There are solo vocal parts for **soprano, tenor, baritone and bass** as well as the chorus. The characters and their voice types are listed below.

Characters and vocal parts for Mozart's opera *Don Giovanni*

Don Giovanni – baritone

Donna Anna – soprano

Donna Elvira – soprano

Zerlina – soprano

Don Ottavio – tenor

Leporello – bass

Masetto – bass

Commendatore – bass

The **librettist** writes the written text for the opera, known as the **libretto**.

These lead roles were difficult to perform, with many demanding solo sections. In opera, melodic solo songs sung by characters are called **arias**. The speech-like dialogue between arias is called **recitative**.

Listen to Mozart's **aria** 'Là ci darem la mano' and follow the music provided. This is a duet for Mozart's characters Don Giovanni (baritone) and Zerlina (soprano). This beautiful melody is balanced and ordered but overflowing with beautiful melodic patterns. What musical features can you identify on the score?

Aria: _____

Recitative: _____

'Là ci darem la mano' from *Don Giovanni* by Mozart

Là ci darem la mano

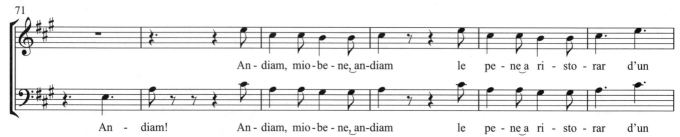

1 Describe the **motif** heard during the rest in Don Giovanni's opening phrase (bar 4). _____

2 Identify the bar in which we hear Zerlina's voice for the first time. _____

3 Identify the five types of **rest** used in the score and indicate the value of each of these. _____

_____

4 Describe one melodic and one rhythmic change in the music from bar 49. _____

_____

5 In bars 72–77 Don Giovanni and Zerlina are singing in

a) unison   b) harmony   c) canon.

Lyrics to Là ci darem la mano

Don Giovanni	Give me thy hand, oh fairest, Whisper a gentle 'Yes', Come, if for me thou carest, With joy my life to bless.
Zerlina	I would, and yet I would not, I dare not give assent, Alas! I know I should not ... Too late, I may repent.
Don Giovanni	Come, dearest, let me guide thee.
Zerlina	Masetto sure will chide me!
Don Giovanni	Danger shall ne'er come nigh thee!

Zerlina	Ah ... that I could deny thee!
Don Giovanni	Let's go! Let's go!
Zerlina	Let's go!
Both	With thee, with thee, my treasure, This life is nought but pleasure, My heart is fondly thine.

English translation by Natalie MacFarren (1826–1916)

Read and discuss the lyrics. What do we know of the story from the lyrics? _____

_____

Listen again, following the lyrics and consider how the music depicts the characters, their relationships and their emotions? Comment below and refer to the music in your answer.

_____

_____

If you search online for 'YouTube – Mozart – La Ci Darem La Mano (English Subtitles)', you should find a performance by Rodney Gilfry and Liliana Nikiteanu with English subtitles allowing you to follow the story. You will also hear the difference between **recitative** and **aria** during this performance.

In Mozart's opera there is a ballroom scene in which there are two different **ensembles** on stage and the **orchestra** in the pit playing simultaneously. Interestingly the three ensembles are playing three different dances in differing metres:

◆ a minuet in 3/4,

◆ a contradance in 2/4, and

◆ a peasant dance in 3/8.

Combining two or more different time signatures simultaneously is known as **polymetry**. In groups of three compose, prepare and perform a rhythm piece using polymetry.

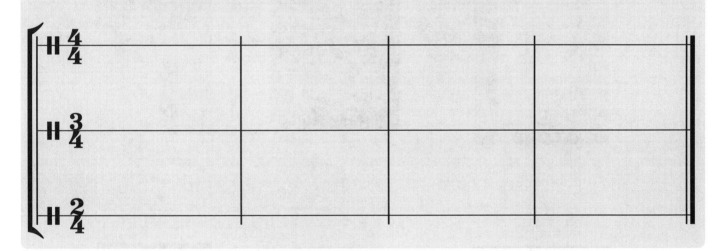

Research and explain these forms, which all involve **vocalists**.

Genre	Definition
Motet	
Cantata	
Oratorio	
Operetta	

Our voices

Everybody's voice is unique; no two voices will sound exactly the same. However, we can categorise all voices into 'types of voices' based on the **range** of notes we can sing.

There are six classifications or categories into which our voices should fit. Vocal range is the number of pitches we can sing clearly from lowest to highest. With vocal training, many people can develop and extend their **range**.

Voice type is a little more complex than **vocal range** as it takes into account the tone and **timbre** of your voice. Categorising voices in this way became important during the Classical period, particularly for performance of opera. Below is a chart which identifies the six voice types we typically categorise singers by and their typical vocal **range**.

Voice	Soprano	Mezzo soprano	Contralto/Alto
Range			
Performer	Maria Callas	Cecilia Bartoli	Kathleen Ferrier

Voice	Tenor	Baritone	Bass
Range			
Performer	José Carreras	Bryn Terfel	Matti Salminen

Use this information to complete the grid below

Voice type	Range	Lowest note	Highest note	Performer
Soprano				
Mezzo soprano				
Contralto/Alto				
Tenor				
Baritone				
Bass				

Sometimes when we are singing, we worry we won't 'hit the right note' or feel we sound funny when we try to sing high or low pitches; if this happens to us, we might end up thinking we can't sing very well. This is rarely true, and these technical problems with singing are often caused by singing songs which are outside our **vocal range** or natural changes in our bodies.

For this reason, it is important to know what your **range** is and which voice type you are, especially if you are singing in your school choir or choosing songs to sing for your practical exam!

Vocal range – where does each voice fit?

Research the main vocal parts – Bass, Baritone, Tenor, Alto, Mezzo and Soprano.

Label each of the six keyboards below and indicate the vocal range of each of the six vocal types we have learned about by colouring in the keys.

Female

Voice type:_____   Range:_____

Voice type:_____   Range:_____

Voice type:_____   Range:_____

Male

Voice type:_____   Range:_____

Voice type:_____   Range:_____

Voice type:_____   Range:_____

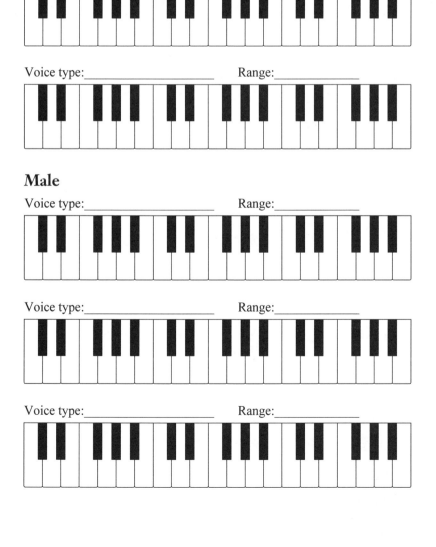

Groups of voices are combined together to form a **vocal ensemble** or **choir**. The most common mix for an ensemble is groups of soprano, alto, tenor and bass voices. Solo voices may also combine to sing duets, trios or quartets.

A chamber choir

A **chamber choir** can have between eight and forty singers and typically performs classical or sacred music. Choirs may sing with or without instrumental accompaniment. Most choirs are led by a conductor, also known as a choir master or choral director.

The four common sections, soprano, alto, tenor and bass, sing in four-part harmony, but there are no limits to the layers of harmony that can be created with a talented choir.

Thomas Tallis, whom we read about earlier in this unit, composed a forty-part Renaissance motet called *Spem in alium*, which was performed by eight choirs each in five-part harmony.

Spem in alium
by Thomas Tallis

 Listen to this work. Quieting our minds for a few moments each day can have a really positive impact on our wellbeing. This music is calming and easy to listen to. Close your eyes and allow your mind to rest as you listen to it.

When you are ready, listen to this excerpt again and focus on how the different voices sing and then are silent as other voices take over. The parts move from a small number of singers to many, but the mood of the piece doesn't change.

1 What period does this music belong to? _____

2 *List* the dates for this musical period. _____

3 What type of work is it? _____

4 What language is it sung in? _____

5 *Explain* what is meant by the term **'sacred music'**. _____

6 Is this piece accompanied? _____

7 *Identify* and *describe* the **texture** of the music in this excerpt. _____

_____

8 *Explain* the term **through-composed**. _____

9 Name another piece you have studied by the same composer.

_____

10 *Comment* on the role of the conductor in conducting a large-scale ensemble such as this one. *Indicate* the skills needed to direct a performance.

_____

_____

_____

_____

_____

Investigate a community vocal ensemble group and write a brief note on their role in your local community. Mention their performances and the benefits their singing has on members of the community.

_____

_____

_____

_____

_____

_____

_____

_____

Investigate and briefly *explain* the following terms

Aria	
Duet	
Recitative	
Falsetto	
Vibrato	
Passaggio	

What stuck with you?

Evaluate your learning in this chapter. List what stuck with you and new key words.

Key Words

_____

_____

_____

Art Songs

Much vocal music continued to be composed in the Romantic period, and opera and choral works still feature during the Romantic era. Composers such as Schubert wrote a great deal of music for voice accompanied by piano. These songs are known as art songs.

Art songs are usually poems set to music by well-known composers. Composing musical interpretations of poetry developed in nineteenth-century Germany. These works were called **lieder**. Some composers wrote groups of songs around a specific theme – love and nature were the most common choices – known as **liederkreis** in German or **song cycles** in English. The development of the piano coincided with the popularity of art songs.

Franz Schubert

German composer Franz Schubert set many poems written by the German poet Johann Wolfgang von Goethe. Schubert wrote over 600 art songs. Listen to one of his most well-known lieder 'Gretchen am Spinnrade', composed for soprano voice and piano accompaniment. Schubert was seventeen when he composed this song.

'Gretchen am Spinnrade' by Schubert

Gretchen and her spinning wheel

Schubert took inspiration for this song from Goethe's famous work *Faust*. *Faust* is a tragic two-act play written in the late 1700s. Schubert uses clever **compositional techniques** to **illustrate** Gretchen working at her spinning wheel waiting for her beloved Faust. She sings of her heartache in the opening lines.

As you listen to the song, notice how the higher pitched right-hand piano part mimics the spinning wheel and the lower pitched notes heard in the left hand represent the treadle.

A **minor tonality** creates a sad and gloomy **mood**, illustrating how Gretchen longs for Faust, but the mood becomes brighter when she begins to talk about him and the left-hand piano motion is replaced by block chords. The removal of the rhythmic left hand could suggest Gretchen's loss of contact with reality, she has stopped working at the spinning wheel as she daydreams of her beloved Faust.

From here on, the tension in the music increases as the song develops towards a climax. Schubert moves the melody to a **higher pitch** and increases the **tempo** and **dynamic** to illustrate Gretchen's feelings as she remembers a kiss shared with Faust. But, as with all day dreams, reality returns and so does the steady rhythmic left hand illustrating the treadle on her spinning wheel.

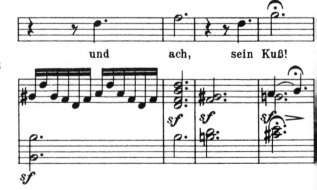

The song ends as it began, with a sense of monotony and the sad mood created by the piano part. Together these features illustrate Gretchen's heavy heart.

Gretchen am Spinnrade

My peace is gone

My peace is gone,
My heart is heavy,
I will find it never
and never more.

Where I do not have him,
That is the grave,
The whole world
Is bitter to me.

My poor head
Is crazy to me,
My poor mind
Is torn apart.

My peace is gone,
My heart is heavy,
I will find it never
and never more.

For him only, I look
Out the window
Only for him do I go
Out of the house.

His tall walk,
His noble figure,
His mouth's smile,
His eyes' power,

And his mouth's
Magic flow,
His handclasp,
and ah! his kiss!

My peace is gone,
My heart is heavy,
I will find it never
and never more.

My bosom urges itself
toward him.
Ah, might I grasp
And hold him!

And kiss him,
As I would wish,
At his kisses
I should die!

Work in pairs to identify and define ten musical symbols from the sheet music.

Name/Draw	Define
1	
2	
3	
4	
5	
6	
7	
8	
9	
10	

Translated from German to English by Lynn Thompson.

1 *Examine* the impact the music here has on the depiction of Gretchen, her relationship with Faust and her emotions. Write a summary on how Schubert reveals all of this to us throughout his composition. Refer to the score in your answer.

2 Consider the role of the piano accompaniment in this piece. *Suggest* reasons why this piece of music was chosen to match the text.

Programme note activity

Compile a programme note for this art song and address the following points.

◆ When did Schubert compose this piece?

◆ What was happening in Germany at the time it was composed?

◆ Is this piece typical of that time?

◆ *Describe* the most interesting part of the piece.

◆ *Identify* some aural signposts to listen out for.

◆ *Discuss* your favourite part of the song.

What stuck with you?

Evaluate your learning in this chapter. List what stuck with you and new key words.

Key Words

Female Composers

In Unit 6 of *Sounds Good 1*, we explored traditional Irish music. In Ireland, singing has always gone hand in hand with our love of storytelling. Ireland is filled with poets and storytellers.

Little is known of female composers, especially Irish female composers. Why do you think this might be? Can you name a female composer from anywhere in the world, from one of the historical periods of music?

Ina Boyle

Ina Boyle an Irish composer grew up in Enniskerry Co. Wicklow. Born in 1889, she spent much of her adult life mastering the skills of composition. She wrote many **art songs**, and Trinity College's Manuscripts and Archives Library has over seventy pieces of art music composed for voice and piano by Boyle in its possession. Boyle used a wide variety of poetry to inspire her art songs from William Shakespeare to William Butler Yeats.

Only two of her art songs were based on Gaelic texts. 'Sleep Song', composed in 1923 was a setting of an ancient Gaelic text which was translated by Padraig Pearse.

Listen to the song on your CD. Listen out for the well-known Irish expression 'Deirín Dé' in the lyrics.

'Sleep Song'
by Ina Boyle

Despite having some of her works published and support from composers like Vaughan Williams, Boyle's work hasn't received much attention in Ireland. None of her songs using Irish texts were ever published.

Listen to Eimear Noone's 'Zelda's Lullaby' released in 2017.

Listen to Jennifer Walshe's '13 Vices' released in 2017.

Compare and contrast these pieces using a venn diagram.

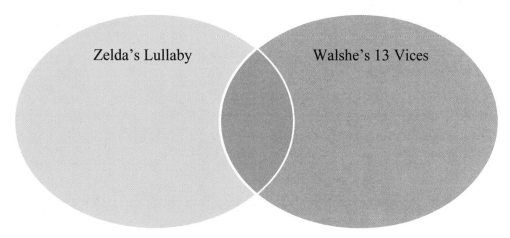

Zelda's Lullaby

Walshe's 13 Vices

Research and write an article about a living Irish female composer. Discuss how society's recognition of their work has changed over time and possible challenges which still face them. List examples of their work.

In the 1800s, female composers were more likely to compose art songs for performance in a recital setting than large symphonic suites for performance in large concert halls. Investigate the possible reasons for this with your classmates.

Examine and discuss the role of women in the history of music.

Investigate the life and work of **one** of the following female composers.

Clara Schumann

Marianna Martines

Amy Beach

Irish people rarely know of our historical composers. Other art forms in Irish culture such as literature, theatre and traditional Irish music and dance have enjoyed worldwide recognition. So why have our composers gone unnoticed?

John Field

In *Sounds Good 1* you researched harpist and composer Turlough O'Carolan, and earlier in this book you read how Irish composer John Field was a key influence in how Chopin composed the nocturne we listened to.

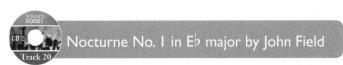
Nocturne No. 1 in E♭ major by John Field
Track 20

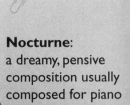
John Field

Have a listen to John Field's Nocturne No. 1 in E♭ major.

John Field was a pianist, composer and teacher born in Dublin in 1782. His father was a renowned violin player at the Theatre Royal. He moved to London and continued his music education under **Muzio Clementi**. Field is best known as the inventor on the nocturne. Very few composers have invented their own **form**! He was highly regarded by contemporaries.

He loved to compose decorated melodic lines that often feature **chromatic** passages. He was known for including **ostinato** patterns in his piano music and used piano **pedals** to add depth to melody lines. His eighteen Nocturnes were extremely influential for the Romantic composers, but so too were his piano concertos. An interesting feature of his compositions is his preference for the keys of C major and E♭ major. A vast number of his works were composed in these two keys.

Nocturne: a dreamy, pensive composition usually composed for piano

Mícheál Ó'Súilleabháin

In November 2018, Mícheál Ó'Súilleabháin, one of Ireland's leading Irish musicians and composers passed away aged 67. He has been described as a visionary and exceptional musician who combined Classical and Irish musical traditions. He was born in Clonmel, Co. Tipperary in 1950, and, after returning to school to do his Leaving Certificate, he began his formal music studies at University College Cork in 1969. He became a lecturer at UCC in 1975. During his time in UCC, he was influenced by another important Irish composer, **Seán Ó Riada**, and later took up his role as Professor of Music there. Both composers shared an interest in classical and traditional Irish music. One of his most recognisable compositions is the beautiful solo piano piece 'Woodbrook'.

Explore the works of two Irish composers. Research their life and influences, listen to their compositions and use their scores to investigate their composing style.

Distinguish and explain the similarities and differences between the compositions you have listened to. Write an article detailing your findings for publication in *HotPress* Magazine.

Use the Venn diagram below to plan and draft your article.

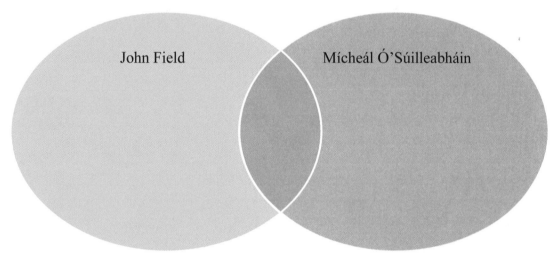

John Field

Mícheál Ó'Súilleabháin

Write your article in the space provided.

Irish Composers of Harp Music

Turlough O'Carolan

Turlough O'Carolan

Turlough O'Carolan was born in Nobber, Co. Meath in 1670. His father was a blacksmith, and when Turlough was fourteen his family moved to Roscommon where his father had taken up employment on the McDermott-Roe family's estate. Mrs McDermott Roe was particularly fond of Turlough. When he was seventeen, he lost his sight after falling ill with smallpox. Mrs McDermott Roe provided him with harp lessons to train as a harpist as a means of making a living.

When he was twenty-one, he left with his horse and a guide to travel across Ireland composing and performing his tunes. He composed songs and instrumental music, but, during O'Carolan's lifetime, traditional music was shared in an **oral tradition**, making it difficult to preserve his music. His composition 'Sí Bheag, Sí Mhór', which means 'Big Hill, Little Hill', refers to a site in Co. Meath where, according to folklore, two battling giants were turned into two hills by a wizard. O'Carolan's concerto is another of his well-known compositions. He was influenced by Baroque composers like Corelli and Vivaldi. O'Carolan often dedicated his compositions to the **patrons** he was performing for. He called these **planxties**, and 'Planxty Irwin' is still a commonly known piece of music among Irish musicians. Much of his music has survived due mainly to the efforts of collectors like Edward Bunting, who collected and preserved music in Ireland.

Write a note on Edward Bunting and the role of collectors in preserving music for future generations.

Name one other **collector** of traditional Irish music. _____

How has the preservation of music changed since Bunting's time?

'Eleanor Plunkett'

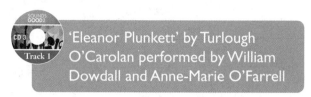

'Eleanor Plunkett' by Turlough O'Carolan performed by William Dowdall and Anne-Marie O'Farrell

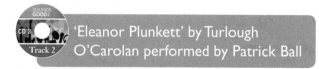

'Eleanor Plunkett' by Turlough O'Carolan performed by Patrick Ball

Listen to two different **arrangements** of Turlough O'Carolan's **slow air** 'Eleanor Plunkett'. Eleanor Plunkett belonged to a Catholic family who were evicted from their home during the Cromwellian Plantations. She was the only surviving member of her family.

Compare these pieces of music in the grid below. Make references to the features of traditional music, elements of music and other influences. The sheet music will help you to follow the performance.

Eleanor Plunkett

As you listen identify and insert the phrase marks. Try to identify the form of the song.

Compare and contrast One song – two interpretations	
Song title	**Style**
Version 1 performers	**Version 2 performers**

Unique to version 1	**Common elements**	**Unique to version 2**

Irish Songwriters

We listened to Ina Boyle's art song 'Sleep Song' earlier in this unit and have explored the creative efforts of our native composers. So what about our songwriters in the popular tradition? There are many Irish **songwriters** and performers who have reached a worldwide audience. Can you name two of your favourite song writers?

1 _____

2 _____

Songwriters compose lyrics and/or accompanying music for songs in the popular tradition.

Dolores O'Riordan

Glen Hansard

Christy Moore

Bob Geldof

Niall Horan

Imelda May

You might be surprised how many songwriters you know from the list below.

Bob Geldof	Hozier
Luka Bloom	Niall Breslin
Niall Horan	Christy Moore
Glen Hansard	Enya
Imelda May	Mundy
Dolores O'Riordan	Bono

and the list goes on…

Choose **four** songwriters from this list and identify one of the songs they have released. Use this information to complete the grid below.

	Songwriter	Genre	Song title
1			
2			
3			
4			

James MacCarthy was born in Cork in 1953 and now lives in Kilkenny. As a singer-songwriter he has spent much of his life in the music industry. He has been composing songs since the early 1970s. His songs have been recorded by many Irish artists including Mary Black, Christy Moore, The Corrs and Westlife. Some songs you may be familiar with include Christy Moore's hit 'Ride On', 'No Frontiers' sung by the Corrs or Mary Black's iconic Irish ballad 'Katie'.

In 1998 MacCarthy released an album with well-known musicians Tommy Fleming, Mary Black, Christy Moore and Mary Coughlin all performing his songs. The album is called *Warmer for the Spark*.

Phill Coulter

Phil Coulter is another Irish singer-songwriter who has enjoyed huge success over his career. Born in Derry in 1942, Coulter was part of a musical family. His father was a fiddle player and his mum a pianist. One of his most famous songs is 'The Town I Love so Well', which tells of the Troubles in Northern Ireland. When he completed his studies in Ireland, Coulter moved to London where he wrote music for legends like Van Morrison and Tom Jones.

He also wrote the UK's winning Eurovision entry in 1967 'Puppet on a String' which was sung by Sandie Shaw. His most treasured song is 'Scorn Not His Simplicity', which was later recorded by Luke Kelly.

Continue to research the works of these two songwriters. Choose one song each has written and compare them to each other. Gather information about the songs you have chosen and access some sheet music to help you compare the two songs. Identify and describe the differences and similarities you can identify between the songs.

Provide a summary of your findings in the grid below.

Songwriters	James MacCarthy	Phil Coulter
Song		
Year of composition		
Performer/s of the song		
Genre		
Song type		
Theme/mood		
Key signature		
Instrumentation		
Form		
Aural signpost		

Create a list of songs you would use to create a **playlist** to celebrate Irish composers and performers.

Playlist title:			
	Song	**Artist**	**Reasons this song is suitable for this playlist**
1			
2			
3			
4			
5			
6			
7			
8			

Discuss the difficulties faced by Irish composers and musicians today. Are they supported and celebrated? *Explore* the realities of trying to establish yourself as a musician in Ireland. Does our local and national media promote our talented composers and musicians?

Indicate your findings on the discussions you share in the Think–Pair–Share chart below and feedback your thoughts to other members of your class for further discussion.

Questions	What I think	What my partner thinks	What we will share
A good song has			
Musical features we hear			
1	1	1	1
2	2	2	2
3	3	3	3
Suggested songs for listening to			
1	1	1	1
2	2	2	2

Research the organisations in Ireland that aim to promote and support music as part of the Arts. Write about their efforts in the space provided below.

What stuck with you?

Evaluate your learning in this chapter. List what stuck with you and new key words.

Key Words

Reflection and Evaluation Sheet

Unit title:

Learning Outcomes (LOs) I worked with:

Music I listened to:

_____

Learning and exploring

I really enjoyed…

_____

Something interesting I learnt…

_____

My biggest challenge was…

_____

I overcame this by…

_____

One improvement I have made is…

_____

Traffic-light your learning

Learning Outcomes	😞	😐	🙂	✔
1.7				
1.8				
1.9				
1.13				
1.14				
2.4				
2.5				
2.9				
3.2				
3.3				
3.7				
3.10				
3.11				

Learning

Key words	Action verbs

Key skills

_____

I got better at x skill by _____

_____

This unit reminded me of learning about… _____

What still puzzles me is…

_____

_____

Feedback and goal setting…

_____

_____

_____

Rate your learning ⭐⭐⭐⭐⭐

Composing Lab

In this unit

We will explore your creative talent in an imaginative and innovative way and develop our working knowledge of how music is constructed as a means of communicating musical ideas. You will have a chance to use your working knowledge of music to create short musical motifs and soundscapes, bringing your ideas to life! This unit includes planning, researching, creating, practising, presenting, evaluating and reflecting on music. Composing activities have been designed with the Compositional Portfolio in mind. Gathering and compiling evidence of our learning and reflecting on ways in which we can move our learning forward is essential.

Checklist	LO	Intended learning
☐	1.2	**Create** and **present** a short piece, using instruments and/or other sounds in response to a stimulus.
☐	1.3	**Design** a harmonic or rhythmic accompaniment, record this accompaniment and **improvise** over this recording.
☐	1.6	Listen to and **transcribe** rhythmic phrases of up to four bars and melodic phrases of up to two bars.
☐	2.2	**Create** a musical statement (such as a rap or an advertising jingle) about a topical issue or current event and share with others the statement's purpose and development.
☐	2.3	**Adapt** excerpts/motifs/themes from an existing piece of music by changing its feel, style, or underlying harmony.
☐	2.4	**Rehearse** and **present** a song or brief instrumental piece; **identify** and **discuss** the performance skills and techniques that were necessary to **interpret** the music effectively.
☐	2.7	**Create** and **present** some musical ideas using instruments and/or found sounds to **illustrate** moods or feelings expressed in a poem, story or newspaper article.
☐	3.4	**Compose** and perform an original jingle or brief piece of music for use in a new advertisement for a product, and record the composition.

The Composing Lab in *Sounds Good 1* began with the statement 'There is only one real happiness in life, and that is the happiness of creativity.' Can you recall who said this? Do you think he has a point?

Creativity is the use of imagination and new original ideas to create something new and innovative.

In an age where many questions can be answered simply by looking them up online, creativity is becoming one of the most highly valued and important human talents. Using our imagination to spark ideas and create new concepts is something our computer simply cannot do. Composers are bursting with creativity; jotting down their ideas for compositions or melodies on paper when they come to mind is something they simply must do. Our creativity is something to be celebrated!

Isaac Newton's creative imagination assisted him in formulating his ideas about gravity. After a falling apple hit him on the head, he began to wonder about why this was so. He questioned why apples fall in a **perpendicular** way and not to the right, to the left or upwards. This thought process sparked original ideas which soon led him to develop his theory on gravity.

What is important to note here is that Newton would not have been so quick to discover gravity if he hadn't first developed such an immense knowledge of physics and math.

A perpendicular line is a straight line at 90° to a given line, plane or surface. The apple fell perpendicular to the tree's branch.

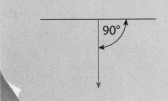

Gravity is a force which tries to pull two objects toward each other. Earth's gravity is what keeps you on the ground.

Like Newton, the greatest composers have developed an in-depth knowledge of compositional theory, which allows them to create the music they have imagined. Compositional skills are an important part of our learning. Coupled with your creative instincts and innovative ideas, your compositional skills will enhance the composing work you do in this unit.

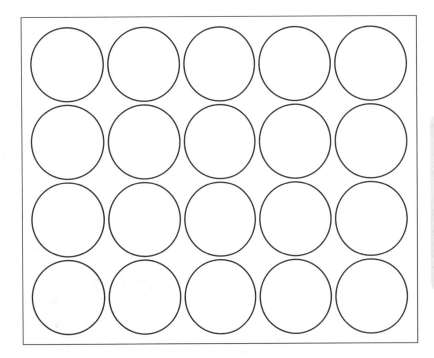

Creativity challenge

Test your creativity by turning the 20 circles below into recognisable objects. You have two minutes to do it! Share your ideas with others when you have finished.

Responding to Rhythm

Rhythm is an important component of any piece of music. It gives motion to the music we listen to. We indicate rhythm using symbols that specify the relative length – or time value – of the notes we place on the stave. Remember, rhythm is not the same as beat, but a more complex pattern which is heard within the beats.

Aural memory – rhythm clap back

Listen to the following rhythm patterns and clap back the pattern you hear. Can you guess the time signature? Use garage band to record clap-back rhythms patterns in 2/4, 3/4, 4/4 and 6/8 and practise clapping back.

Define 'improvisation'

Call and response clapping

Call and response is a musical form where the first part or musician poses a **question**, which a second part or musician presents an **answer** to. It is a form of **dialogue** between two musicians or parts. To do this, you will rely on your **improvisation** skills.

Work in pairs. The first person should clap a two-bar rhythm pattern in 4 (8 beats) and the other person should answer this pattern by creating an answering rhythmic pattern. Continue back and forth to create a rhythmic dialogue of call and response.

Repeat this exercise in groups, keeping to a pulse of four. This is a fun way to invent rhythms together! Who can fit the most complex pattern into a short space of time?

Loop: a loop is repeating section of recorded sound to create ostinatos or add layers to a composition

Activity

Create a rhythmic statement on the rhythm line below.

Record your rhythmic pattern using software which allows you to **loop** it and *improvise* over it using other **rhythmic patterns** as it plays.

Make notes on the process in the space below. What worked well?

What software did you use to record your rhythm? _____

Reading Rhythms

Rhythm recap

Each note value has its own symbol. You developed your knowledge of note values in *Sounds Good 1*. Can you remember the symbols used to indicate rhythm on the stave? Complete the revision grid below.

Note name	Note symbol	Value	Other (US) name
	𝅝		
Minim			
		1 beat	
			Eighth note

Dotted rhythm

Dotted notes often occur in written music. *Explain* how a dot after a note changes the value of the note.

_____

_____

Indicate the symbol for the following note values.

Symbol	Value
	6
	3
	1½
	¾

Sound and silence

Composers use both sound and silence in their compositions. The symbols used to indicate silence on the score are called **rests**. Each note value has an equivalent rest. Can you remember these?

Circle the rests in the music below and label them.

Classify the rests we have learnt about in the grid below.

Name of rest	Symbol	Note value

Composing a call and response

Call and response is a musical **form** which uses dialogue. A melody sung or played is answered by a subsequent phrase. It is commonly found in church music and African music. Search for 'call and response demonstration – YouTube' for an example of how it works.

 Work in pairs to compose an eight-bar **call and response** rhythmic piece in 3/4. Remember, when one part poses a rhythmic question, the other part is silent and vice versa.

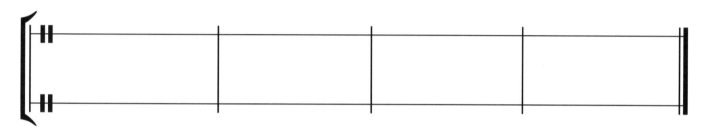

Rehearse and perform your composition for your classmates.

If percussion instruments are available to you, choose two percussion instruments which have contrasting **timbres** to perform your rhythm piece on.

What is **timbre**?

_____

Explain the form call and response, and research composers and pieces of music which use this form. Make notes on your findings below.

> Search online for 'YouTube – Sister Act Oh Happy Day HD' from *Sister Act 2* for an example of call and response singing.

Musical maths

Complete these musical sums.

1 ♩ + ♩ + ♩ + ♩ = _____

2 𝅝 + ♩ + ♩ = _____

3 ♪ + ♪ + ♪ + ♪ = _____

4 𝅗𝅥 + 𝅗𝅥 + ♩ + ♩ = _____

5 ♪ + ♪ + ♪ = _____

6 ♩ + 𝅝 + 𝅗𝅥. = _____

7 ▬ + 𝄽 = _____

8 ▬ + ▬ = _____

9 𝄽 + 𝄽 + ▬ = _____

10 𝄾 + 𝄾 + 𝄾 + 𝄽 = _____

Peer assessment

Design your own musical maths and test your partner, write them below. Use addition, subtraction, division and multiplication to make them a little trickier than the ones above.

a) _____   b) _____

c) _____   d) _____

Check your partner's answers once they have finished, and work out any mistakes together.

Time signature

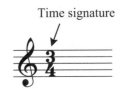

Time signatures

Your rhythm piece on page 159 uses the time signature 3/4 to organise the rhythmic pattern you composed. We learnt much about time signatures in Unit 4 of *Sounds Good 1* and in Unit 4 of this book.

A time signature consists of two numbers, placed at the beginning of a piece of music. The top number tells us how many beats are in each bar and the bottom number tells us the duration or time value of each beat.

We explored the patterns used by **composers** to communicate the **pulse** and **tempo** of a piece of music to the musicians who play it. We practised demonstrating these patterns to conduct pieces of music in 2/4, 3/4, 4/4 and 6/8. Revise Unit 4 and complete the grid below.

Time signature	Typical bar of rhythm	Conducting pattern
4/4		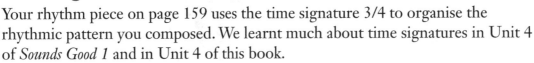
3/4		

Time signature	Typical bar of rhythm	Conducting pattern
$\frac{2}{4}$		
$\frac{6}{8}$		

Music and geometry

Graphic-score composers use very interesting ways of presenting information to musicians, often using physical or visual representations of rhythm and pitch rather than using standard notation. We explored some of these ideas in *Sounds Good 1*. Name a graphic-score composer and one of their compositions.

A **polygon** is a two-dimensional shape formed using straight lines. The number of straight lines used to create the shape is used to name the shape. A hexagon is an example of a polygon.

Design a polygon to represent the metres 3, 4 and 6 in your copy book and colour them in.

Can you name a shape that is a non-polygon? _____

Sight-clapping

Sight-clapping is a form of **sight-reading**. Read the pattern carefully and try to imagine how it should sound before clapping it. Try these, remembering to count yourself in!

Common time

Exercise 3 uses **C** as its time signature. This symbol is called **common time** and is another way to denote 4/4 on a stave. Common time is another way of indicating there are four crotchet beats per bar.

In Unit 4 of this book you were introduced to 6/8. Sight-clapping rhythms in this time signature can be tricky. Look at the image below which reminds us of the differences between 6/8 and 3/4. It shows where the emphasis is placed. Rehearse and clap back both examples below.

Now try this one.

You may find it helpful to write the numbers for each quaver underneath each bar. After clapping these, go back and draw a line under the **emphasised beat** in each bar. Clap them again, ensuring you place the emphasis on the correct beat of the bar.

$\frac{2}{4}$	2 beats per bar	1 2 1 2 1 2 1 2 1 2 1 2
$\frac{3}{4}$	3 beats per bar	1 2 3 1 2 3 1 2 3 1 2 3
$\frac{4}{4}$ or C	4 beats per bar	1 2 3 4 1 2 3 4 1 2 3 4 1 2 3 4
$\frac{6}{8}$	6 quavers per bar	1 2 3 4 5 6 1 2 3 4 5 6

Dotted rhythms

Clapping dotted rhythms can be tricky. Rehearse and clap the exercise below. Use numbers to count out the beats in each bar as you clap the rhythm. Insert them under the rhythm pattern to help you if you wish.

Compose a four-bar rhythm pattern in 4/4 using the dotted rhythm in two of the bars and clap it out.

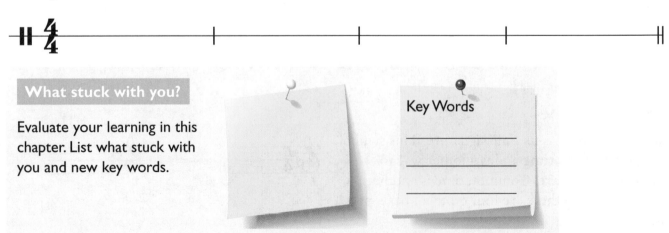

What stuck with you?

Evaluate your learning in this chapter. List what stuck with you and new key words.

Key Words

_____

_____

_____

Listening to Rhythm

Identifying rhythmic patterns

Listen carefully to three rhythmic patterns and determine whether you hear rhythm a) or b) in each case. Play each track three times.

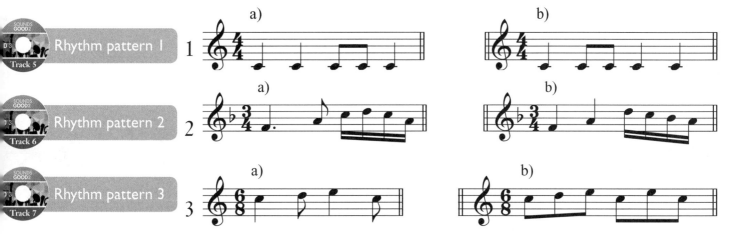

Rhythm pattern 1 — Track 5

Rhythm pattern 2 — Track 6

Rhythm pattern 3 — Track 7

Rhythmic dictation

Complete the following two-bar rhythmic patterns. The first bar is given for you. Play each pattern three times.

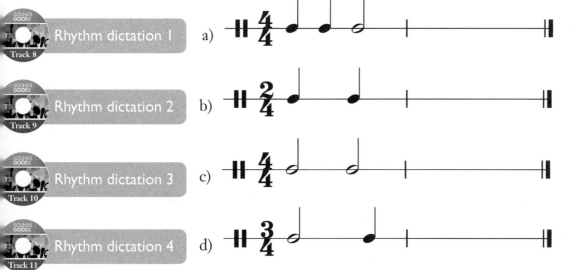

Rhythm dictation 1 — Track 8 — a)

Rhythm dictation 2 — Track 9 — b)

Rhythm dictation 3 — Track 10 — c)

Rhythm dictation 4 — Track 11 — d)

Now try to notate these two-bar rhythmic patterns. For each exercise:

◆ Play each track four times.

◆ The time signature is identified for you.

◆ Exercise a) includes a dotted-crotchet and quaver.

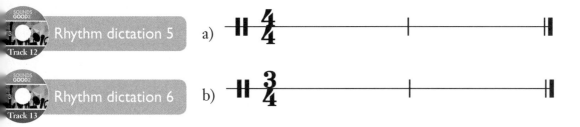

Rhythm dictation 5 — Track 12 — a)

Rhythm dictation 6 — Track 13 — b)

Transcribe the following rhythmic patterns. Play each pattern three times.

Track 14 c)

Track 15 d)

Track 16 e)

Track 17 f)

Performing Rhythm Patterns

Longer rhythm patterns will need to be rehearsed. Study the rhythm parts below, consider the role dynamics play in the performance of this rhythm. Perform both patterns using a rhythm instrument of your choice.

Define the terms:

rit. _____

cresc. _____

mf _____

Pattern 1

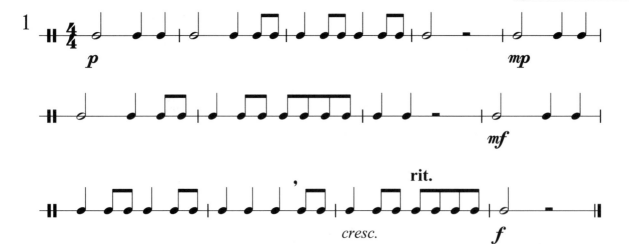

Pattern 2

3 Compose a rhythmic statement in 6/8

Performing together

Paired clapping exercise. Work in pairs to rehearse and perform together.

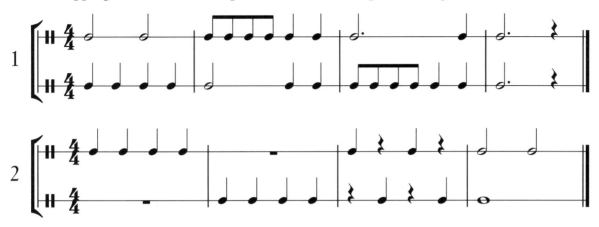

Clap and tap for fun!

Multi-tasking is a good way to improve concentration. Try performing this short ostinato in two parts. Clap the top line and tap the bottom line with your foot, playing both parts simultaneously.

Compose your own two-part **ostinato**.

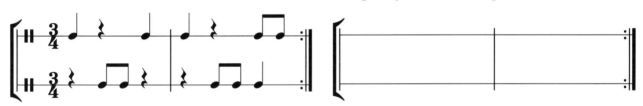

Evaluate your learning in this chapter. List what stuck with you and new key words.

Key Words

Composing a Rap

Rapping, also known as MCing, is vocal performance using a rhythmic style of speech or rhyme which is performed alongside a back beat or ostinato accompaniment.

Can you name a rap artist?

_____

Create a musical rap about a topical issue or current event.

Rap lyrics

A topical issue is a subject which is currently relevant to society. Usually there are two sides to the matter, so it takes some thinking to understand the different viewpoints. A topical issue can often be presented as a question. Here are some examples of topical issues.

1 Are zoos ethical?
2 Global warming
3 Ireland's homeless crisis
4 Child labour

Suggest two other topical issues.

1 _____

2 _____

Choice of topic and the time signature are very important.

Topic	Time signature

Creative steps

1 Pick a topic you care about.

2 Brainstorm the concepts, key words and theme words. Then write down all the **rhyming words** you can think of that are relevant to the topic you have chosen.

3 Set a metronome going or tap the beat while you think about your lyrics. Don't be afraid to **freestyle** with your **lyrics** to get the creativity going. Keep note of them by jotting these ideas down.

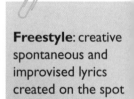

Freestyle: creative spontaneous and improvised lyrics created on the spot

Writing a rap is a process of trial and error. Use **lyrics** that are catchy but real. Write your lyrics in the space below.

Jotter: rhyming words, key words and other ideas	Lyrics

Back beat

Once you have decided on your lyrics, you must choose a back beat. Ideas for these can be found using the app Drum Genius. It is a library of drum loops for all styles and genres.

Compose a **rhythmic ostinato** or **melodic ostinato** to accompany your rap.

You could record yourself tapping or clapping your ostinato or create a sound file using an app like GarageBand. Use the drums setting to record your ostinato, making use of the high hat and bass drum sounds for a funky beat. Alternatively, compose a melodic ostinato. **Loop** your recording to accompany your lyrics.

Rap and refine!

As you *rehearse* your rap, *refine* it. Try rapping your song alongside your chosen ostinato to work out what changes it may need. Cut out any words that are not necessary; only use the words that are needed to make your point, nothing more. Don't be afraid to add a pause or two; this can help to enhance a certain point in the song.

 When your rap is ready, perform it for your classmates.

Insert your final draft below.

Rap title	Topical issue
Lyrics	Explain the purpose of this rap

Ostinato

Offer feedback to your classmates on their work and *discuss* their choice of topical issue. Why was this issue important to them and what is their message?

Reflecting on this learning experience

Explain why did you choose to write about this topical issue.

_____

Identify one **lyric** you like and *explain* how it reflects your topical issue.

_____

What part of this activity did you enjoy and why?

_____

Outline which part of this activity you found challenging and why.

_____

Describe what helped you to overcome these challenges?

_____

Did your classmates write about other interesting topics? Name two.

1 _____

2 _____

Investigate the rap genre and write about one rapper who has written lyrics about a topical issue similar to the one you chose. *Transcribe* some of their lyrics below.

Hip hop is more complex than sunglasses and gold chains! The first hip hop beats were created by experimenting with scratching vinyl records. MCs were party hosts who spoke over the beats. They were the first rappers.

Topical issue:	Rapper's name
Lyrics	Info:

Advertising Jingles

Suggested slogans for advertisements which are concerned with the topic of **peace** are listed in the grid on page 169. Before adding pitches, we must compose **rhythmic patterns** to match the words.

Consider the syllables in the words and where the emphasis naturally lies in these statements. Compose a rhythm pattern and insert it on the rhythm line printed alongside each set of lyrics.

A space is given at the bottom of this grid for you to compose your own short slogan. Write it alongside its rhythmic pattern in the space provided.

Slogan	Rhythm patterns
Power to the peaceful	
Human kindness grows where peace lives	
Peaceful places for our children to roam	
Keep a peaceful place in your heart	
Write your own slogan	Compose a rhythm pattern for this slogan below:

Composing Ostinatos

In Unit 2 we explored the rhythmic feature of syncopation. *Define* the term **syncopation**.

_____

Identify a musical **genre** which uses syncopation. _____

Name a song you have listened to which uses syncopation.

_____

Compose a two-bar rhythmic pattern which uses some syncopation on the rhythm line below.

Define the term **ostinato**. _____

 Using found sounds, record and playback this ostinato for your classmates. Alternatively, *rehearse* and perform it on percussion instruments that are available to you.

What stuck with you?

Evaluate your learning in this chapter. List what stuck with you and new key words.

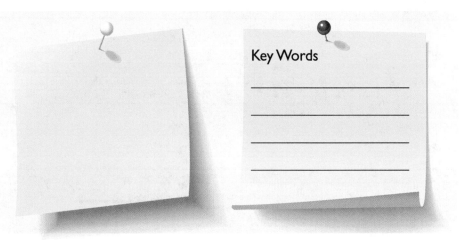

Key Words

_____
_____
_____
_____

169

Changing time signatures

Marching music is usually written in 2/4, while 3/4 is used for waltzes. 4/4 is used both in classical and popular music for all sorts of purposes. Time signatures can be complicated and sometimes change within a piece of music.

'Classical Gas' by Mason Williams is a piece of instrumental music which was released in 1968. The song won three Grammy Awards the following year. 'Classical Gas' has seventeen time-signature changes throughout the two-and-a-half-minute song. It switches between 3/4, 4/4, 5/4 and 6/4.

Listen to a version of this music by searching online for 'Glenn Campbell – Classical Gas – YouTube'

Classical Gas

Mason Williams

'All You Need Is Love' by The Beatles is another example of a song which uses changing time signatures. The main verse pattern contains a total of twenty-nine beats, split into two bars of 7/4, a single bar of 8/4, followed by a one-bar return to 7/4 before the pattern is repeated. Other well-known songs which have changing time signatures include 'Lucy in the Sky with Diamonds' by The Beatles and 'Take Five' by Dave Brubeck.

Unusual time signatures

5/4, 6/4 and 7/4

Most **popular music** is written in 4/4, a time signature you are now very familiar with. You may also find you can count the beats 1, 2, 3, 4 quite easily as you listen to or play music in this time signature. In the same way, 3/4 is relatively easy to identify and to perform. Composers who change time signatures in their music tend to make use of less well-known time signatures, as is the case for each of the pieces mentioned above.

A relatively small amount of music is written in more unusual **time signatures** such as 5/4, 6/4 and 7/4.

English rock band **Radiohead** formed in 1985. Their electronic rock song '15 Steps' is written in 5/4 and remains in 5/4 for the full song. The use of 5/4 gives the song a strangely syncopated feel. Search online for 'YouTube – Radiohead – 15 Step – Live From The Basement [HD]'. Listen to the song and try to identify the count of five crotchets in the rhythm using the number line below.

Research and identify two more pieces of music with unusual time signatures:

Piece	Composer
1	
2	

Radiohead

1 2 3 4 5 **1** 2 3 4 5 **1** 2 3 4 5

American rock band **MGMT** formed in 2002. Their hit song 'Electric Feel' is written in 6/4. This time signature gives the music a bouncy, upbeat feel. Search online for 'YouTube – MGMT – Electric Feel'. Listen to the song and try to identify the count of six crotchet beats in each bar. Use the number line below to help you.

MGMT

1 2 3 4 5 6 **1** 2 3 4 5 6 **1** 2 3 4 5 6

English rock band **Pink Floyd** formed in 1965. Their song 'Money' is in 7/4. This time signature gives the song a jazzy feel. Listen out for the use of **found sounds** and the very cool **bass riff**! Search online for 'YouTube – Pink Floyd – Money (Official Music Video)'. Listen to this song and try to identify the count of seven crotchets using the number line below.

1 2 3 4 5 6 7 **1** 2 3 4 5 6 7 **1** 2 3 4 5 6 7

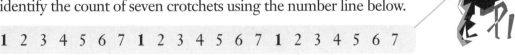

What stuck with you?

Evaluate your learning in this chapter. List what stuck with you and new key words.

Key Words
_____
_____
_____

Melody is the magic that occurs when pitches are added to a rhythmic pattern. When songs run through our heads over and over, it is the melody we have memorised first. Often, we are missing some of the lyrics and find ourselves replacing them with something else. A good example of the power of melody is when children are learning to sing their ABCs. Many young children have learnt this before starting school; the reason for this is the catchy melody. Young children have memorised the melody even though the letters are often muddled up when they sing it. Interestingly, it is the melody that helps them to correct this mistake over time. Experiment! Try to sing the alphabet to the tune of 'Happy Birthday'. Not easy!

> " Melody is the tune. Pitch is how high or low the sound is "

Pitch

Musical alphabet

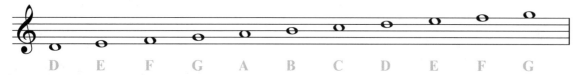

D   E   F   G   A   B   C   D   E   F   G

Pitches in music are assigned to a stave to help us identify the notes of the melody written by composers.

Do you use a menmonic for remembering these notes?   Lines: _____

Label the pitches on the staves below.   Spaces: _____

a)

....

b)

....

c)

....

Ledger lines

In pairs, identify the names of the notes on the ledger lines in this exercise.

a)

....

b)

....

C Major

In *Sounds Good 1* we composed melodies in the key of C major. Here is the scale of C written on a stave for you to look at.

C   D   E   F   G   A   B   C

On the stave below, using semibreves, rewrite this scale an **octave lower** on the bass clef descending.

Define the term **octave**.

Scales are very important in music! Exploring the scale of C major in more detail will help you to understand the other major scales composers often used.

A scale is a collection of different pitches, organised around a central pitch called the tonic.

Major scales are defined by the interval pattern; that is, how the gaps (intervals) between the notes are arranged.

Scale degree numbers indicate the order of pitches in a scale when **ascending**. The tonic note is always called 1̂. Each **octave** of a major scale is made up of eight consecutive notes, also known as the degrees of the scale. The eighth note has the same name as the tonic and is exactly one octave above it. Label the notes on the stave below.

> **Interval**: the difference in pitch between two sounds

 Major scales follow a specific interval pattern of **tone-tone-semitone-tone-tone-tone-semitone**. This is sometimes easier to understand when you look at a piano keyboard. Use your whiteboard from *Sounds Good 1* to help you with this.

Each degree of the major scale is shown here for you. 'S' short for 'semitone' shows a half step, as there is no black key falling between it and the next note. 'T' stands for 'tone' – this is equivalent to two semitones.

It is not just C major that works like this. **All major scales follow the same pattern**.

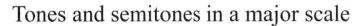
Tones and semitones in a major scale

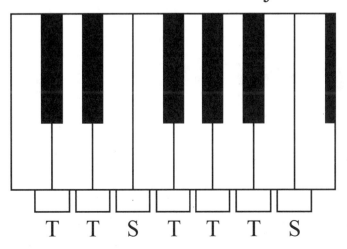

T   T   S   T   T   T   S

Let's recap!

A major scale consists of eight notes (the first and last note have the same name and are one octave apart). It is arranged in a pattern of tones (steps) and semitones (half steps). So how do we construct all the other major scales?

Simply start with the name of the scale (also known as the **tonic**), follow the tonic with a whole step, then another whole step, a half step, a whole step, another whole step, yet another whole step and finally a half step. This will bring you back to the tonic one octave above where you started.

Check back on your key of C; the notes of the C major scale are C D E F G A B C. Using your whiteboard to help you, follow the motion of the C major scale below.

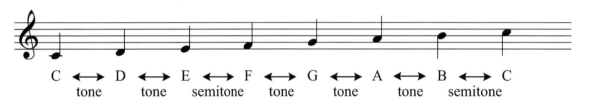

- ◆ C to D is a full tone.
- ◆ D to E is a full tone.
- ◆ E to F is a semitone.
- ◆ F to G is a tone.

- ◆ G to A is a tone.
- ◆ A to B is a tone.
- ◆ B to C is a semitone.

It is sometimes useful to remember that the two semitones in a major scale always fall between scale degree numbers $\hat{3}$ and $\hat{4}$, and $\hat{7}$ and $\hat{8}$.

Melodic dictation in C major

Musical memory is an important part of musicianship. Dictation is tricky to begin with but over time you build up the skills needed and your musical memory will improve.

Transcribe the melodies you hear on the staves provided. Play each exercise a few times until you have mastered it.

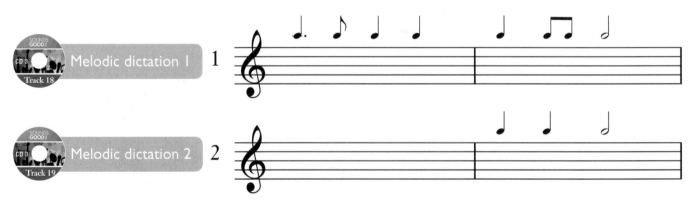

Developing and adapting melodic phrases in C major

Below is the opening phrase of Johann Hummel's Allegro in C Op. 5 No. 2.

Play this melody on your recorder or another instrument and consider ways we can *adapt* this **motif** to develop the ideas presented in it.

Rewrite the melody in 2/4 on the stave below.

Further *adapt* this theme by making further changes to it on the stave below.

Other Major Keys

G major

Here is a keyboard template. Work in pairs. Beginning from G, identify each note of the scale using your guide for tones and semitones. The seventh note can be tricky! You should have landed on a black key. What does this mean?

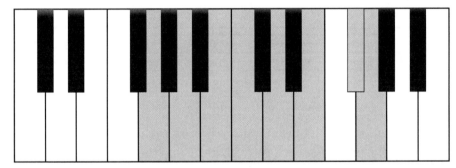

Take a look at the scale of G written out for you. A sharp sign (♯) has been placed before the high F, the seventh note of your scale. This black key is F♯ and is a semitone higher in pitch than the F found on the white key, known as F natural (F♮).

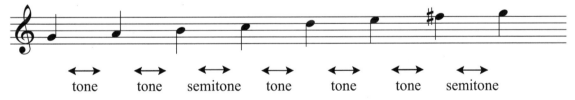

The piano's black keys

As we mentioned earlier, the musical alphabet runs from A to G. Pianos typically have eighty-eight keys. The alphabet pattern repeats in groups of eight notes (octaves), and there are five black keys that fall within each octave. Black keys always appear in consecutive patterns of two and three. These black keys represent separate pitches or notes. The black keys share the same name as the closest white key to it but with the **addition of a suffix (sharp or flat)**. This also means that each black key has two names! The note becomes

◆ a **sharp** when the black key is to the right or higher than the white key

◆ a **flat** when the black key is to the left or lower than the white key.

To return to the original note following a ♯ or ♭ we use a **natural** sign ♮.

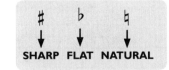

When we read sheet music we may find one of these suffixes placed **before a note** in the melody. A sharp means to raise the pitch by a semitone, while a flat means to lower a pitch by a semitone.

Write out the scale of G major ascending and descending, inserting suffixes where necessary.

Here's how G major looks with and without a key signature.

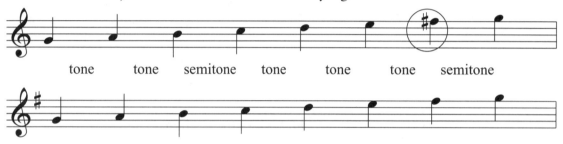

tone   tone   semitone   tone   tone   tone   semitone

Compose a four-bar melody in the key of G on the stave below. Don't forget to insert your key signature at the beginning and to end on the key note G (doh).

Composing in G major

When writing melodies in the key of G major, composers don't insert a sharp **before** each F used in the piece. Instead the F♯ is represented at the beginning of the piece, between the treble clef and the time signature. This is called the **key signature** and indicates to musicians before they start playing what pitches need to be used in the piece.

Below is the opening phrase of Tchaikovsky's 'Morning Prayer Op. 39'. Identify and circle the F♯ in this theme.

Listen to the theme below played on the piano. It will be played three times for you. Insert the missing notes in bars 3 and 4, marked x on the score. Then answer the questions.

Theme to 'Morning Prayer'

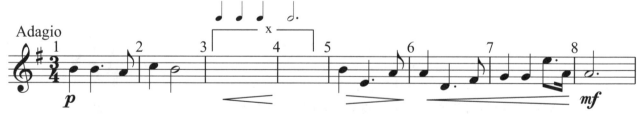

1   *Explain* the **tempo** marking. _____

2   How many times is **dotted rhythm** used in this theme.? _____

3   *Identify* the **range** of the melody. _____

4   *Suggest* a suitable instrument for performing this excerpt. _____

5   *Explain* what is 'p' short for? _____

F major

F major is another commonly used key signature. 'Go Your Own Way' by Fleetwood Mac and Queen's 'We Are the Champions' were written in this key.

As before, use the keyboard template to identify the degrees of the scale and label the keyboard below and shade them in.

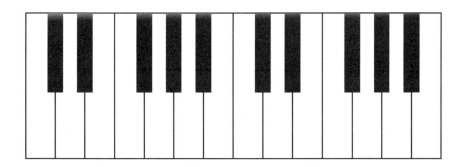

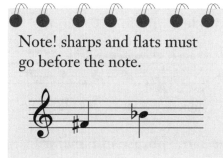

Note! sharps and flats must go before the note.

Insert the notes on the stave below and insert any sharps or flats needed.

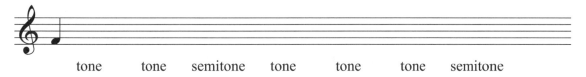

tone   tone   semitone   tone   tone   tone   semitone

Compose a four-bar **answering phrase** in the key of F on the stave below. Don't forget to listen to the opening melody and consider how the melody moves. **End on the key note F.**

F major four-bar melody

Answering phrase

Melodic dictation in F major

Listen and transcribe the short melody onto the stave below.

Transposing

Sometimes composers will decide to change the key of a piece of music. This may be to accommodate a change of instrument – some instruments need the music to be written at a particular pitch – or to ensure a vocalist is able to sing the notes of the melody comfortably. Taking a piece of music and changing it into another key is known as **transposition**.

Here 'Twinkle Twinkle' has been transposed from C major to F major.

Twinkle Twinkle in C major

Twink-kle, twink-kle, lit-tle star,   how   I   won-der what you   are.

The same phrase in F major

D major

The Eagles' 'Hotel California' and Avicii's 'Wake Me Up' were composed in the key of D. Most pieces of traditional Irish music are written in this key; if you have ever owned a tin whistle, it was most likely a D whistle.

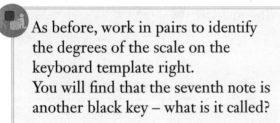

As before, work in pairs to identify the degrees of the scale on the keyboard template right.
You will find that the seventh note is another black key – what is it called?

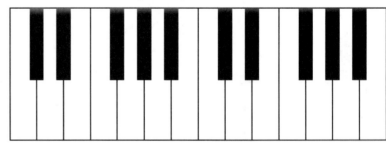

Insert the notes of the D major scale using semibreves on the stave below, ascending and descending.

Listen to this four-bar melody in D major on the CD, then compose an **answering phrase**.

Four-bar melody

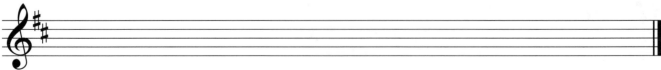

Canon in D is a very famous piece of music, written by Johann Pachelbel for three violins and cello. Pachelbel was a composer from Germany. The melody and harmonic patterns in this composition have influenced many later composers, including Handel, Haydn and Mozart. There are two things to note in this piece – the first is that the **form** of the piece is canon.

Define the term 'canon'. _____

Distinguish the texture. _____

Have a listen to it. I bet you have heard it before. Follow the music printed below as you listen. Notice the opening melody in bars 3 and 4. You will also hear a change in texture.

 Another feature of this work is Pachelbel's use of ostinato throughout the piece. You can hear it played in the two bars of rests at the beginning of the piece. Listen to it on the CD.

Define the term 'ostinato'.

Performing the ostinato

Write out the scale of D major and use it to help you identify the solfa pattern for the ostinato above. Rehearse and sing the ostinato along with your CD.

Adapting the ostinato

Use the staves below to adapt the two main **motifs** used by Pachelbel in his canon by changing the feel, style or other features.

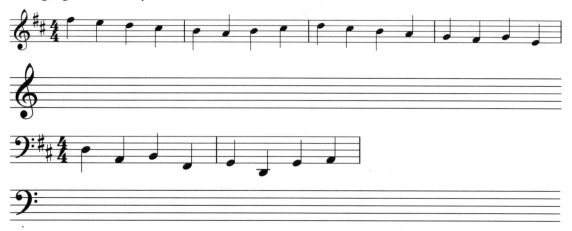

Composing a canon

In order to compose a piece of canon, what do we need to know and what decisions do we need to make?

Comment on the performance skills needed to perform as part of a canon.

In *Sounds Good 1* we performed canons and rounds. A canon begins with a single unaccompanied melody. The second and third performers enter after a set distance, usually a few bars after the previous part started. As each part enters and the melodies blend together, harmony is created.

The opening voice or instrument is called the 'leader', and all the parts sing or play the same line as the leader has done before them. Many traditional songs are sung in canon, in *Sounds Good 1* we sang 'Row, Row, Row Your Boat'. 'Three Blind Mice' also works well.

Another extremely well-known song is 'Frère Jacques'. This French song has a simple melody, but when performed as a three-part canon it sounds interesting. Do you think you could compose a three-part canon using this melody?

Here is 'Frère Jacques' in D major.

When performed in canon this song is typically performed at a **two-bar distance**.

 Work together to transcribe this melody as a three-part canon with a two-bar distance between performers. Watch out for the clef used for the third part! What vocal part reads from this clef?

Record your performance and listen back. Evaluate your performance together and identify and discuss the **performance skills** and **techniques** that were necessary to interpret the music effectively.

When you have completed the composition, insert the lyrics and rehearse and *present* this song to an audience.

1 *Discuss* the need for **dynamics** and articulation in performance.

2 *Suggest* suitable dynamics for this song and insert them on the score.

3 *Refine* the details and repeat your performance of this piece.

What would happen if you tried to play this piece on the recorder? What is the lowest note on the descant recorder? How would the highest note be written? Write these two notes next to each other on the stave below with a straight line joining up the note heads. Look at the example provided for the guitar to help you. This is how we show the **range** of an instrument.

Guitar range

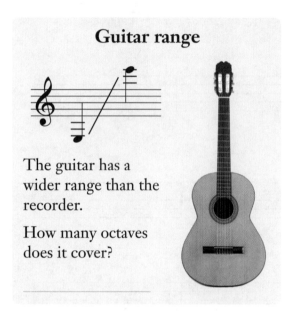

The guitar has a wider range than the recorder.

How many octaves does it cover?

Recorder range

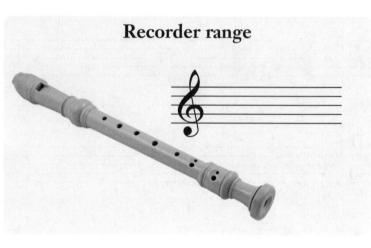

Transposing music for recorder performance

In order for a recorder **ensemble** to be able to play your 'Frère Jacques' canon, you will need to **transpose** it into the key of F major. Look back at the scale of F major that you wrote out on page 177. *Use* it to help you transpose the tune of 'Frère Jacques' into F major. Write your transposition below. Don't forget to *insert* the right **key signature** and the **time signature**.

Insert numbers or symbols to show where each recorder part should enter to perform this canon and insert the lyrics.

When three parts play in canon the texture of the music is _____.

'Adiemus' was written by Welsh composer Karl Jenkins in 1995. Jenkins, a composer of advertising music composed this commissioned piece for Delta Airlines. The vocals are not real words but a collection of sounds designed to complement the music.

◆ Search online for 'YouTube – Karl Jenkins – The History of Symphonic Adiemus'.

Performance skills and techniques are important aspects of performance. Search online for 'YouTube – Kilkenny Presentation Girls Choir – Up For the Match – RTÉ One'. This choir's director Veronica McCarron prepared this performance of 'Adiemus' with her students. Watch and appraise the performance using the appraisal sheet below.

Performance Appraisal Form

Title of piece _____

Composer _____

Performer _____

For each aspect of the performance, tick the first, second or third column.

	Consistently good	Good, but some mistakes	Could be improved
Musical qualities			
Correct notes			
Good rhythmically			
Good tempo			
Use of dynamics			
Use of articulation			
Control of instrument or voice			
Overall style			
Presentation			

Indicate what you liked best about this performance.

_____

_____

_____

Identify what you have learnt from this performance that you can apply to your own performances.

_____

_____

_____

B♭ Major

Prince's 'Purple Rain' and Queen's 'Bohemian Rhapsody' were composed in this key.

Prince

Queen

As before, use the keyboard template to identify the degrees of the scale.

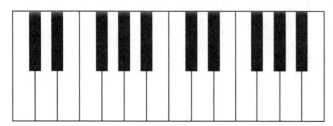

Insert the notes on the stave below and insert the suffixes once you have decided whether any of the notes need a sharp or flat sign.

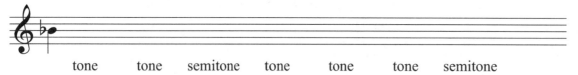

tone   tone   semitone   tone   tone   tone   semitone

Composing in B♭

Study the opening bar of a melody in B♭ major below. Compose a rhythm pattern and melody to complete this four-bar melody. End on the key note of B♭.

Compose a rhythmic accompaniment for this melody on the rhythm line below.

Combine your B♭ melody with the rhythmic accompaniment you have composed on the stave provided below. Ensure you align the rhythm patterns correctly so that they correlate.

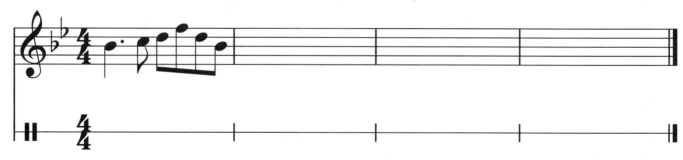

Let's recap!

Name the five major keys we have worked with in this unit

1 _____   4 _____

2 _____   5 _____

3 _____

Explain the term **key-note**.

_____

Write out **two-octave** scales on the staves below. The key signatures are indicated next to the treble clef.

Moveable doh

Add tonic solfa labels doh re mi fah soh lah ti doh to each of the scales above. What do you notice? Each scale begins with doh. This is understood as 'moveable doh' because the pattern stays the same despite the note you start on. Tonic solfa begins with the tonic of each key and makes it easier for singers to sing the various pitches with or without sharp or flat suffixes.

Gather the information needed to complete this grid from your labelled scales above.

	Doh	Soh	Tonic/Keynote	Piece of music in this key/Composer or artist
C major				
G major				
F major				
D major				
B♭ major				

What stuck with you?

Evaluate your learning in this chapter. List what stuck with you and new key words.

Key Words

You are going to create and present some musical ideas using instruments and/or found sounds to illustrate the mood and feelings expressed in the poem 'Midterm Break' by Seamus Heaney.

'Midterm Break' was written by the acclaimed Irish poet Seamus Heaney following the death of his younger brother, who was killed by a car in 1953. This is a poem about death and family grief. Heaney was only fourteen when the funeral took place, but I think you will agree he has captured the atmosphere in his home on the day of the funeral in a very special way.

Listen to the poem being read aloud to you and follow the lines of each stanza.

'Midterm Break' by Seamus Heaney

Midterm Break

I sat all morning in the college sick bay
Counting bells knelling classes to a close.
At two o'clock our neighbours drove me home.

In the porch I met my father crying—
He had always taken funerals in his stride—
And Big Jim Evans saying it was a hard blow.

The baby cooed and laughed and rocked the pram
When I came in, and I was embarrassed
By old men standing up to shake my hand

And tell me they were 'sorry for my trouble'.
Whispers informed strangers I was the eldest,
Away at school, as my mother held my hand

In hers and coughed out angry tearless sighs.
At ten o'clock the ambulance arrived
With the corpse, stanched and bandaged by the nurses.

Next morning I went up into the room. Snowdrops
And candles soothed the bedside; I saw him
For the first time in six weeks. Paler now,

Wearing a poppy bruise on his left temple,
He lay in the four-foot box as in his cot.
No gaudy scars, the bumper knocked him clear.

A four-foot box, a foot for every year.

Seamus Heaney

Listen again and identify which **words** or **ideas** you could **illustrate** by means of musical motifs using **found sounds** or **instruments**.

Record your ideas and give details of the motifs you would create in the space below.

Record some of these sounds and use garage band to synchronise the sounds with a person reciting the poem. Listen back and refine your work.

With your teacher, choose another poem or newspaper article and write a short melody to represent the main **mood** or theme in it.

Insert your melody on the stave below and evaluate your composition in the space provided.

Why do composers feel compelled to compose?

Composers are masters of melody. Their compositions have the power to communicate with others in a meaningful way. Melodies help to preserve memories for those who attach their thoughts to the music they listen to. Composers use melodies to bring **illustrative music** to life and evoke emotion or create tension.

For many composers, the creative process is one of escape and brings them great joy and satisfaction. Composers believe their music can tell the stories of the real world; indeed, it is sometimes the strongest way of expressing the world we live in. Sometimes, for some composers, writing their melodies is a means of accessing 'another place' that is otherwise hidden and allows them to create musical pictures of imagined worlds.

Search online for 'YouTube InSight #1 Maria Minguella – Boom'.

Consider the role **imagination** plays in composition. Complete a Think–Pair–Share Sheet with another student and feedback your ideas to your classmates.

Name		Date
Question or topic: Does imagination play a role in composition?		
What I think...	What my partner thinks...	What we will share...

Composing melodies is great stimulation for our minds; it allows us to consider our thoughts and feelings about something and express these through music, supporting our wellbeing.

Composing activity 1

Choose a photograph or image that is really important to you. Create and present a short piece using instruments and/or other sounds in response to your image.

 Transcribe your eight-bar melody in a major key of your choice on the stave below. Use **tempo** and **dynamic** markings to illustrate the **mood** or feelings you wish to highlight. Remember to insert the **key signature** and the **time signature** in the right places. You should draft and refine your melody on your *Sounds Good 1* whiteboard before you write your **final version** on the stave below. Give your composition a title and use the copyright symbol © to protect your creative work.

Composing activity 2

Compose, perform and record an original **jingle** or brief piece of music for use in a new advertisement for a product.

Begin by creating an advertising slogan. Assign a **rhythmic pattern** to the words you have chosen and, finally, add a catchy **melodic motif** to complete your jingle.

Notate your advertising jingle in the space below. Ensure you insert the **lyrics** correctly under the completed jingle.

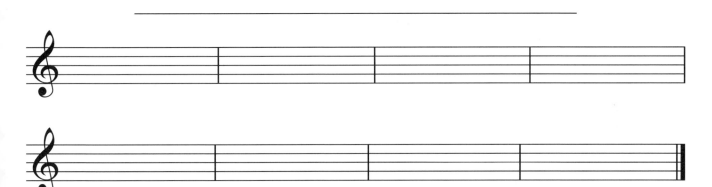

Completed melodic statement

Perform and record your composition. Listen back and evaluate your advertising jingle.

Key Word	Definition

What stuck with you?

Evaluate your learning in this chapter. List what stuck with you and new key words.

Key Words

Reflection and Evaluation Sheet

Unit title:

Learning Outcomes (LOs) I worked with:

Music I listened to:

Learning and exploring

I really enjoyed…

Something interesting I learnt…

My biggest challenge was…

I overcame this by…

One improvement I have made is…

Traffic-light your learning

Learning Outcomes	🙁	😐	🙂	✓
1.2				
1.3				
1.6				
2.2				
2.3				
2.4				
2.7				
3.4				

Rate your learning

Learning

Key words	Action verbs

Key skills

I got better at x skill by

This unit reminded me of learning about…

What still puzzles me is…

Feedback and goal setting…

Unit 6

Creative Lab

In this unit

Unit 6 is a creative space designed to move your learning and skills forward. A greater understanding of how melody is constructed and how sounds are layered to create texture and harmony is explored here. Engaging with the activities in this unit encourages you to compose harmonic support for your creations using chord progressions. Learning to revise and refine music to perform for and with others is important in this unit. In doing so we learn how to make informed musical decisions and judgments about our work.

Checklist	LO	Intended learning
☐	1.1	**Compose** and perform or play back short musical phrases and support these by creating rhythmic/melodic/harmonic ostinato to accompany them.
☐	1.3	**Design** a harmonic or rhythmic accompaniment, record this accompaniment and **improvise** over the recording.
☐	1.4	**Indicate** the chords that are suitable to **provide** harmonic support to a single melody line.
☐	1.12	**Indicate** where chord changes occur in extracts from a selection of songs.
☐	1.13	**Compare** different interpretations or arrangements of a piece of Irish traditional or folk music, paying attention to musical elements and other influences.
☐	2.2	**Create** a musical statement about a topical issue or current event and share with others the statement's purpose and development.
☐	2.3	**Adapt** excerpts/motifs/themes from an existing piece of music by changing its feel, style or underlying harmony.
☐	2.6	**Design** a rhythmic or melodic ostinato and add layers of sound over the pattern as it repeats, varying the texture to create a mood piece to accompany a film clip or sequence of images.
☐	2.8	**Analyse** the chordal structure of excerpts from a range of songs and compile a list of songs with similar chordal structures and progressions.
☐	3.9	**Investigate** the influence of processing effects (e.g. distortion, reverb, compression) on the recording process; select some recordings and **evaluate** the use and effectiveness of such effects within them.

While participating in new learning experiences throughout this book and *Sounds Good 1*, you have had many opportunities to explore the varied genres and historical periods of music. It is important to consider how each of these has fed into the development of others. We can trace links from one genre to another, and identify how one genre has influenced another.

Talk trios

In groups of three, identify who will be person A, person B and person C. Person A and person B discuss the two statements below and person C will feedback details of the discussion to the remainder of the class.

	Statement
Person A + B Discuss	Topic 1: The **Romantic** composers were masters of **programme music**. How has their efforts influenced the **film music** industry of today? Topic 2: Could we argue that **songwriters** such as Paul McCartney or Bono owe much to Schubert?
Person C	Present their arguments to the class as part of your group.

In Unit 5 you composed melodies in various keys and metres, for different purposes. In this unit you will expand your knowledge of composition. Melody was the first element of Western music to develop, and it wasn't until many years later that **harmony** was added. **Baroque** composers like Bach and Handel moved music forward in leaps and bounds. Bach filled his music with ornate and complex melodies and harmony. The composers that followed in the **Classical era** stripped much of this away and focused on the melodic line, supported by simpler **harmony**. The **Romantic** composers added more pitches to their harmony preferring to use **chromatic** harmony, going beyond the classical rules. Remember the Romantic composers were concerned with evoking and illustrating emotion in their music. Adding **chromaticism** and creating **dissonance** helped them with this.

> **Dissonance**: tension or disharmony caused by pairing notes together which clash or fail to harmonise.

What is Harmony?

Harmony occurs when two or more pitches are sounded together simultaneously.

A **melody** is made up of single pitches in succession, written from left to right. Once we add an additional pitch to a note we have harmony. If you can visualise a melody as horizontal and harmony as vertical, this may help you to understand how they are different from each other but work together.

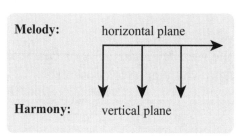

Harmony

Singing in harmony

You have already experienced singing in harmony when you performed in a **round**. You can do this now using 'Row, Row, Row Your Boat' or you can revisit 'Hava Nashira' on page 160 of *Sounds Good 1*.

Classical composers Mozart and Haydn based much of the harmony in their compositions on three or four chords!

Listen to the opening bars of the Overture to *The Magic Flute* on your CD. Mozart uses three majestic **chords**, each one fuller than the one before and separated from it by a **rest** to add to the drama. The number three is significant in this opera and these opening bars provide an example of how Mozart used three chords to introduce a **motif** that would be interwoven throughout the work.

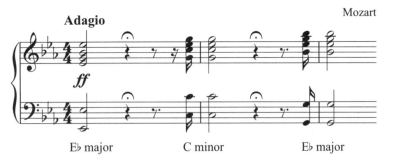

> How is the key signature of E♭ major associated with the number three?

> **Excerpt from Overture to *The Magic Flute* by Mozart**

Mozart knew that these three **chords**, used together to create a **chord progression**, would resonate with the members of his audience, making his music memorable. This would encourage people to return to hear the performance again.

Mozart composed his final opera *The Magic Flute* in 1791. It is probably the most famous **opera** to include spoken dialogue alongside the singing; this type of opera became known as **Singspiel** (literally meaning 'song-play') and represents the beginning of a new genre which developed to include musicals! The **Overture** to *The Magic Flute* is performed by the orchestra before the curtain opens, composed to set the scene and to get the audience into the right frame of mind for the stories that are about to unfold.

Name a modern musical and the composer of the musical score.

> Watch a performance of this work by searching 'YouTube – Mozart The Magic Flute overture Neville Marriner'.

Name your favourite song or character from the musical you have named above and explain why you have chosen this.

Songwriters of today such as Chris Martin, lead singer of Coldplay, and Lady Gaga know the power of chord progressions too! The chord progressions used in many of our favourite hits were tried and tested by some of the greatest composers in the world and have been around for a long time.

Could we say Schubert designed the first pop songs? He did write over six hundred **art songs**! Schubert used memorable melodies and set his songs out in verse and chorus form. He used piano accompaniment, and much of what the piano played was based on a repeating chord progression too. Many of these features remain the hard-and-fast rules of songwriting today.

Elton John

Listen to some songs by Elton John or Nina Simone to hear examples of these features.

Name a recently released pop song which features a vocalist accompanied by piano that is in verse–chorus form?

_____

Why do you think the piano has been such a popular choice of accompaniment?

_____

_____

List three other instruments often used to accompany vocalists.

1 _____

2 _____

3 _____

Nina Simone

Composing with Chords

Up to now, we have been busy creating and composing melodies. These are suitable for soloists to perform, but most of the music we listen to is based around a melody with an **accompaniment**.

Accompaniment is a musical part which has been composed to support the **melody** of a song or instrumental piece. The accompaniment can be provided by another single player or an **ensemble** of performers, such as an orchestra. Common instruments used to accompany melodies are piano or guitar; they often play **chord progressions**.

An **accompanist** is a musician who accompanies a **soloist**. Suggest a reason why accompanists need to have excellent **sight-reading** and **improvisation skills**.

_____

_____

Choose **two** pieces of music with your teacher and *identify* how the melody line is supported by the accompaniment. *Describe* the accompaniment in each case, referring to the elements of music you have studied.

	Title of piece	Composer	Description of the accompaniment
Piece 1			
Piece 2			

What are chords?

So, what are chords and how do they work? When two or more notes are played together at the same time they sound a **chord**. If you hit two notes on the piano at the same time, you are playing a chord. Try singing a different note to the person sitting next to you at the same time – you have made a chord! In either case, the two notes have a certain distance between them. The distance between two notes of a chord is better known as an **interval**. We learned about intervals in Unit 5 when we explored semitones, tones and octaves!

Working out intervals seems tricky at first. Count the letter names from the bottom note to the top note, as when you identify the **range** of two notes. It is important you don't forget to count the note itself when you are trying to identify the interval.

An example of the intervals in C major is available to listen to on your CD. You will hear the notes individually and then together. Each interval will be played in succession as shown on the stave below.

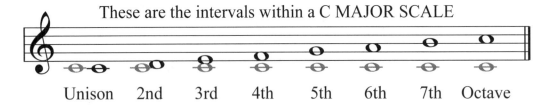

These are the intervals within a C MAJOR SCALE

Unison   2nd   3rd   4th   5th   6th   7th   Octave

Intervals

Count the interval out from the bottom note to the top. Use the keyboard on your whiteboard to help you visualise the chord. Complete the grid below, the first box is completed for you.

Notes	C–C	C–D	C–E	C–F	C–G	C–A	C–B	C–C
Interval	unison							

The quantity name is given below the scale above for you; this tells us the interval between two notes. However, each interval also has a quality name which is used to describe the sound that the two notes make. When the interval is wider than an octave, it is called a compound interval, but it is named in the same way by counting the distance between the notes e.g. a twelfth or a fifteenth.

A good way to help us to recognise intervals is to sing them.

Sing the repeated two-note opening to the *Jaws* theme and you are singing the **interval** of a second. If you start singing 'Somewhere over the Rainbow' from *The Wizard of Oz*, the opening two notes that you sing to the word 'some-where' are an **octave** apart. A tune you know very well is 'Twinkle Twinkle'; the interval between these two words is a **fifth**! Try the exercise below in C major.

doh   re   doh   me   doh   fah   doh   soh   doh   la   doh   ti   doh   doh'
major 2nd   **major 3rd**   **perfect 4th**   **perfect 5th**   **major 6th**   **major 7th**   **octave**

Can you give another example of a particular interval that occurs in a famous song?
Name of song _____ Interval _____

Work in pairs to identify the following **intervals**. Write your answers below each bar.

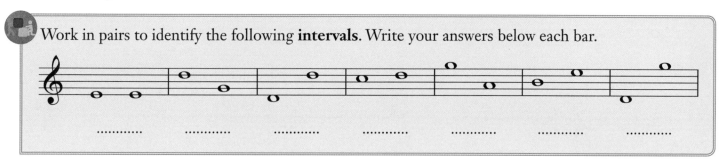

....

Complete the following **intervals** by adding the missing note in each bar.

| Second Lower | Octave Lower | Fifth Higher | Third Higher | Sixth Higher | Fourth Lower | Unison |

Listen to the intervals on the CD. Using your ear, try to identify the distance between the two notes. You will hear the interval played three times. Each interval begins with doh.

Intervals 1 — CD 3 Track 29
Intervals 2 — CD 3 Track 30
Intervals 3 — CD 3 Track 31

	1st note	Note name	2nd note	Note name	Interval
1	Doh	C			
2	Doh	C			
3	Doh	C			

Counting in semitones

Investigate the intervals shown here. At first glance, it appears that both intervals are a third. Using the piano keyboard count the number of **semitones** between the two examples below.

doh re mi fah soh la ti

You will have noticed that the interval from E to G spans three semitones (E → F, F → F♯, F♯ → G) and counting from F to A was four semitones (F → F♯, F♯ → G, G → G♯, G♯ → A). Intervals can also be made wider or smaller where there is a flat (♭) or sharp (♯) in the key signature, meaning the interval can be larger or smaller than it first appears.

What do we call a scale that moves in semitones? _____

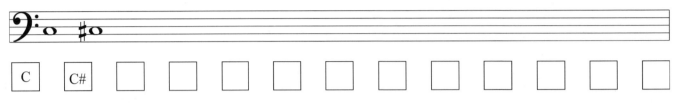
Insert the C major ascending chromatic scale the stave below. Label each pitch name in the scale.

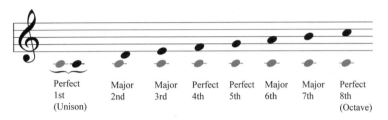

| C | C# | | | | | | | | | | | |

The scale below labels the intervals by their quantity and their quality names.

Perfect 1st (Unison)   Major 2nd   Major 3rd   Perfect 4th   Perfect 5th   Major 6th   Major 7th   Perfect 8th (Octave)

Whilst two notes are enough to make a chord, it is more common for chords to have three notes. Three-note chords are called **triads**.

Triads and chords

A triad is a chord made up of three notes. The notes are stacked in thirds, one on top of the other. Triads can be built on each note of a scale. We call the note in the scale the **root** and build the triad from there, adding two further notes, each a third above the previous note.

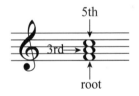

Look at the example shown for the chord of F major. The root names the chord (F), the third is placed a third above the root (A) and the fifth is a fifth higher than the root (C). Using the F major scale laid out for you below, build the triads for each note on the stave. Count out the third and fifth notes starting from the root note each time.

F major triads

F   G   A   B♭   C   D   E   F

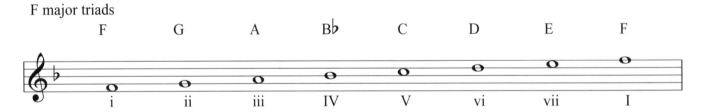

i   ii   iii   IV   V   vi   vii   I

Triadic compositions

We've learned that melodies move in varies different patterns and directions. We use words like ascending, descending, by step or by leap to describe melodic movement. A **triadic melody** uses the notes of a triad in succession. This can happen in one bar, over the course of several bars or throughout a piece. Look at the example below.

Example A: triadic melody

These successive leaps are in the same triad

Example B: Not triadic

These are not

Oh,   say,   can   you   see,

Example A is the first phrase of 'Star Spangled Banner' which we worked with in Unit 4. Name these pitches and you will notice each note is part of the C major triad. The notes used in example B are not part of a triad.

Why do you think many composers use the notes of triads to construct melodies?

Bach based the opening melody of his Brandenburg Concerto No. 5 – Allegro on the **tonic** or **doh triad**, D major.

Identify the notes of the doh triad in D major: _____   _____   _____

Activity 1

Investigate the opening violin **motif** on the stave below and circle notes which are **not** part of the doh triad.

Adapt this motif by transposing it into a different key.

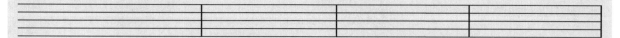

Suggest a suitable instrument to perform this _____.

Activity 2

When melodies are based on triads or chords composers often develop the same melody in the next phrase. The phrase below is in C major. Work in pairs to identify the triads used in each bar.

Use the same triads, in the same order to compose an answering phrase for this opening tune, on the staves below.

Activity 3

Compose a mood piece for <u>four parts</u>.

This four-bar composition should reflect your choosen mood and must be based on the triads **Doh, Fah and Soh**. Choose a **key signature** and **time signature** for this piece and begin to draft and re-draft your work using your music whiteboard.

Your composition should include **two** melodic parts, **one** part which uses **pedal notes** and **one** rhythmic ostinato. The instruments you choose should reflect the nature of the part (rhythmic or melodic) and the clefs you have inserted, treble or bass.

Write a detailed description of this task and the mood you have choosen to reflect. Comment on the the key moments of learning in this task and reflect on how you overcame any difficulties in the space provided below.

Naming triads

In the F major triads exercise on page 198, the triads have been labelled using three different systems:

◆ pitch names   ◆ tonic solfa   ◆ Roman numerals.

These are equally valid ways of identifying chords. Chords are most often named by their **root** name (usually the bottom note). The root note of the chord determines the **chord symbol**.

Triads can also be recognised by the **solfa** labels: doh, fah or soh triads etc.

Roman numerals are commonly used to label things in a particular order, such as **chord progressions**. It is important to notice that some of the labels appear in capitals (I, IV, V) and the others use lower-case letters (ii, iii, vi, vii).

Using your scale on page 198 to help you, insert the letter names of the notes of each of the triads in F major in the **chord box** (right).

Fifth							
Third							
Root							
Chord symbol	F			B♭			
Tonic solfa	doh	re	mi	fah	soh	lah	ti
Roman numeral	I	ii	iii	IV	V	vi	vii

Complete the exercise below indicating the chord symbol (root), tonic solfa and the Roman numeral label for each triad. Use your completed chord box to help you.

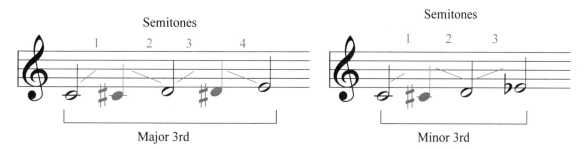

Chord symbol   _____   _____   _____   _____   _____   _____   _____   _____

Tonic solfa   _____   _____   _____   _____   _____   _____   _____   _____

Roman numeral   _____   _____   _____   _____   _____   _____   _____   _____

It is likely that, when you experimented with making a two-note chord earlier on piano or by singing with your classmates, some combinations sounded sweeter on the ear than others. There is a reason for this.

Triads are built using intervals of a third, but we have just learnt on page 197 that sometimes the interval is wider when we count the **semitones** between notes. So, there are two types of thirds: **major thirds** and **minor thirds**.

Major thirds are made up of two notes that are four semitones apart. C to E is a major third. If there are only three semitones, it is a minor third (C–E♭). This shows how flats and sharps affect intervals.

Major 3rd   Minor 3rd

The interesting thing is that each triad has one of each, a major and a minor third! What is really important is identifying which comes first.

The triad of C major is built using a major third and then a minor third. Go back to the keyboard on page 197 to check this.

Major triad

◆ C–E is four semitones = major third

◆ E–G is three semitones = minor third

When the major third comes first it is recognised as a **major triad**.

In C major, the triad of D is different. The notes of the D triad in C major are D–F–A. D–F is three semitones and F–A is four semitones. Therefore, the minor third comes first, making this a **minor triad**.

Minor triad

Identify another major triad in C major _____.

Identify another minor triad in C major _____.

Look at the G triad below and identify whether it is a major or minor triad.

Pitches	Interval	Major/Minor
G–B		
B–D		

Identify the intervals below by their quality and quantity name.

Major triads are easy to spot in a labelled scale or chord box because major triads are written using capital Roman numerals (I, IV and V). These are known as **primary chords**. Also known as the doh, fah and soh triads, they are the same in every major key.

Minor triads are identified by lower-case roman numerals (ii, iii and vi) or by the solfa names re, mi and lah.

I hope you have spotted that one triad has not been accounted for yet: vii or ti! This is a **diminished chord** and there is one in every key. It is the exception to the rules above because it is built using two minor thirds. It has a **dissonant** sound, meaning it doesn't sound quite as nice as the others. Composers often save these chords to create a certain mood or a feeling of unease.

Listen and compare the **major, minor** and **diminished** versions of the G chord on your CD. This will help you to understand what the labels can tell us about how certain chords or triads will sound.

◆ G major

◆ G minor

◆ G diminished

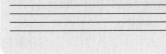

Major, minor and diminished triads

In Unit 5 we worked with the five major keys C, G, F, D and B♭ major. Complete the following activities in the grid on the next page.

◆ Insert a one-octave ascending scale in the given key using semibreves.

◆ Build the triads for this key on the root notes and label each triad correctly using tonic solfa.

◆ Use the triads to help complete the chord box.

◆ Identify the minor chords by inserting 'm' next to the chord symbol for minor chords.

◆ Identify the diminished chord by inserting 'dim' next to the chord symbol.

> Experiment with trying to identify the intervals of the school bell or a message or alarm tone on your phone. Insert it on the stave below if you can identify the pitch.

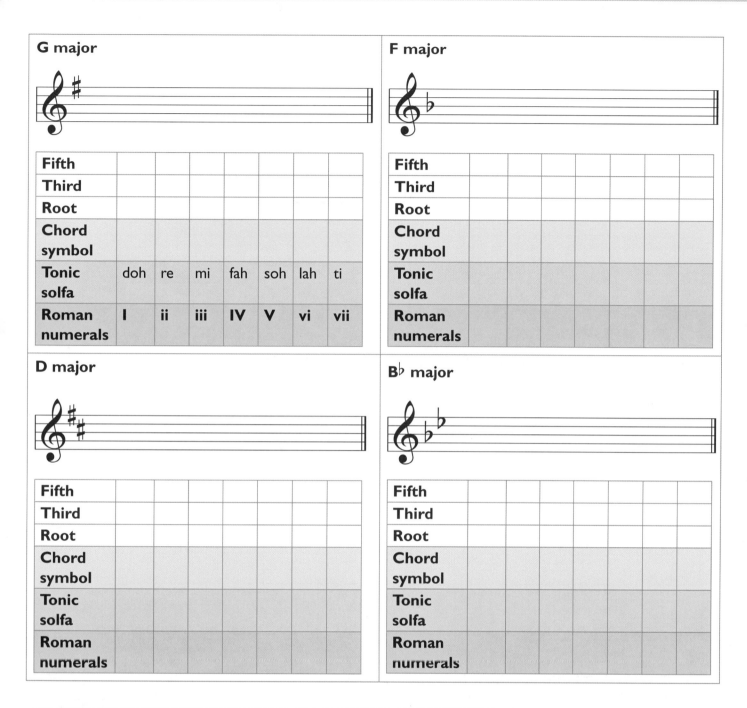

G major

Fifth							
Third							
Root							
Chord symbol							
Tonic solfa	doh	re	mi	fah	soh	lah	ti
Roman numerals	I	ii	iii	IV	V	vi	vii

F major

Fifth							
Third							
Root							
Chord symbol							
Tonic solfa							
Roman numerals							

D major

Fifth							
Third							
Root							
Chord symbol							
Tonic solfa							
Roman numerals							

B♭ major

Fifth							
Third							
Root							
Chord symbol							
Tonic solfa							
Roman numerals							

What stuck with you?

Evaluate your learning in this chapter. List what stuck with you and new key words.

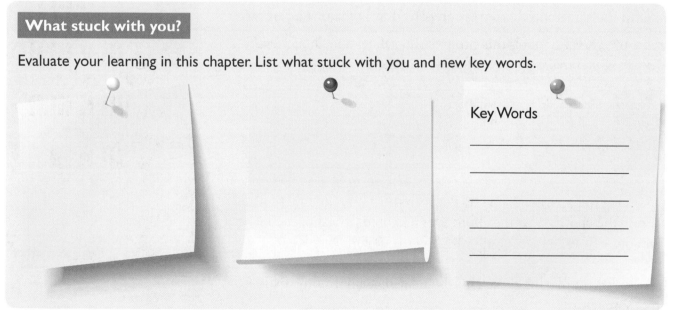

Key Words

_____
_____
_____
_____
_____

Chord Progressions

What are Chord Progressions?

A **chord progression** is a series of chords played in succession or in a repeating sequence.

The same chord progressions are used again and again in popular music. The most common chords used are **I, IV** and **V**; these are also called the **primary triads**. Research and identify two three-chord and two four-chord songs and list them below.

	Three-chord songs	Four-chord songs
1		
2		

The songs you have identified most likely use chords **I, IV, V and vi** in the key the song was composed in. Many composers and songwriters have written masterpieces using these chords as the basis for their melody. Looking back at our major keys, complete the grid below by identifying the chord symbols and pitches for each of these chords.

Major keys	I	Notes	IV	Notes	V	Notes	vi	Notes
C major	C	C–E–G						
G major			C	C–E–G				
D major								
F major								
B♭ major							GM	G–B♭–D

In Western music, the chords I and V are the most common. Many **folk songs** and tunes use the chords I, IV and V as the basis for their melody and accompaniment.

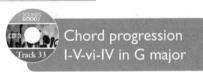
Chord progression
I-V-vi-IV in G major

Listen to the progression I-V-vi-IV in G major played twice. The piano chords are shown for you on the right.

Listen to the same chord progression played in D major played twice.

Indicate the chord symbols this progression relates to. Then *identify* the notes which make up each of these chords.

Roman numeral	I	V	vi	IV
Chord symbol	D			
Notes				

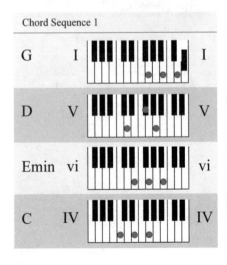

Chord Sequence 1

G   I   I

D   V   V

Emin   vi   vi

C   IV   IV

Working in pairs, use the piano keyboard on your whiteboard to locate the chords. Play the chord progression on a piano, keyboard or app such as GarageBand for both G major and D major.

Experiment with playing these chords and *design* a harmonic ostinato using these chords.

Chord progression
I-V-vi-IV in D major

Record your progression and *transcribe* your progression onto the stave below by inserting the notes of the triads.

 Working in groups, use this harmonic progression as the basis for a new composition. Create a piece for performance. Play, record and loop your chord progression and *experiment* by *improvising* over it to create more layers.

◆ Add a rhythm line for clapping, body percussion or performance on a percussion instrument.

◆ Use a melody instrument to create a **triadic melodic line** based on the harmonic progression of chords.

◆ Add a vocal line with lyrics you have composed yourselves. Transcribe your work into your compositional portfolio.

Reflect on and *evaluate* the creative process you engaged in. Comment on the role you played below.

  Chord progression I-V-vi-IV in C major

Listen to the progression I-V-vi-IV in C major, played twice.

 Identify the chords and indicate on your music whiteboard where the notes of the chord lie on the piano keyboard.

The progression vi–IV–I–V in C major consists of the chords **Am–F–C–G**.

Chord progression vi–IV–I–V in C major

Listen to these chords played on piano twice. Does this chord progression remind you of any songs?

Block and broken chords

There are two common ways to play chords: as **block chords** or as **broken chords**.

◆ When musicians play block chords, the notes of the chord are played together at the same time.

◆ When musicians play broken chords, the notes are played one at a time.

Listen to the opening phrase of Mozart's Sonata in C. This is an example of **broken chords** accompanying a **melody**.

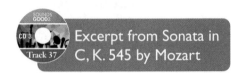

Excerpt from Sonata in C, K. 545 by Mozart

Identify the **pitch** names of the left-hand **broken chords**. Using these pitches and the pitches in the right hand work out the chord progression used in this phrase. Insert Roman numerals or chord symbols into the boxes laid out for you below.

Theme from Sonata in C, K. 545

Allegro

Mozart

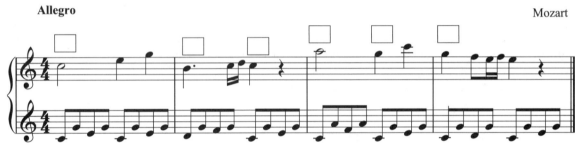

Chords are used by composers as a plan or framework which enables them to decide on the melody notes for their composition. Circle the notes in the melody that are part of the chord progression for this phrase. These are known as **harmony notes**; they ensure the melody moves according to the chord progression the composer is using.

Triadic movement

The first three notes of Mozart's melody are an example of **triadic movement**. Triadic melodies use the notes of the triad and often begin with the **root** before moving through

the other notes of the triad. You will recognise most triadic melodies because they move in thirds. Name another piece of music we have studied based on **triadic movement**.

Compose a four-bar **triadic melody** using the chord progression **I–IV–V–I** in B♭ major. Insert it on the stave below. Use a **chord box** to help you.

Unessential notes

The other notes which make up the melodic line are called **unessential notes** because they do not appear in the chords used. Their purpose is to decorate the melody. There are two types of unessential notes we need to know about: passing notes and upper/lower auxiliary notes. **Passing notes** are notes which connect the notes of the chord. **Upper or lower auxiliary notes** are notes

Passing notes marked with asterisk

Auxiliary notes marked with asterisk

which move up or down by step between two repeated notes. There are no unessential notes in bar 1 of Mozart's Sonata, as each note is part of the chord of C. Circle the unessential notes in bars 2 and 4 of Mozart's opening motif.

> Look back at Bach's cello suite on page 126 for examples of these.

Suggest two reasons why unessential notes are an important part of any melody.

1 _____

2 _____

Transcribe the melody of the first phrase from Mozart's Sonata on the stave below, right hand only. Then use the chord progression to identify which **block chords** you need to insert for the piano accompaniment onto the bass clef. Create a rhythmic ostinato to accompany the piano part and insert it on the rhythm line below the stave. Make sure you line up the beats carefully.

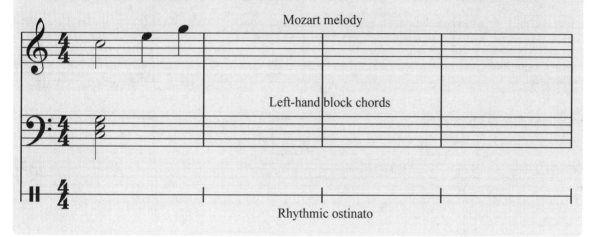

Investigate the melody of Beethoven's 'Ode to Joy' from his Symphony No. 9 printed below. It is in the key of C major and the chord progression is shown for you. Circle the **unessential notes** in the melody line.

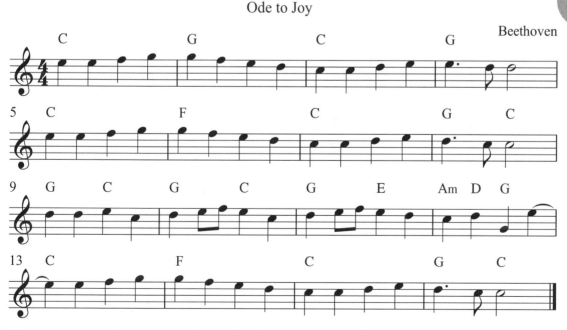

Many versions of this song exist, each with its own variation on the chords, rhythm and melody. Research and listen to **two** other interpretations of this well-known song.

Using your research as inspiration *adapt* this piece by changing its **rhythm**. Pencil in your ideas on the score above.

Once you have adapted the rhythm, transpose the melody from C major to G major on the staves provided below. Changing the key will have an impact on the chords as well as the notes. You will need to use the chord box to help you complete this task.

When you have transposed your melody and identified your new chord symbols, use the **root** of each chord to help you compose a simple left-hand accompaniment for the melody, so a pianist can play this piece. Ensure you align your treble and bass stave notes correctly.

Task preparation

Include a scale of C and G in your rough work. You will need a G major chord box to help you identify the chords needed.

Composing a melody using a chord progression

Many composers report that inspiration for their melodies comes to them in all sorts of circumstances, but for most, there is a plan or a structure decided at the beginning of the creative process that helps them to shape their melody. This is often a **chord progression** like those we have just been looking at. Using a chord progression to **compose** a **melody** can seem tricky at first, but once you get going there will be no stopping you!

Let's work with the chord progression **I–IV–V–I** in F major.

Insert the chord symbol and the notes of the chord in the grid.

Progression	I	IV	V	I
Chord symbol				
Notes				

Explore the melody line below and discuss in pairs how the melody has been developed using the progression **I–IV–V–I**. Where are the essential and unessential notes? Circle the harmony notes and draw a triangle around any passing notes or upper/lower auxiliary notes. Identify and indicate where the chord changes occur in this phrase.

Composing answering phrases

Some melodies use answering phrases to develop a melodic statement. A question is presented and it is followed by an answer. These phrases typically reflect the chord progression of the initial phrase.

Use the melody above as your question and compose an answering phrase based on the chord progression I–IV–V–I above. The melody and rhythm of your answer should be similar to that of the question. Don't forget to end on doh!

> Use a chord box in F major to help you with this task.

Question

Answer

Paired composition

Using the chord progression **I–vi–IV–V**, compose a four-bar melody in 3/4 in D major. Once completed, switch copies with one of your classmates, allow them to compose a suitable answering phrase to your question! Use a chord box to help you with this task.

Question

Answer

This task allows for an element of 'Chance'. What composers often provide the opportunity for chance music in performances of their compositions?

Group songwriting

Work together in groups of three or four.

◆ Compose a short **verse** or statement about a topical issue or event of your choice.

◆ Add a suitable **rhythmic pattern** to the syllables set out in your **lyrics**.

◆ Compose a **melody** for your song using the progression **I–IV–vi–V–I** in B♭ major. Transcribe it on the stave on the next page.

◆ Compose a **block-chord** accompaniment and a **rhythmic ostinato** to complete your song.

◆ Stay focused and work together to identify the emphasised syllables in your lyrics and to place these syllables on the essential harmony notes from the chords you are using.

◆ Make use of the **unessential** notes between **harmony** notes where necessary.

◆ Insert the **lyrics** underneath the **melody** and ensure you align the syllables and notes correctly.

◆ *Refine* your composition by adding **dynamics**, **articulation** and don't forget to end on the tonic note doh!

Use the chord box provided to assist you with this task.

								Lyrics
Fifth								
Third								
Root								
Chord symbol								
Tonic solfa	doh	re	mi	fah	soh	lah	ti	
Roman numeral	I	ii	iii	IV	V	vi	vii	

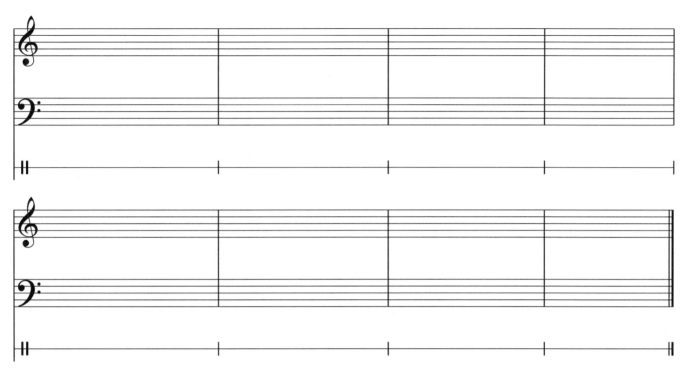

Choose a trio of instruments to play the melody line, chordal harmony and percussion parts.

Role	Instrument
Melody	
Harmony	
Rhythm	

Record or input the parts using GarageBand or other software available to you and play back your composition. As you listen to it, *appraise* your melody by considering its strengths and/or weaknesses and reflect on ways in which you could *refine* your work. Make notes on your thoughts below.

_____

_____

_____

_____

You might decide to submit this composition as part of your CBA 1.

What stuck with you?

Evaluate your learning in this chapter. List what stuck with you and new key words.

Key Words

_____

_____

_____

Backing Chords

Some composers add chords to accompany melodies they have written rather than shaping a melody around a chosen chord progression. By adding chords, composers can cater for all the voices or instruments the piece has been designed for. These chords are called **backing chords**, and they are typically played by piano or keyboard to support the **soloist**.

It is important we use a chord box to assist us when trying to identify chords to accompany a melody line. The chords which are best suited to the melody you are working with are the chords which include notes that match the melody. We know from what we have learnt about unessential notes that not every note in the bar will appear in the chosen chord, but you should aim to match as many as you can. The chords **iii** and **vii** are particularly dissonant and can clash with the melody. <u>These chords should be avoided.</u>

Cadences

Before you choose which chords to use to accompany the melody, you will need to identify a **phrase plan**. Each phrase will need a cadence. A **cadence** is a progression of two chords which create a resting place at the end of each phrase or at the end of the piece of music, similar to placing a comma or full stop in your English sentences. To create a cadence there are pairs of chords which can be used together to create a good sense of rest. There are four types of cadence; two of them sound more final than the other two. Each of these will be played for you on your CD.

Finishing cadences

◆ A **perfect cadence** is created using **chord V followed by chord I**, i.e. soh moving to doh.

◆ A **plagal cadence**, also known as the 'amen cadence' due to its common use in liturgical music, is created using **chord IV followed by chord I**.

Cadences	
Perfect V – I	G – C
Plagal IV – I	F – C
Imperfect ii –V	DM – G
Interrupted V – vi	G – AM

Non-finishing cadences

◆ An **imperfect cadence** creates a comma rather than a full stop to a musical phrase and must end on chord V.

◆ An **interrupted cadence** also creates the feel of a comma in a piece of music. It is created using **chord V followed by chord vi**.

Complete the grid to identify the chords used to create each of the cadences in the major keys we have engaged with. Two have been completed for you.

Key	Perfect	Plagal	Imperfect	Interrupted
B♭ major	F – B♭			
D major		G – D		
F major				
C major				
G major				

Complete the following exercises by exploring the two melodies provided below.

◆ Use a chord box to identify suitable chord progressions to accompany the melody. Draw this on your whiteboard.

◆ Label the chords correctly; remember the same chord <u>should not be repeated in succession</u>.

◆ Do not use the chords **iii and vii**.

◆ To find the **cadence** point, you must identify any places of rest in the melody. This might be where you would breathe if you were singing the piece or playing it on the recorder. Long notes or rests can indicate a resting point/pharse ending.

◆ Use **chord symbols** instead of Roman numerals in your answers. Ensure you use the correct combinations to create cadences at the end of phrases.

◆ End with a **finishing cadence**.

'The West Wind'

a)

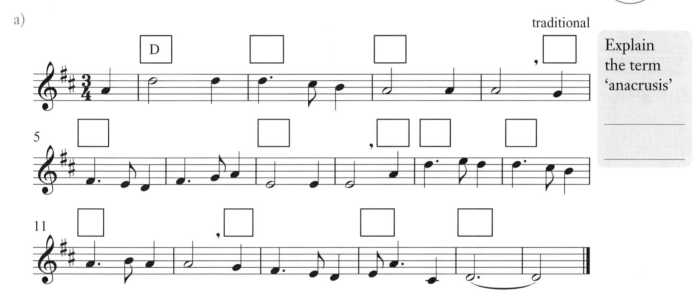

Explain the term 'anacrusis'

_____

_____

b) Once you have indicated an appropriate chord progression for the melody of the 'Song of Western Men', below, choose suitable long notes from the chords you have decided on and add them to the bass stave to create a piece of music for piano. Ensure you take care to align the bass notes accurately with the treble line.

'Song of Western Men'

'God Defend New Zealand'

This is one of two national anthems for New Zealand. Can you name the other national anthem?

Originally a poem written by Irish-born Thomas Bracken, these lyrics were set to music in 1876 by Joseph John Woods. The Maori lyrics were added two years later. In 1940 the New Zealand government bought the **copyright** for this hymn and adopted it as their national anthem. This **hymn** used to be sung in English, but at the 1999 Rugby World Cup match between New Zealand and England, players sang only the Maori verse of this hymn. As a result of debates that followed, one English and one Maori verse should be performed.

Listen to an instrumental performance of this song on piano. Try to identify where the chords are changing as you listen and use a pencil to mark these points on the music printed below. The song will be played three times for you.

God Defend New Zealand
National Anthem of New Zealand

Thomas Bracken, 1870s
Thomas H.Smith, 1878

John Joseph Woods, 1876

Complete a chord box to help you to identify what chords have been used. Work with another member of your class to decide on the position of the chords and insert the chords you feel are correct.

'The Minstrel Boy'

Analyse the chord structure of this **Irish folk song** written by Irish poet and song writer Thomas Moore. 'The Minstrel Boy' is a **patriotic song** that is widely believed to tell of Moore's friends who died during the Irish Rebellion in 1798. The medieval Irish tune 'The Moreen' is the underlying **melody** used in this song. This song is poignant and became a **hymn** for soldiers who went on to fight in the American Civil War and World War I. We still hear this song performed at the funerals of those who have lost their lives serving their country.

Folk songs tell of everyday events. Research another Irish folk song and share with others the story told in the song. Play a piece of the song for your classmates.

Consider the progressions used to accompany this melody and try to recognise the cadence points. Use a chord box in G major to help you analyse the chords used. Insert phrasing to indicate where the phrases begin and end.

The Minstrel Boy

CD 3 Track 40 — The Minstrel Boy

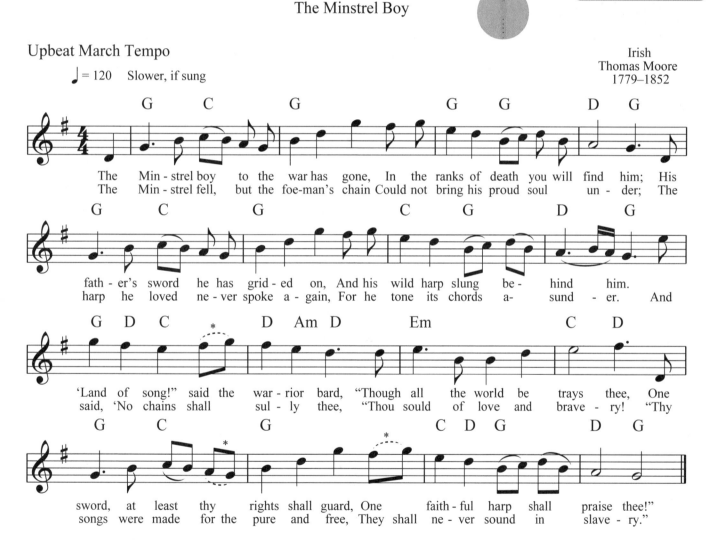

Upbeat March Tempo

♩ = 120 Slower, if sung

Irish
Thomas Moore
1779–1852

Listen to two different arrangements of this song. Search on YouTube for these performances:

1 Jack Lukeman – 'The Minstrel Boy'

2 'The Minstrel Boy' – Ceiliúradh at Royal Albert Hall, April 2014

Compose a short blog post distinguishing between these two performances for an Irish tourism website which hopes to promote Irish music. Mention the motion picture this song features in.

Today's blog title		
		Time

Produce a programme note for this song.

Title	
Composer	
Era (period)	
Genre:	
Expression or mood	
Tempo	
Dynamics	
Rhythm	
Melody	
Other points of interest	

Design, type and print your programme note. Insert an appropriate image and include information on how to listen to this song online.

Identify the chord progression used in the first phrase of this song.

Folk songs

Earlier in this unit, we explored the use of four chords I, IV, V and vi which are used in many popular songs. *Investigate* well-known folk songs from different countries and *analyse* the chord progressions used in these songs. *Provide* details of your three examples below.

Folk song	Country of origin	Type of song	Chord progression
1			
2			
3			

What stuck with you?

Evaluate your learning in this chapter. List what stuck with you and new key words.

Key Words

_____

_____

_____

Processing Effects

In the course of our learning journey we have discovered that many composers and songwriters use melodies, harmonies, ostinatos and chord progressions to compose their music. Music producers use a different set of tools to create their recordings. These are known as audio or **processing effects**.

Inputs

Pan

Mute

Master fader

Channel faders

Master output

Producers use these recording techniques to shape sounds and create the finished product for musicians recording their music in recording studios. Processing effects are a process of manipulating sounds after they have been recorded.

Listen to how these effects change the sound of the chord progression on your CD.

Panning

Panning is a processing effect which splits the sound between speakers. It is used to create the illusion of sound moving from one side of the stage to another or from one speaker to another. Sometimes when we hear panning occur through our headphones we think one of them has stopped working for a moment as the sound switches from one ear to the other.

Reverb

Reverb is short for the word reverberation. Reverb occurs all the time when sound waves bounce off the various objects around us before hitting our ears. Not all sounds can travel directly into our ears; instead there are echoes which create reverb. Reverb happens in our natural surroundings; think of the echo that you hear in tunnels or caves. Digital reverbs use technology to generate multiple echoes resulting in reverb. Reverb sounds like an echo and adds a fullness to the sound.

Distortion

Distortion is created by overloading the speaker and creates a harsh sound. This distorts the original clean sound, making it sound heavy and fuzzy. Distortion is commonly used with electric guitars or synths.

Compression

Compression balances the dynamic range of the various instruments or parts recorded on a track so that you can hear the whole track comfortably. It reduces the volume of the loudest parts and amplifies the quietest parts. This improves the quality of the sound when you turn up the volume.

With your teacher, select some recordings and *evaluate* the use and effectiveness of such effects within them. Give a brief description of two examples you have listened to below.

	Piece of music	Processing effect	Description (refer to the music)
1	Title	1 _____	_____
	Composer	2 _____	_____
	Genre	3 _____	_____
2	Title	1 _____	_____
	Composer	2 _____	_____
	Genre	3 _____	_____

What stuck with you?

Evaluate your learning in this chapter. List what stuck with you and new key words.

Key Words

_____

_____

_____

_____

Reflection and Evaluation Sheet

Unit title:

Learning Outcomes (LOs) I worked with:

Music I listened to:

Learning and exploring

I really enjoyed…

Something interesting I learnt…

My biggest challenge was…

I overcame this by…

One improvement I have made is…

Traffic-light your learning

Learning Outcomes	☹	😐	🙂	✓
1.1				
1.3				
1.4				
1.12				
1.13				
2.2				
2.3				
2.6				
2.8				
3.9				

Rate your learning

Learning

Key words	Action verbs

Key skills

I got better at x skill by _____

This unit reminded me of learning about… _____

What still puzzles me is…

Feedback and goal setting…

Unit 7 Performing

In this unit

Music is the expression of the people. Performance provides us with a way of sharing this with others. All pieces of music are composed to be heard! Performing with others is an enjoyable and collaborative activity. In unit 7 we begin to develop the important skill set needed for performance. Engaging in activities like singing, recorder playing, sight-reading and body percussion has helped us to discover our own talents as performers. By participating in the learning experiences in this unit you will gain experience in performance, giving you confidence in your performance skills. You may decide to present some of these performances for your practical exam.

Checklist	LO	Intended learning
☐	1.1	**Compose** and perform or playback short musical phrases and support these phrases by **creating** rhythmic/melodic and harmonic ostinato to accompany them.
☐	1.5	Read, **interpret** and play from symbolic representations of sounds.
☐	1.7	Perform music at sight through playing, singing or clapping melodic and rhythmic phrases.
☐	1.8	**Rehearse** and perform pieces of music that use common structural devices and textures.
☐	1.9	**Demonstrate** an understanding of a range of metres and pulses through the use of body percussion or other means of movement.
☐	2.1	**Experiment** and **improvise** with making different types of sounds on a sound source and notate a brief piece that incorporates the sounds by **devising** symbolic representations of these sounds.
☐	2.5	Prepare and **rehearse** a musical work for ensemble focusing on cooperation and listening for balance and intonation; **refine** the interpretation by considering elements such as clarity, fluency, musical effort and style.
☐	2.10	**Develop** a set of criteria for **evaluating** a live or recorded performance, use these criteria to complete an in-depth review of a performance.
☐	3.9	**Investigate** the influence of processing effects (e.g. distortion, reverb, compression) on the recording process; select some recordings and evaluate the use and effectiveness of such effects within them.

In *Sounds Good 1* we shared fun experiences making music together. The learning experiences in Unit 7 explored the idea that everyone is a performer in the making. Would you tend to agree with that statement now?

Through our opportunities to rehearse and perform together, we began to develop our creativity and some of the other important skills needed to progress as music-makers!

Can you recall these skills? *List* two in the grid opposite and *briefly describe* how you developed these particular skills.

We learnt that making music is good for our health. Music has been contributing to the wellbeing of man since the beginning of time. The earliest thinkers, known as philosophers, spoke of the importance of music performance. Plato said in 300 BC that music is law. He said that music 'gives soul to the universe, wings to the mind, flight to the imagination, and charm and gaiety to life and to everything'. His sentiments are proven by the fact that no geographical place, culture or community has existed without music.

Performing with others is fun and rewarding.

Describe an experience you shared with your classmates rehearsing and performing together. *Outline* details of the performance.

Skill	How you developed this skill

_____

_____

_____

_____

_____

_____

_____

_____

_____

_____

_____

_____

_____

_____

Philosophy comes from the Greek word 'philosophia' meaning 'love of wisdom'. It is the study of knowledge, truths and nature and often focuses on questions like 'What is the meaning of life?' or 'Why are we here?'

Singing brings joy to so many people! There are many reasons to sing alone and to sing together with others.

Here are some of the benefits singing offers:

◆ Singing boosts the immune system.

◆ Singing is a workout which improves lung capacity.

◆ Singing improves posture.

◆ Singing improves the quality of our sleep.

◆ Singing lowers stress levels.

◆ Singing improves our brain function and alertness.

◆ Singing releases feel-good hormones which help to lift our mood.

◆ Singing introduces us to others, increasing our circle of friends.

◆ Singing with others develops our communication skills.

◆ Singing with others combats stage fright and helps boost our confidence.

Jazz singer Ella Fitzgerald once said "The only thing better than singing is more singing!"

Warming Up

Develop a short guide for a new singer on how to physically warm up their body before they sing. *Outline* three steps you would advise them to take. Look back to Unit 7 of *Sounds Good 1* for ideas.

Step 1: _____

_____

Step 2: _____

_____

Step 3: _____

_____

Breathing

Breathing provides the fuel for singing. *Suggest* tips can you share about how to breathe when you sing.

_____

_____

_____

_____

_____

Phonation fun!

Phonation means to make a sound. It aims to relax the tongue and throat to improve the sound of our voice. It is also a fun way to stretch or loosen out our vocal chords. Breathing effectively from the diaphragm is important for these exercises. Place your hand on your tummy as a reminder to breathe from here.

Activity 1

Consider how we blow out our birthday candles. Breathe in and begin by blowing out but then move to an 'ooo' sound. This will help you to feel the breathing muscles turning on.

Activity 2

Keeping in the birthday mood **hiss** 'Happy Birthday' together. To do this, you do not use words or pitches – simply stick to the 'ssss' sound.

Activity 3

a) Consider the unvoiced sounds in the grid below and experiment with creating them.

b) Draw a visual representation of the sounds you have made in the grid below.

Ssssssss	
Sshhhooooo	
Haaaaaaaa	
Yaaaaaaaa	
Whoooosh	
Whissssssh	
Wheeeez	

Activity 4

You will need a regular drinking straw to blow through. With the straw placed in your mouth, try to perform a **pitch glide**. Beginning as low as you can, slide up through the pitches until you reach the top of your range and then slide back down.

Ensure no air is escaping through your nose or around the straw itself.

Together choose a song everyone knows and try to vocalise it together through the straw.

Can you name an instrument which works in the same way?

Vowel Singing

Do you remember our vowel sounds guide from *Sounds Good 1*? Look back at page 156 and compete the vowel sounds info box below.

Vowel	Sound when being sung

Work in pairs to *design* a singing warm-up using the important vowel sounds. *Transcribe* it on the staves below and write the vowel sounds under the notes. Take care to align each syllable vertically under its note. Present your warm-up to the class.

What stuck with you?

Evaluate your learning in this chapter. List what stuck with you and new key words.

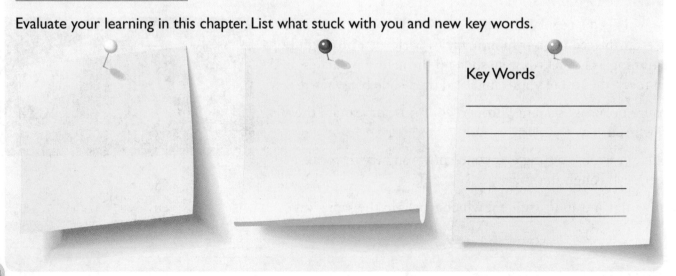

Key Words

Sight-Reading Rhythms

Define the term '**sight-reading**'.

_____

_____

In order to be able to sight-read or sight-sing a melody accurately, you need to be able to read the rhythms that have used.

Clap or play the following examples together

Listen to these patterns on your CD and clap them back. Step a **pulse** with your feet whilst you complete this activity.

Adding melody to rhythm

Choose one pattern in 2/4 and one in 3/4 from above and compose a melody to accompany the rhythm pattern in the key signature provided.

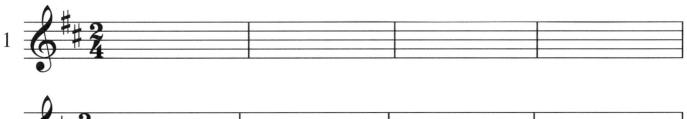

Tonic Solfa

In *Sounds Good 1* we learned about solfeggio singing, a method of naming pitches.

Let's remind ourselves of how it goes by singing it together.

Check in with your learning		
I can sing this tonic solfa scale **ascending**	Yes ☐	No ☐
I can sing this tonic solfa scale **descending**	Yes ☐	No ☐
I can sing it **ascending and descending** in one breath	Yes ☐	No ☐ Almost ☐

doh
ti
la
soh
fah
mi
re
doh

Label the C major scale below using solfa.

Sight-singing with solfa

Sight-sing the following short phrases.

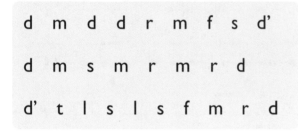

d m d d r m f s d'

d m s m r m r d

d' t l s l s f m r d

Using solfa with notation

Activity 1: Choose one of the sight-reading solfa melodies above and *transcribe* it onto the stave below. Give each pitch a **minim** value and compose in the key of G major.

Activity 2: On the stave below, write out the **descending** scale of B♭ major, one octave and place the solfa names below the notes.

Activity 3: Insert the Doh, Fah and Soh **triads** from D major on the stave below.

Activity 4:

a) Write out the scale of C major **ascending** one octave with the solfa names below the notes.

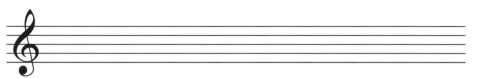

Define the term 'round'.

_____

_____

Explain the texture of a round?

_____

b) Split your class into three groups. Sing this ascending scale with each group beginning **two** sounds later than the next.

Discuss what you notice as the three parts sing together.

Transcribe this three-part vocal exercise on the staves below. Give each pitch a **minim value**.

The **repeat signs** show which bars should be performed several times.

Rehearse and perform this **round** together.

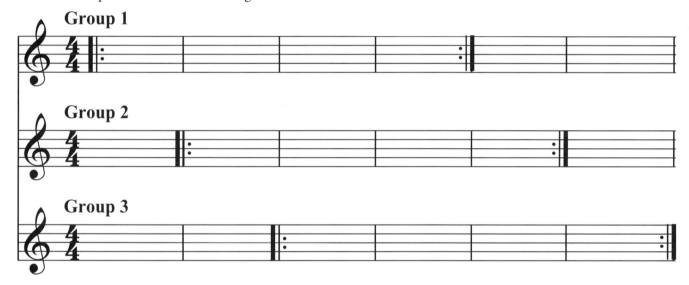

Moveable doh!

When composing using different **key signatures** the **tonic** note is always doh. _Insert_ the major scales named below and label each pitch in the scale using solfa. Don't forget to include the key signature each time.

G major

D major

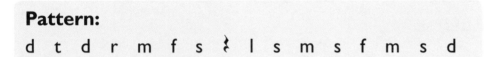Paired Work Activity

Pattern:

d t d r m f s ⅔ l s m s f m s d

On the stave below *transcribe* the following solfa pattern in **G major**. *Use* the scale of G major and the solfa labels in the box above to help you.

d t d r m f s ⅔ l s m s f m s d

Now you need to work together to *compose* a four-bar rhythm pattern in 4/4 to match this short melody.

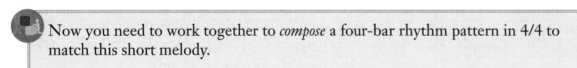Sing it together and *explore* the different ways you would like it to sound. *Use* your music whiteboard to help you to draft and redraft the rhythm you want to use for the melody before you write it on the stave below.

To complete your composition, *compose* a one-bar **ostinato** in 4 to accompany this short melodic phrase; write it on the rhythm line making sure it is correctly aligned with the melody.

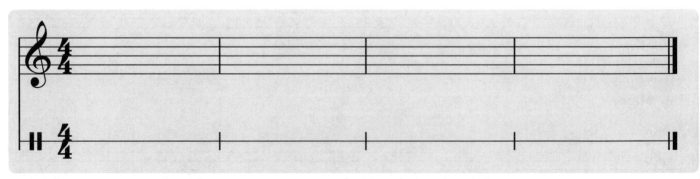

Use the music software accessible to you to record and play back what you have created. If you are using Audacity or GarageBand explore the use of **reverb or distortion**.

Critique the recording you have made. *Identify* aspects are you pleased with. Which aspects would you like to change and why?

_____

_____

_____

_____

_____

_____

_____

Using Distortion

Distortion will make your recording sound more gritty or fuzzy by altering the shape of the sound waves. Also look for the 'drive' or 'overdrive' controls to experiment with this effect.

Comment on the value of **processing effects**. Have they enhanced your work and if so, how?

_____

_____

Mention the software or **apps** you used for this activity and explain the process.

_____

_____

Using Reverb

Adding reverb can make your piece sound as though it was recorded in a larger room by adding an echo effect.

A similar composition could be added to your compositional portfolio in written, digital or audio format.

What stuck with you?

Evaluate your learning in this chapter. List what stuck with you and new key words.

Key Words

_____

_____

_____

_____

Body percussion or body music has existed for as long as we have and predates any musical instruments. Percussion instruments are typically played by hitting, shaking, scraping or striking them with another object. These techniques can be used on the human body too. Breathing in or out to produce sound is also considered body music!

Body percussion is a fun way of being active and creative. In *Sounds Good 1* we explored various ways in which we can create body sounds. Complete the body percussion bank below. Suggest ways in which our hands and feet can provide a rhythmic element to music.

Body Part	Description
Hands 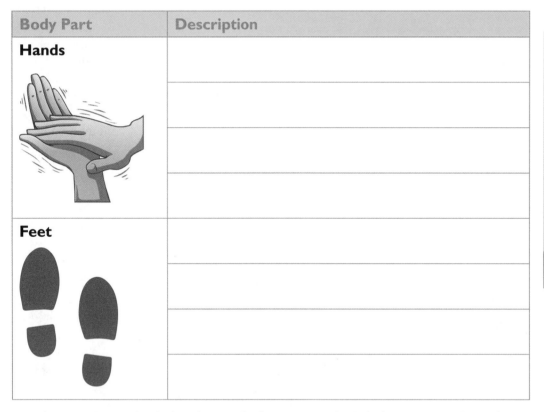	
Feet	

Let's Recap!

Writing body percussion patterns can be done in three different ways:

◆ on a rhythm line

◆ using words or letters

◆ using images or symbols

Try this together! Check the clues at the beginning which help you to perform the pattern.

Body percussion is fun to perform on our own, but it can be a really effective way of accompanying a song we are singing. Can you remember the percussion parts used in 'Thula Kliezo' from *Sounds Good 1*?

Collaborate with your classmates to *devise* a body percussion composition for each of the metres we have explored.

 Use your whiteboard to compile your ideas. Notate your rhythm patterns on the rhythm lines below and **indicate the body actions** for each beat underneath the corresponding rhythmic value.

Rehearse and perform these patterns together.

Group performance

In this unit we have further developed our performance skills, and this task requires us to put these skills to work. We will perform the musical **motif** on page 232 as an **ensemble**. To do this we must **communicate** and **cooperate** effectively. **Listening** to each other and valuing each other's opinions will be helpful in completing this task.

On page 232 is a three-part piece for performance. There are two vocal parts and one for percussion. The vocal parts have been written for you, but you must collaborate to *compose* a two-bar rhythmic ostinato for performance using body percussion.

 To begin, *identify* the steps you should take to complete this task and let the creating begin! Identifying the **roles** required to perform a musical work, assign them to members of your group and begin to *rehearse it* together as an ensemble.

> "No-one can whistle a symphony. It takes a whole orchestra to play it."
>
> H.E. Luccock

List the roles you have identified here.

Role	Name(s)

Take a moment to explore and perform the vocal parts before you begin composing your ostinato. Then discuss what you feel will work best.

Your body-percussion pattern is a **two-bar ostinato** which should repeat to accompany the vocal parts. Once you have composed your ostinato, write it on the rhythm line below, then *design* a body percussion pattern on the score on the next page for the conductor to use when directing your performance.

Add a title to your composition and record the names of those in your group as the arrangers.

arr. by

Rehearsing and performing

Listening and communicating with each other during your rehearsals is very important.

After each rehearsal, *evaluate* and *discuss* how you think it sounds.

Adapt the performance if you feel it needs to be *refined*.

Is your **pitch** accurate? Does the **rhythm** fit? What **dynamics** would be effective and where? Do you need to refine your composition in any way?

Make a note of any changes you decide on here.

_____

_____

_____

 As a group, perform your piece for the class. You might consider compiling this composition as part of your compositional portfolio.

Evaluate your performance

Reflect on your performance. *Evaluate* your participation in this activity. Write a short note below and *indicate* what have you learnt about yourself.

_____

_____

Building a success criteria for performance

Create a success criteria for performance. Discuss and agree on what makes a great performance. Identify the elements and features of performance we aspire to include in our own performances.

Unit:		Date:			
Learning goals:		**Learning Outcomes:**			
Success criteria I can…			😊	🤔	🙁 😐
Feedback: Strengths: Areas for improvement: Goals:					

In *Sounds Good 1* we used a performance appraisal form to evaluate live performances. Look back at the criteria set out to review performance and create your own appraisal form in the space below. Invite a member of your school community to perform for your class. Use the criteria set out on your appraisal form to complete an in-depth review of the performance. Include suggested feedback you would offer to support this performer in developing his/her performance.

What stuck with you?

Evaluate your learning in this chapter. List what stuck with you and new key words.

Key Words

'Bring Me Little Water, Sylvie'

'Bring Me Little Water, Sylvie' is a lovely American **folk song**. It has a beautiful memorable melody and is typically performed **a capella** with **body percussion** for accompaniment.

Records suggest the earliest performance of this song dates back to 1936, when it was performed by American folk musician Huddie Ledbetter. As is often the case with folk songs, the composer is not known, and it is not clear whether Ledbetter is the composer of the original or whether he has based his version on an older one. However, during his performance of this song he would tell audiences that the song was about his Uncle Bob, who whilst out ploughing the fields, would call out to his wife Sylvie to bring him some water.

Research the meaning of **a capella** and list two well-known songs which make use of this style of singing.

Name two well-known Irish folk songs we have listened to:

1 _____

2 _____

A capella:	Song title	Artist/composer
	1	
	2	

Finding the pulse and the rhythm

 Listen to the song. Once you have learnt the tune, hum it in your head and clap what you feel is the **pulse**. Is it fast or slow? Follow the sheet music on page 236.

Now try to clap the **rhythm** of the song. The rhythm pattern is different to pulse. Rhythm is more complex and often fills in the spaces between the pulses. You should be clapping the rhythm of the words you are singing. Sing and clap together to help you. The lyrics for verse one are here to help with this task.

'Bring Me Little Water, Sylvie'

Verse 1
Bring me little water, sylvie,
Bing me little water now.
Bring me little water, sylvie,
Every little once in a while.

Body percussion

The rhythmic pattern below has been designed by Evie Ladin to accompany this performance. There are two patterns to learn.

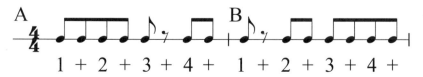

Practise clapping this pattern. The placement of the **rests** can make it tricky. Repeat the pattern over and over.

Counting in patterns 1 to 8 as you learn each body movement will help you coordinate the movements. Each number represents an action.

I have explained the actions in the grid below. Have fun!

A	1	2	3	4	5	6	7	8
	Clap	Right chest	Left chest	Right stomp	Clap	𝄾	Brush thigh backwards	Brush thigh forwards
B	1	2	3	4	5	6	7	8
	Right stomp	𝄾	Clap	Left stomp	Clap	Clap	Right stomp	Clap

Search online for
◆ 'Moira Smiley teaches Bring Me Little Water Silvy'
◆ 'performance by the United States Navy Band: Bring me Little Water Sylvie'.

The melody for the vocals is transcribed below. Work together to coordinate the vocals and the body percussion. Take it one phrase at a time.

traditional African American

Body percussion is a fun way to accompany singing, but it won't always be suitable and can distract performers from their singing. *Experiment* and *improvise* with making different types of sounds on a sound source and replace the body-percussion part for this song with a rhythmic motif. Notate your brief motif (incorporating the two 8-beat patterns) by *devising* symbolic representations of these sounds.

A	1	2	3	4	5	6	7	8
						⁊		

B	1	2	3	4	5	6	7	8
		⁊						

Alternatively *rehearse* and perform the pattern on a rhythmic instrument to accompany the singers.

Singing a Capella

Explain the term **harmony** and describe how it created.

_____

_____

_____

_____

Chords help us to choose harmony notes when composing vocal parts for an **ensemble** performance. It is especially helpful when writing a piece of a capella music. A **capella** is solo or group singing without the use of any instrumental accompaniment.

Listen to 'Adeste Fideles' sung **a capella**.

Describe the **texture** of this piece.

CD 3 Track 49 'Adeste Fideles'

The phrase 'a capella' itself is Italian; translated it means 'in the style of the chapel', which shows its origins in church vocal music. **Gregorian chant** as used in the early Roman Catholic Church is an example of a capella singing. Gregorian chant developed in Europe during the ninth and tenth centuries. It was originally sung by men and boys in church choirs or by monks or nuns in monasteries or convents when celebrating the mass.

Listen to this piece of Gregorian chant. *Describe* the texture of this piece.

CD 3 Track 50 Three Easter Allelujahs

What do these pieces have in common? What is different about them? Complete the Venn diagram below.

Adeste Fideles   **Three Easter Allelujahs**

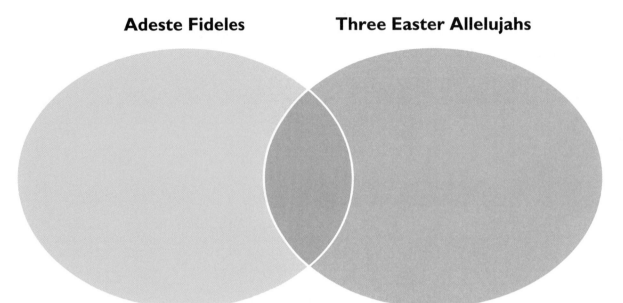

We learned about ensembles in Unit 5. Over the past century a capella has developed and styles such as **barbershop** have grown in popularity. Barbershop **quartets** are vocal ensembles for four male singers. Singers perform a capella in close four-part harmony. The **harmony** notes form chords making the performance homophonic. Each of the four singers has their own role; the lead takes the main melody and the other parts sing above or below the melody line.

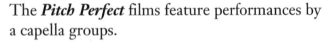
Listen to this barbershop performance of 'Swing Low, Sweet Chariot'.

'Swing Low, Sweet Chariot'

The *Pitch Perfect* films feature performances by a capella groups.

In Unit 6 we explored harmony and chord progressions. We explored many songs which feature the same chord progressions. Compile a list of songs which use the four-chord progression I–V–vi–IV.

1 _____   5 _____

2 _____   6 _____

3 _____   7 _____

4 _____   8 _____

More contemporary versions of a capella music can be heard when musicians add close vocal harmonies, beatboxing or vocal percussion to their performances. Research the Pentatonix and listen to their performances.

'Caravan of Love'

In November 1986, a British Indie-Rock group called The Housemartins released an **a capella** version of 'Caravan of Love' which was first released by the American trio The Isley Brothers in the 1970s. It is one of very few a capella songs to reach number one in the UK charts. Watch a performance of this song online by searching 'The Housemartins – Caravan of Love (Live) – YouTube'.

The Housemartins formed as a group in the 1980s and had a relatively short run. The lyrics of many of their songs were about social politics and had reflected their religious beliefs. After the band broke up, two members went forward to set up a new band called The Beautiful South. The band's bass player, Norman Cook, later became known as Fatboy Slim, a very successful DJ in the 1990s.

Apart from noticing the a capella vocals, you may also have noticed that 'Caravan of Love' uses a **harmonic ostinato** which is based on the **chord progression** I–vi–ii–V. The song was written in A major for four parts. In the introduction we hear this progression clearly with three parts singing the notes of the chords on 'Ah' and a rhythmic pattern sung in the lower fourth part.

Explain the following terms:

◆ harmonic ostinato

◆ chord progression

_____

_____

_____

_____

Earlier in this book, we learnt about commonly used chord progressions. The four-part vocal exercise below is based on the progression I–vi–ii–V. Rehearse and perform it together.

Using the four-part stave below, compose a similar exercise based on the most commonly used progression in popular music: I–V–vi–IV.

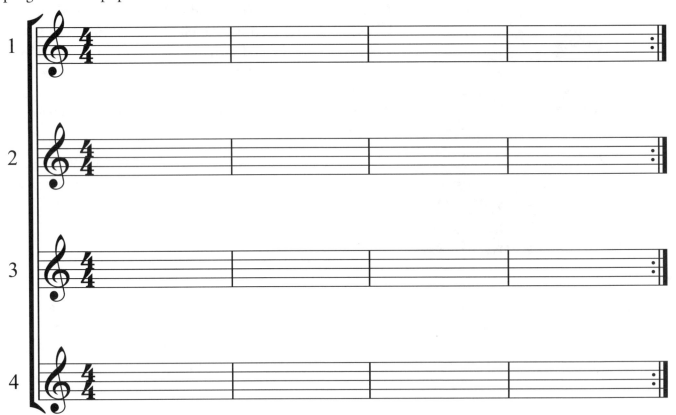

Cover Songs

Live Lounge is a segment on BBC Radio 1 which features well-known artists as guests. Typically these musicians perform one of their own songs and an acoustic cover of another well-known hit. Artists perform songs from **genres** very different to their own, which makes for some really interesting adaptations of the original tracks. These covers have been produced, compiled and released as compilation albums by the Sony music label since 2006.

Compare different interpretations or arrangements of original songs which have been covered by artists on Live Lounge. *Distinguish* between the versions of the well-known hits below.

You can watch performances of these songs to help you by searching on YouTube.

	Song title	Original artist	Cover artist
1	'These Days'	Rudimental	George Ezra
2	'Let Her Go'	Passenger	Birdy
3	'Graceland'	Paul Simon	Chris Martin (Coldplay)

Song title	'These Days'	Search for
Original artist	Rudimental	'Rudimental – These Days – Jess Glynne, Macklemore & Dan Caplen (Live at Abbey Road)'
Cover artist	George Ezra	'George Ezra – These Days (Rudimental cover) – Live Lounge'

Song title	'Let Her Go'	Search for
Original artist	Passenger	'Passenger – Let Her Go (Official Video)'
Cover artist	Birdy	'Birdy – Let Her Go (Passenger) – Live Lounge'
Song title	'Graceland'	Search for
Original artist	Paul Simon	'Paul Simon – Graceland – Live'
Cover artist	Chris Martin (Coldplay)	Chris Martin – Paul Simon's Graceland – Live Lounge'

Design a listening map or use a **Venn diagram** to make notes as you listen to these songs.

 Research and listen to one other **cover version** of a well-known song. Play the original and cover versions of the song and give a short presentation for your classmates, identifying the similarities and difference between the two performances.

Use the grid below to gather the main points of information for your presentation.

Song:		
Original artist:		Cover artist:
Similarities	Differences	Other points of information

Choose one phrase from a piece of music you have enjoyed listening to in one of the two *Sounds Good* books. *Transcribe* it on the stave below.

Piece/Song:	Composer:

Experiment with this phrase by making changes to the **melody** and *adapt* it by changing the **rhythm, melody, harmony** or the style of the music. Make notes on the process in the space below and reflect on the skills which helped you to complete this task. Insert the final draft of your cover version on page 242.

'Wild Mountainside' by John Douglas

Listen to a performance of this song by Eddi Reader by searching online for 'Eddi Reader – Wild Mountainside'. Rehearse and perform this song on your recorder using the CD to accompany you.

Wild Mountainside accompaniment

List two songs composed in F major

1 _____

2 _____

Verse 1

Beauty is within grasp,

Hear the highlands call.

The last mile is upon us,

I'll carry you if you fall,

I know the armour's heavy now

I know the heart is tired,

It's beautiful just over,

The wild mountainside.

Verse 2

Snow is falling all over,

Out of clear blue sky,

Crow is flying high over.

You and I are going to wander

High up where the air is rare

Wild horses ride.

It's beautiful just roaming

The wild mountainside.

Wild and free we roam,

Only a mile to go.

Wild and free we roam,

Only a mile to go.

Verse 3

Beauty is within grasp,

Hear the highlands call.

The last mile is upon us,

I'll carry you if you fall,

I know the armour's heavy now

I know the heart inside,

It's beautiful just over

The wild mountainside.

It's beautiful, let's go over

The wild mountainside.

John Douglas

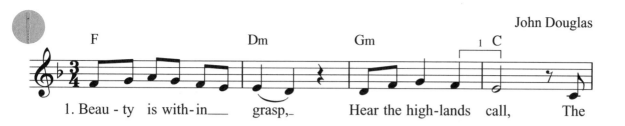

1. Beau-ty is with-in— grasp,_ Hear the high-lands call, The

last mile is u-pon_ us,— I'll car-ry you_ if you fall,— I

know the ar-mour's hea-vy now, I know the heart is tired, It's

Fine
(after v.3)

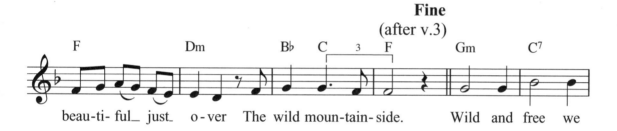

beau-ti-ful_ just_ o-ver The wild moun-tain-side. Wild and free we

D.C. al Fine

roam,———— On-ly a mile to go.————

Activity

Complete the F major chord box below and use it to identify the cadences marked on the score (⌐———⌐).

Fifth							
Third							
Root							
Chord symbol							
Tonic solfa	doh	re	mi	fah	soh	lah	ti
Roman numerals	I	ii	iii	IV	V	vi	vii

Cadence Point	Type of Cadence
1	
2	
3	
4	

243

Songs for Group Performance

In *Sounds Good 1* you practised singing in harmony when you sang 'Thula Klizeo' in two parts. On the pages that follow, you will find songs that you can sing together in one or more parts. Rehearse these in groups and perform them for others including your peers, your parents and your teachers.

'The Moon' by Andy Beck

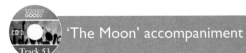

'The Moon' accompaniment

O moon, shi-ning in the night, O moon, are you

O moon, shi-ning in the night, O moon, are you

lis-ten-ing? O moon, sil-ve-ry and bright, come a-gain to-mor-row night,

lis-ten-ing? O moon, sil-ve-ry and bright, come a-gain to-mor-row night,

come a-gain to-mor-row night. Night-time will soon be done,

come a-gain to-mor-row night. Night-time will soon be done,

bring-ing the mor-ning sun. Where will you go? What will you do?

bring-ing the mor-ning sun. Where will you go? What will you do?

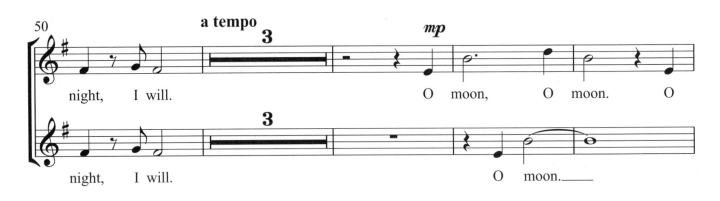

50

night, I will. O moon, O moon. O

night, I will. O moon.____

57

moon, O moon. O moon. Moon.

O moon.____ O moon. Moon.

Summarise the role you played in the performance of this song.

_____

_____

_____

_____

What stuck with you?

Evaluate your learning in this chapter. List what stuck with you and new key words.

Key Words

_____

_____

_____

_____

_____

Here's a reminder of all the recorder fingerings you learned in *Sounds Good 1*, and some new ones.

In *Sounds Good 1* we learned how to play the recorder. Try these traditional pieces and perform them for your class.

'Sally Gardens'

'Down by the Sally Gardens' is a pretty poem written by William Butler Yeats. The words were set to music by Hubert Hughes using the tune 'The Moorlough Shore' in 1909.

It was down by the Sally Gardens, my love and I did meet.
She crossed the Sally Gardens with little snow-white feet.
She bid me take love easy, as the leaves grow on the tree,
But I was young and foolish, and with her did not agree.

In a field down by the river, my love and I did stand
And on my leaning shoulder, she laid her snow-white hand.
She bid me take life easy , as the grass grows on the weirs
But I was young and foolish, and now am full of tears.

Down by the Sally Gardens, my love and I did meet.
She crossed the Sally Gardens with little snow-white feet.
She bid me take love easy, as the leaves grow on the tree,
But I was young and foolish, and with her did not agree.

traditional Irish

1 What type of song is this? _____

2 The form of the verse is   AB   AABB   AABA   ABBA (circle the correct form).

3 Look at the key signature. What key is this song in? _____

4 Does the music begin on the first beat of the bar? Explain your answer.

_____

5 Identify which phrase(s) end(s) with repeated notes.

Phrase 1   2   3   4 (circle the correct number(s))

6 Identify which phrase(s)which begin(s) with a leap.

Phrase 1   2   3   4 (circle the correct number(s))

7 Identify a bar which has an octave leaf in it. Bar number _____

'Deck the Halls'

'Deck the halls' is a traditional Christmas carol. The melody dates back to the sixteenth century and comes from the Welsh carol 'Nos Galan'. The lyrics were written by Scottish musician Thomas Oliphant in 1862. The words 'fa la la' are sung at the end of each line much as they were in the earlier Welsh carol. These words were often used in the refrain of medieval ballads.

traditional

1 This song in in AABA form common to American popular songs. Identify and label the phrases on the score.

2 What key is this song in? _____

3 The time signature is split common, explain what this means.

_____

4 Insert the lyrics 'Fa la la la la' onto the score wherever they should appear.

5 Name the rest used in bar 1 and explain its purpose.

_____

Melody

1 This piece is in

   simple time   compound time   free rhythm   (circle the correct answer)

2 The melody is in the key of _____

3 How many phrases are there? _____

4 Mark where any repeated phrases occur.

5 Identify the texture of this piece. _____

6 Insert suitable dynamics for this performance.

Preparing a Song for Performance

Make sure you know the basic facts about the music you want to perform:

- Time signature
- Tempo
- Key, key signature and range
- The name of the composer and the lyricist

It is also helpful to have an understanding of the background of the piece. Find out as much about the music as possible.

We often receive a printed programme when we go to a **live** performance. What information is usually included? Why do composers and performers choose to share this information with us? Every piece of music has a unique combination of elements which can be appreciated. Sharing information about the composer, the inspiration for their work, the story or mood of the music, the instruments chosen and things we should listen out for can all be identified and explained to us in a programme note.

Choose one of the songs you have performed this year and write a short programme note for it. Good research skills will be required! Include background information, features of the melody, and a musical signpost or point of interest we should listen out for.

Song title	Composer	Genre
Information		
Points of interest		

Performance project

Choose a piece of music you would like to perform. Research and perform it and write about your findings below. Give reasons why you have chosen this music. Discuss the musical features you think listeners might enjoy.

_____

_____

_____

Include a line of the melody on the stave below if you can.

The Performance Exam

Keep a note of suggestions, ideas and advise for your performance exam in year 3.

Reflection and Evaluation Sheet

Unit title:

Learning Outcomes (LOs) I worked with:

Music I listened to:
_____

Learning and exploring

I really enjoyed…
_____

Something interesting I learnt…
_____

My biggest challenge was…
_____

I overcame this by…
_____

One improvement I have made is…
_____

Traffic-light your learning

Learning Outcomes	🙁	😐	🙂	✓
1.1				
1.5				
1.7				
1.8				
1.9				
2.1				
2.5				
2.10				
3.9				

Rate your learning

Learning

Key words	Action verbs
_____	_____
_____	_____

Key skills
_____

I got better at x skill by _____
_____

This unit reminded me of learning about… _____
_____

What still puzzles me is…
_____
_____

Feedback and goal setting…
_____
_____
_____

Unit 8

The Ukulele

In this unit

Learning to play a musical instrument is a rewarding activity. Learning the ukulele supports what we have learnt about harmony and chords in this book. It will support your creative endeavours and offer an insight into performing skills and performance techniques. Demonstrate your knowledge of musical elements. Begin to compile a list of possible songs for use in your performance exam.

Checklist	LO	Intended learning
☐	1.4	**Indicate** chords that are suitable to provide harmonic support to a single melody line.
☐	1.7	Perform music at sight through playing, singing, or clapping melodic and rhythmic phrases.
☐	1.12	**Indicate** where chord changes occur in extracts from a selection of songs.
☐	2.1	**Experiment** and **improvise** with making different types of sounds on a sound source and notate a brief piece that incorporates the sounds by **devising** symbolic representations for these sounds.
☐	2.4	**Rehearse** and **present** a song or brief instrumental piece; identify and **discuss** the performance skills and techniques that were necessary to **interpret** the music effectively.
☐	2.5	Prepare and **rehearse** a musical work for ensemble focusing on cooperation and listening for balance and intonation; **refine** the interpretation by considering elements such as clarity, fluency, musical effect and style.
☐	2.6	**Design** a rhythmic or melodic ostinato and add layers of sound over the pattern as it repeats, varying the texture to **create** a mood piece to accompany a film clip or sequence of images.
☐	2.8	**Analyse** the chordal structure of excerpts from a range of songs and compile a list of songs with similar chord structures and progressions.
☐	2.10	**Develop** a set of criteria for **evaluating** a live or recorded performance; **use** these criteria to complete an in-depth review of a performance.
☐	3.5	**Devise** and perform examples of incidental music that could be used in a variety of contexts or environments.
☐	3.9	**Investigate** the influence of processing effects (distortion, reverb and compression) on the recording process select some recordings and **evaluate** the use and effectiveness of such effects within them.
☐	3.10	**Discuss** the principles of music property rights and **explain** how this can impact on the sharing and publishing of music.

The Ukulele

List three songs you enjoyed performing last year:

1 _____

2 _____

3 _____

In *Sounds Good 1* we learned to play the recorder. Many of the skills you established last year will help you to explore and develop the skills needed to play the ukulele. Unlike the recorder, the ukulele has only been around since the late nineteenth century.

Organised emigration of the Portuguese to Hawaii began in 1878. Many immigrants who came to Hawaii were recruited as labourers for the sugar plantations. Historical accounts from their arrival tell of their celebrations on arrival in Hawaii, with many immigrants bursting into song accompanied by their 'machete de braga' or 'braguinha', a small wooden guitar-like instrument.

The Portuguese immigrants quickly introduced their musical culture to the Hawaiian people, in particular the small traditional machete. The ukulele later developed as a Hawaiian adaptation of the migrants' machete. Made using the indigenous wood, Acacia koa, the ukulele instrument made its debut in Honolulu in 1889, played by a **trio** of women including Princess Victoria Kaiulani. Victoria was a niece of King Kalakaua, the Hawaiian patron of the arts. The king was particularly taken with the ukulele and went to great efforts to promote this instrument, often providing opportunities to showcase the instrument at royal gatherings and important events.

The ukulele is iconic for its happy and carefree sound. This small vibrant instrument is made of wood and has a shape similar to the guitar. Typically, ukuleles have four nylon or gut strings, but sometimes extra strings are paired with the main four to increase the volume of the instrument when strummed. Many people are not aware that the ukulele comes in four different sizes: **soprano**, concert, tenor and baritone.

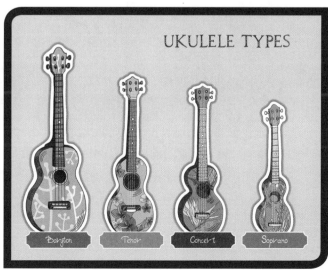

UKULELE TYPES

Baritone   Tenor   Concert   Soprano

Today, this highly portable and inexpensive instrument has gained popularity worldwide. Native Hawaiian singer-songwriter and musician Israel Kamakawiwo'ole helped to revive ukulele playing after its steady decline following World War 2. From the 1990s onwards, ukulele playing has grown in popularity, and musicians such as Israel have released songs which have featured widely in TV and film.

Jake Shimabukuro

Search online for 'Israel Kamakawiwo'ole playing Somewhere Over the Rainbow'.

How we access music has also influenced the worldwide popularity of the ukulele. This little instrument now has a large audience, and, with access to music streaming and online resources such as YouTube, musicians across the globe have learned to play the ukulele. Many ukulele videos have gone viral; popular videos with over 10 million views include Jake Shimabukuro's performance of a George Harrison hit 'While My Heart Gently Weeps' and TEDxMaui's Tamaine Gardner's Ukulele Virtuoso.

 Listen to two different ukulele performances and *compare* and contrast them. Report your findings in the Venn diagram below.

Search online for 'Jake Shimabukuro playing While My Guitar Gently Weeps by George Harrison'.

Search online for 'TEDxMaui's Tamaine Gardner's Ukulele Virtuoso'.

Tamaine Gardner   **Jake Shimabukuro**

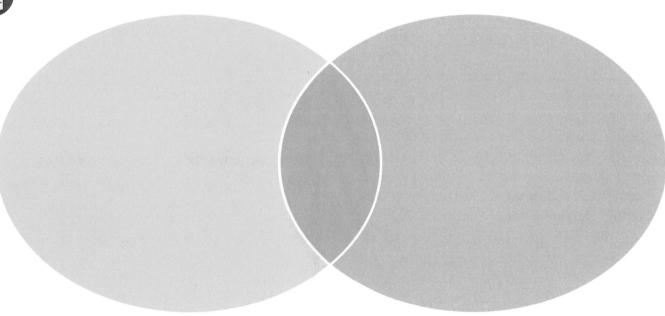

Soprano Ukulele

For use with this textbook you will need a **soprano** ukulele. The soprano is the most common instrument for beginners to learn. Soprano ukuleles should be easy to find and are not too expensive. Before we learn how to hold or strum the ukulele, it is important you become familiar with the different parts of your new instrument. Below is a labelled illustration to help you familiarise yourself with your ukulele.

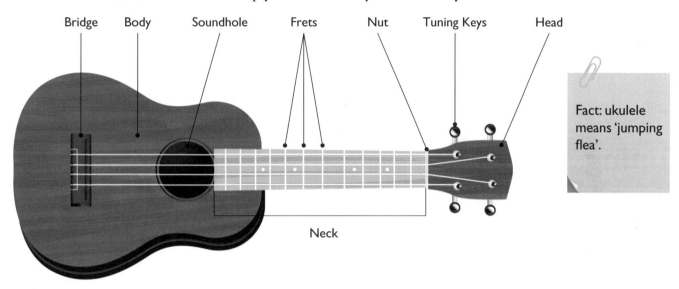

Bridge   Body   Soundhole   Frets   Nut   Tuning Keys   Head

Fact: ukulele means 'jumping flea'.

Neck

The anatomy of the ukulele is slightly different to that of the guitar. The body of the ukulele is made of wood, and you strum the strings above the **soundhole**. The long piece of wood attached to the body is called the neck, onto which the fingerboard or fretboard is added.

The **fretboard** acts as a guide for locating **pitch**. When each string is attached over the fretboard, the metal lines which mark out the frets allow us to locate a pitch or note.

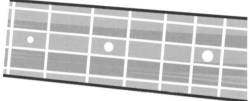

The top of the instrument is called the head, and it holds the four tuning pegs, which have an important job. The tuning pegs allow us to keep the ukulele in tune. The four strings attached to the instrument run along the fretboard and are secured using the tuning pegs.

Each of the four strings differ in thickness. Once the strings are positioned correctly, you must learn to tune your instrument. This can be a frustrating task at first, but it is very important that you can tune the ukulele accurately. The tuning pegs are used to loosen or tighten the strings. Remember, it is normal for the strings to loosen as you play and practise; as the tension in the string loosens, the string goes down in pitch. As a guide, you will mostly have to tighten strings rather than loosen them, but do this gradually, so you don't snap the strings by over tightening them.

Go to ukutuner.com or access Apps for iPad and Android to tune your ukulele.

See the Ukulele Fingerings Cover Flap at the back of *Sounds Good 2* to check your fingerings.

The standard ukulele string tuning is G C E A. The four strings on the ukulele are named after the **pitch** that each string will sound when struck if it is tuned correctly. Learn the names of these strings.

◆ The top string also known as the **4th string**, is G.

◆ The 3rd string is C.

◆ The 2nd string is E.

◆ The bottom string, known as the **1st string**, is A.

A is closest to the floor and G is closest to your chin.

Can you *devise* a mnemonic to help you remember these?

G _____ C _____ E _____ A _____

Tuning

We can tune the ukulele in several different ways. Over time, some people learn to tune their ukulele strings relying on their ear and its ability to recognise the pitches. Typically, however, people invest in an electronic tuner to help them to tune the strings accurately, or they make use of online tuners and tuner apps for their phone or tablet, which are easy to access too. Alternatively, you can play the notes G, C, E and A on a piano. Use the keyboard image to help you to locate these pitches on the piano.

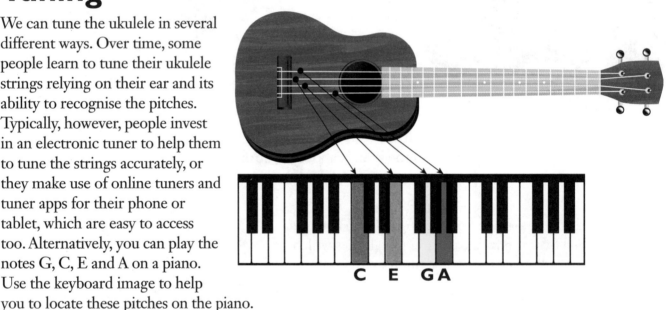

Whilst you listen carefully to each pitch, gently turn the string's peg as you **pluck** the string. You should hear the pitch of that string gradually rise. When we pluck a string in this way and don't obstruct the string by pressing down on the frets or any part of the string, it is known as an **open string**. Continue to check the ukulele's sound against that of the piano. When both sounds match, hey presto, you are in tune! Repeat the process for each of the four strings.

To allow us to do this together, the pitch for each open string is on the *Sounds Good 2* CD.

 Listen to the sound of each string carefully and pluck the string of your ukulele, adjusting the tuning peg until you get a match.

G   C   E   A

Another good trick for quick tuning is to sing the pitches for G, C, E and A. There are two common ways to do this.

You can sing the tonic solfa pattern **soh doh mi lah** or sing the catchy lyric **'my dog has fleas'** to the melody shown here.

'My Dog Has Fleas'

Track 58

Track 59

Now listen to how the four open strings sound when *strummed together*. Strum downwards from the 4th string to the 1st string; you should be in tune. If not, go back and revisit each string. Having your ukulele in tune will ensure you will get the best possible sound for your performance.

Listen to these four pitches played on the open strings G, C, E, A, then play them back on your instrument.

Track 60

The pitches G, C, E and A on open strings played twice each

Posture

Another important factor in achieving the best sound quality is your posture. How you hold the ukulele will affect the sound quality. Rest the ukulele in the crook of your elbow and hold it between your chest and your forearm, high on your body and not down at your waist. The neck of the ukulele should rest comfortably in the curve of your hand between your thumb and forefinger, allowing all four fingers to reach each of the four strings.

To strum the ukulele, you should strum above the soundhole, on the fingerboard, unlike the guitar. Every ukulele is different, but the point where the body meets the neck is usually the sweet-spot for gaining the best sound when you strum.

The most basic ukulele strum would be any combination of up and down strokes with your **thumb** and/or **index finger**. Strumming is a form of rhythm and should be steady and consistent. This may take a while to get used to, and we will learn much more about strumming later in this unit. Do not use a guitar pick when playing your ukulele, even if you feel it may add volume.

Strumming
Track 61

Lastly, mind your posture! Try to stand or sit up straight with both feet on the floor. Avoid slouching over the ukulele; this common mistake can lead to tension in your back and neck. Practising in front of a mirror can help with this as it will allow you to see what you are doing whilst remaining upright.

What stuck with you?

Evaluate your learning in this chapter. List what stuck with you and new key words.

Key Words

_____
_____
_____
_____

Chapter 38

Strumming

Finally, it's time to make some music!

With our ukuleles in tune we can try developing our strumming skills. The up-and-down movement can be tricky to coordinate, so let's begin with the down strum only. The arrows here indicate the four counts or pulses in a bar of 4/4. Rehearse and perform this pattern together.

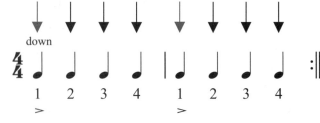

Once you are confident with this pattern try the other variations below.

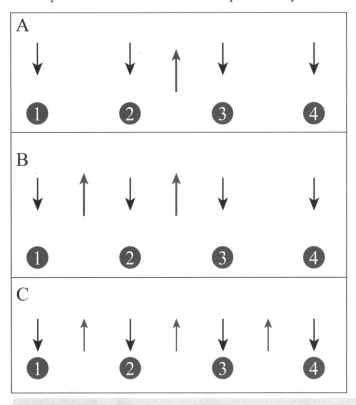

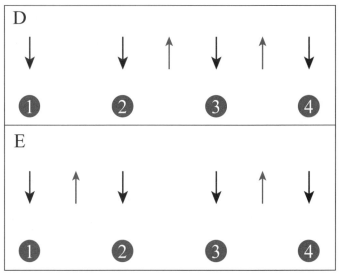

Experiment with and *improvise* making different types of sounds on your ukulele and notate a brief piece that incorporates the sounds created by the up and down strum. Use the up and down arrows to represent these sounds. Your piece should be four bars long and you should indicate the rhythm pattern on the rhythm line below.

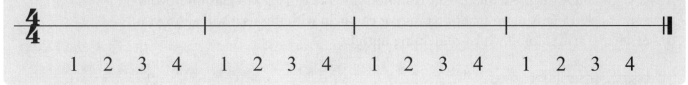

Strumming rhythmic patterns

Learn to strum the following rhythmic patterns on open strings.

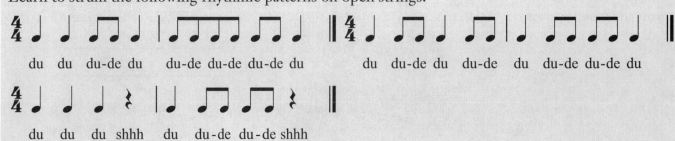

Major Chords

Explain the term **chord**. _____

We have spent time looking at chords in Unit 6. The next skill for us to develop is playing the chords that allow us to strum along with our favourite songs. How chords are played is indicated on chord charts. The ukulele chord chart is a snapshot of your ukulele's **fretboard**. Take a look at the chord chart below and you will recognise the fretboard lines are the horizontal lines and the four ukulele strings run vertically over these fretboard lines. The dots placed on these charts indicate where a finger or group of fingers must be placed on the strings to create a chord.

Sometimes the dots on the chord chart are numbered or coloured. This is to help you with the placement of your fingers. The numbers do not indicate the number fret. Any number placed on a dot is indicating the finger that should be placed there. We will use colour to help us too.

An example of this is shown below for our first chord: the chord of C.

The C Chord on ukulele and strumming pattern

CD 3
Track 62

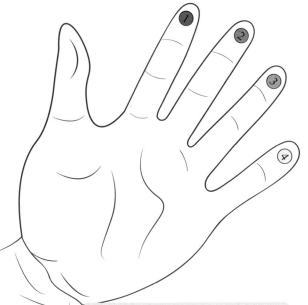

Strings

G C E A   Frets   Dots

Chord of C

C

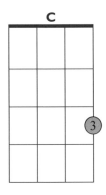

See the Ukulele Fingerings Cover Flap at the back of *Sounds Good 2* to check your fingerings. Open it out to help you.

Rehearse and perform the strumming pattern below.

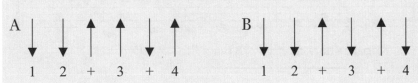

Use strumming pattern A or B below.

Name the notes of the chord

_____

_____

Now you are comfortable with the chord C, let's move on to strumming the chord to a rhythmic pattern like this one in 4/4.

du-de du-de du de du

Compose another suitable bar of rhythm to strum and write it in the box.

Chord of F

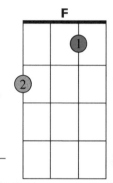

Let's move on! Our next chord is not as easy to play as C, but it's still not too difficult. Our next chord is **F**.

Identify the notes of the F chord

_____

See the Ukulele Fingerings Cover Flap at the back of *Sounds Good 2* to check your fingerings.

  The F Chord on ukulele and strumming pattern

Track 63

Rehearse and perform the strumming pattern below.

Let's Play!

We have learnt a lot of new skills so far. Let's combine them all to prepare and rehearse a musical performance of the Australian **folk song** 'Kookaburra' as a **round**, accompanied by the ukulele. Performing as an **ensemble** means we must stay focused and work together as a team.

 First let's remind ourselves of the tune and sing along.

Kookaburra

Koo-ka-bur-ra sits on the old gum tree,— Mer-ry mer-ry king of the bush is he.—

Laugh, Koo-ka-bur-ra, laugh! Koo-ka-bur-ra, gay your life must be!

This song is typically performed as a round.

1 *Explain* the term **round**.

_____

2 *Describe* the **texture** of rounds.

_____

_____

_____

Rehearse and sing this Australian song in a **round**. You can have up to four parts, but it may be easier to begin with only two. The points at which the later voices should enter are indicated for you by the boxed numbers above the music.

1 Is it easy to perform as a member of a round? *Suggest* the skills and qualities we rely on to help us to perform with others.

_____

_____

_____

2 *Identify* the notes in bars 4 and 5. _____

3 *Explain* the symbol in bars 5 and 6. _____

4 *Identify* the **key signature** of this piece of music. _____

Now that you are familiar with the melody, use the chord indications above the stave to help you to master playing the accompaniment for this song.

Points to help you:

◆ Using a simple down strum for each of the four beats in the bar is a good idea at the beginning.

◆ Coordinating the chord changes will be difficult at first, but with practice you will find this gets easier.

◆ Singing along whilst you strum can be tricky to manage at first, so instead of singing the lyrics you may decide to hum or whistle the melody line as you play the chords.

 In small groups *rehearse* and present this song in a round with ukulele accompaniment to your classmates. The melody can also be played on recorder.

1 *Identify* and *discuss* the performance skills and techniques that were necessary to complete this performance.

_____

_____

_____

2 *Outline* your role in the performance and how performing with others made you feel.

_____

_____

_____

3 *Identify* one other song which can be accompanied using the chords C and F.

_____

Chord of G

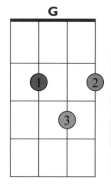

See the Ukulele Fingerings Cover Flap at the back of *Sounds Good 2* to check your fingerings.

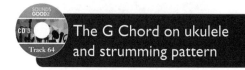

The G Chord on ukulele and strumming pattern

What stuck with you?

Evaluate your learning in this chapter. List what stuck with you and new key words.

Rehearse and perform the strumming pattern below.

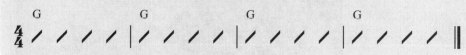

Indicate the dots needed to complete the following chord charts.

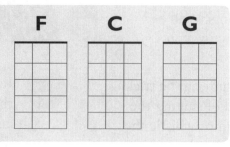

This chord is tricky at first, especially when moving to it from another chord. To help our coordination of this, let's try to play some **chord progressions**.

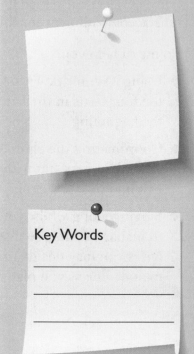

Key Words

_____

_____

_____

Chord Progressions

A **chord progression** is a harmonic series of chords played in succession. We learnt about them in Unit 6. Remember that chord progressions are the foundation of harmony in music. The chords are often represented by roman numerals: I, IV, V, etc., but sometimes we are given the name of each chord: C, F, G, etc. instead. This is how we have labelled our chords in this unit.

> Use your rhythm pattern to play the following progressions; be patient and take your time to begin with. Then, once you are familiar with them, try to incorporate other strumming patterns for each chord movement.
>
> 1 C......F......G......C......
>
> 2 C......G......C......F......C......G......C......
>
> 3 F......G......F......C......G......F......G......C......
>
> Perform the following chord progression using the rhythm provided below. You may need to create a strumming pattern to help you. Draw arrows for up and down strums under each note to help you.
>
>
>
> *Compose* a four-bar rhythm pattern and compose a **chord progression** to accompany it.
>
> Notate it in the box below.
>
>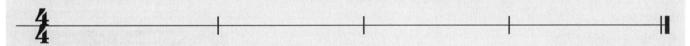

Choosing Chords

> The more songs you play, the more familiar the chords' sound will become. In pairs, work together to *identify* what chords are needed to accompany 'Row row row your boat' below, and 'Yankee Doodle' on page 266. To help you, there is an empty box placed where the chords should change. The first chord is given to help you begin.

'Row row row your boat' uses chords F and G

F ☐
Row row row your boat, gently down the stream

☐ ☐
Merrily, merrily, merrily, life is but a dream

This song is a round too!

Sing and play it in groups.

Chord of D

Below is an example of some ukulele sight-reading. We learnt about sight-reading in *Sounds Good 1*.

The D Chord on ukulele and strumming pattern

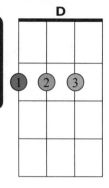

Take your time to consider the time signature. The lines on the stave are there to help you strum along.

Using the stave below, compose a piece of music for ukulele sight-reading in C major. Do this using the chords **C, F and G only**.

See the Ukulele Fingerings Cover Flap at the back of *Sounds Good 2* to check your fingerings.

'Yankee Doodle' uses chords G, D and C

G

Yankee Doodle went to town a-riding on a pony

He stuck a feather in his cap and called it ma-ca-ro-ni

'You Are My Sunshine' by Jimmie Davis and Charles Mitchell

Chorus

C
You are my sunshine, my only sunshine
        F   **C**
You make me happy when skies are grey
        F   **C**
You'll never know dear, how much I love you
      C   **G**   **C**
Please don't take my sunshine away

Verse

C
The other night dear, as I lay sleeping
      F   **C**
I dreamed I held you in my arms
      F   **C**
And when I awoke dear, I was mistaken
   C   **G**   **C**
So I hung my head, and cried
Repeat chorus

Listen to a piano accompaniment and play along on your ukulele

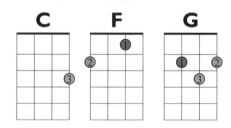

Perform this song in groups, some singing and some accompanying on ukulele. Adding percussion on cajun or playing the melody on a glockenspiel will add a nice variety to your performance.

'Blue Suede Shoes' by Carl Perkins

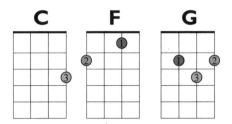

C   C

Well it's one for the money, two for the show

Three to get ready, now, go, cat, go

      F   C

But don't you, step on my blue suede shoes

         G   F   C

You can do anything but lay off of my blue suede shoes

C   C

You can knock me down, step in my face

C   C

Slander my name all over the place

Do anything that you wanna do

But uh uh honey lay off of them shoes

F   C

Don't you, step on my blue suede shoes

         G   F   C

You can do anything but lay off of my blue suede shoes

C   C

Well you can burn my house, steal my car

C   C

Drink my liquor from an old fruit jar

Do anything that you wanna do

But uh uh honey lay off of my shoes

F   C

And don't you, step on my blue suede shoes

         G   F   C

You can do anything but lay off of my blue suede shoes

'Blue Suede Shoes' was first recorded by Carl Perkins in 1955. Elvis's cover of the song became more famous than the original. Explain the term 'cover song'.

_____

_____

George Harrison, a member of The Beatles, was an avid ukulele fan. Watch the music video for The Beatles' song 'Free as a Bird' on YouTube. There's an interesting section that features the ukulele towards the end. This song was recorded in 1977 by John Lennon but wasn't released until 1995! Do some research on this song to find out why!

'Three Little Birds' by Bob Marley

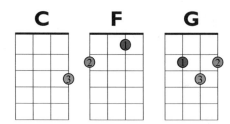

Chorus

      C   C
Don't worry, about a thing

    F   C
Cos every little thing, gonna be alright

        C
Singin' don't worry, about a thing

    F   C
Cos every little thing, gonna be alright

Verse

            C   G
Rise up this morning, Smile with the rising sun

            C   F
Three little birds perch by my doorstep

           C   G
Singin' sweet songs, of melodies pure and true

          F   C
Sayin', this is my message to you-whoo-hoo

Repeat chorus

'Singin in the Rain' by Arthur Freed and Nacio Herb Brown

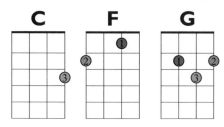

> The last four songs we have performed use the same three chords: **F**, **C** and **G**. Compile a list of songs which use these three chords.
>
> 1 _____
> 2 _____
> 3 _____
> 4 _____

Chorus

    C   F
I'm singin' in the rain

    C   F
Just singin' in the rain

      C
What a glorious feelin'

    G   F
I'm happy again

    C   F   C   F
I'm laughin' at clouds, so high up above

    C   F   C   G
The sun's in my heart and I'm ready for love

Verse

      C   F
Let the stormy clouds chase

    C   G
Everyone from the place

    C   C
Come on with the rain

    G   F
I've a smile on my face

    C   F   G   F
I walk down the lane with a happy refrain

      C   G   C
Just dancin' and singin' in the rain

Songs for Performance

'The Lion Sleeps Tonight' by Solomon Linda

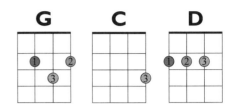

Chorus

G

Ee-e-e-um-um-a-weh, Ee-e-e-um-um-a-weh,

C

Ee-e-e-um-um-a-weh, Ee-e-e-um-um-a-weh,

G   **D**

Wemoweh, wemoweh, wemoweh, wemoweh

Verse 1

G   **C**

In the jungle, the mighty jungle

G   **D**

The lion sleeps tonight

G   **C**

In the jungle, the quiet jungle

G   **D**

The lion sleeps tonight

Chorus × 2

Verse 2

G   **C**

Near the village, the peaceful village

G   **D**

The lion sleeps tonight

G   **C**

Near the village, the peaceful village

G   **D**

The lion sleeps tonight

Chorus

Verse 3

G   **C**

Hush my darling, don't fear my darling

G   **D**

The lion sleeps tonight

G   **C**

Hush my darling, don't fear my darling

G   **D**

The lion sleeps tonight

Chorus

This song was first recorded in 1939 by Solomon Linda, a South African musician. He called the song 'Mbube' (meaning 'lion' in Zulu) originally. This song was covered many times earning lots of money for other musicians, but Linda died almost penniless in 1962. In 2000 it was estimated that the song would have earned 15 million dollars in composer-royalties, but Linda's family had yet to receive a penny. Film maker François Verster made a documentary called *A Lion's Trail* that told Linda's story and was broadcast in 2002. This documentary exposed the music publishing industry's mistreatment of artists and prompted legal action by Linda's heirs. Just before the trial, an out-of-court settlement was reached between the family, Disney and Abilene Music Company. As a result, Linda would be credited as co-composer of the song and his family would be paid the royalties for past and future uses of 'The Lion Sleeps Tonight'.

Revisit the importance of copyright laws in music.

Discuss the principles of music property rights and how they affect musicians like Solomon Linda.

Royalties: a sum of money paid to the creator of a work of art each time it is performed or sold.

Investigate the details of this case. Split your class into groups. Decide who is going to *argue* on behalf of Linda's family and who will *argue* the case for the music publishing industry. Conduct a debate in which you *argue* your case.

Choose one of the songs you have performed this year and write a short **programme note** for it. Include background information, features of the melody, and a point of interest we should listen out for.

 Search online for 'Mbube by Ladysmith Black Mambazo' and 'OBCR The Lion Sleeps Tonight (Full)'. Work in pairs to compare these two interpretations of this song. Evaluate the two performances and identify the skills and techniques used.

Compare and contrast: One song – two interpretations		
Song title: The Lion Sleeps Tonight	**Style:**	
Version 1 performers:	**Version 2 performers:**	
Special to version 1	**Common elements**	**Special to version 2**
_____	_____	_____
_____	_____	_____
_____	_____	_____
_____	_____	_____
_____	_____	_____
_____	_____	_____
_____	_____	_____

Alternating between roles requires different performance skills.

1 *Evaluate* the role of playing the melody on recorder and compare it to the role of playing the accompanying chords on ukulele.

_____

_____

_____

2 *Comment on* the skills needed to perform successfully as a group.

_____

_____

_____

_____

What stuck with you?

Evaluate your learning in this chapter. List what stuck with you and new key words.

Key Words

_____

_____

_____

Looking Back!

In *Sounds Good 1* we learnt to play the songs below on our recorders.

> Work in pairs to play these songs together. Play the tune on the recorder and the chords on the ukulele. Ensure you alternate the part you take. Understanding how **melody** and **harmony** interact is very important for developing your performance skills.

Play along with the accompaniment

Little John

German folk song

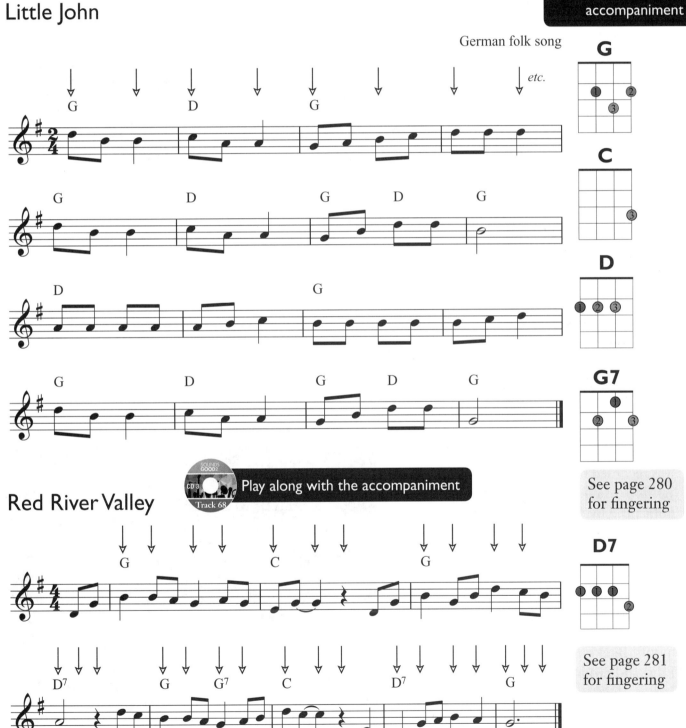

See page 280 for fingering

See page 281 for fingering

Play along with the accompaniment

Red River Valley

The word **minor** may mislead you into thinking that minor chords are less important than the major chords we've learnt about so far. This is not so! A minor chord's sound is often described as sad or mysterious; however, you will still hear them in happy songs.

It is important to be aware that minor chords are identified by placing a small 'm' next to the chord name. They can also be labelled using small roman numerals e.g. vi.

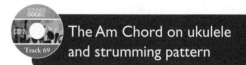
The Am Chord on ukulele and strumming pattern

Chord of Am

Adding the A minor chord to your repertoire will help you to learn and perform lots of new songs.

As you build up your bank of chords, it is really important you practise moving from one chord to another. Progressions and **sight-reading** exercises are very helpful when trying to improve your performance skills.

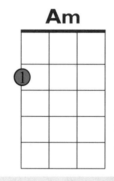

Am

Strumming pattern

See the Ukulele Fingerings Cover Flap at the back of *Sounds Good 2* to check your fingerings.

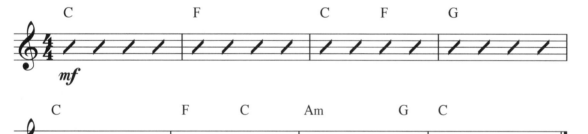

Rehearse and perform this simple chord progression.

'Still Haven't Found What I'm Looking For' was recorded by Irish rock band U2 for their *Joshua Tree* album released in May 1987. It is influenced by American rhythmic patterns and gospel music. These rhythms are heard performed by drummer Larry Mullen and the choir-like backing vocals give it a gospel feel. Lead singer Bono sings in the highest **range** he can. Guitar **overdubs** are used to fill guitarist The Edge's **arpeggio**-like motifs. **Backing vocals** were sung by the Edge and producers Brian Eno and Daniel Lanois. Their voices were **multi-tracked** to sound like a choir. The music video was shot in Las Vegas in 1987 whilst the band were in town to perform their *Joshua Tree* concert.

'Still Haven't Found What I'm Looking For' by U2

Verse 1
C
I have climbed highest mountain

I have run through the fields

     F   C
Only to be with you, only to be with you

C
I have run, I have crawled

I have scaled these city walls

      F   C
These city walls, only to be with you

Chorus
    G   F   C
But I still haven't found what I'm looking for
    G   F   C
But I still haven't found what I'm looking for

Verse 2
C
I have kissed honey lips

Felt the healing in her fingertips

      F   C
It burned like fire, (I was) burning inside her

C
I have spoke with the tongue of angels

I have held the hand of a devil

      F   C
It was warm in the night, I was cold as a stone

Chorus

Verse 3
C
I believe in the kingdom come

Then all the colors will bleed into one

      F   C
Bleed into one, but yes I'm still running

C
You broke the bonds and you loosed the chains

'Carried the cross of my shame

    F   C
Of my shame, you know I believed it

Chorus × 2

Define the following terms:

Arpeggio	
Backing vocals	
Multi-tracking	
Overdubbing	
Range	

'Amazing Grace'

We explored the story of 'Amazing Grace' in *Sounds Good 1*. What can you remember about this song?_____

_____

Let's sing it together!

> Amazing Grace, how sweet the sound
>
> That saved a wretch like me!
>
> I once was lost but know I'm found
>
> Was blind, but now I see.

Piano accompaniment to 'Amazing Grace'

CD 3
Track 71

In pairs, sing and listen to the verse on your CD. Try to *identify* where the chord changes are required. Use your whiteboard to draft and redraft the chord progression to accompany the lyrics. The chords needed to do this are C, F, G and Am.

Insert your final draft in the space below. Take care to place the chords you have chosen carefully, not too soon or too late. *Use* your ukulele to check that the progression you have chosen harmonises with the melody of the lyrics.

_____

_____

_____

_____

The chords C, F, Am and G are used in thousands of hits you will recognise.

Research and *identify* songs which use these four chords and compile a list below.

	Genre	Song title	Artist/Composer
1			
2			
3			
4			

Chord of Em

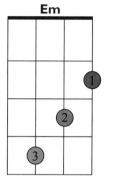

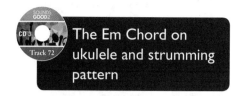

The Em Chord on ukulele and strumming pattern

See the Ukulele Fingerings Cover Flap at the back of *Sounds Good 2* to check your fingerings.

Rehearse and perform the **chord progression** below. Pay attention to the dynamic markings.

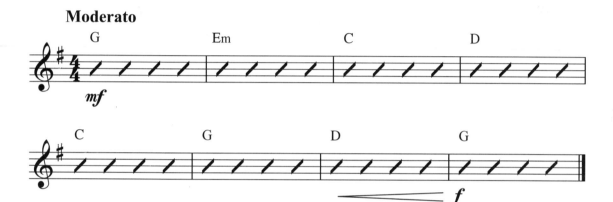

Developing your **sight-reading** skills is important for group playing.

Try to sight-read this progression without preparing it beforehand.

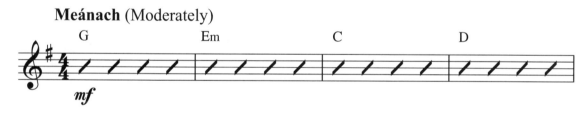

Compose a **rhythmic ostinato** to accompany the chord progression above. *Transcribe* your rhythm on the rhythm line below and assign the chords to each bar as they appear above.

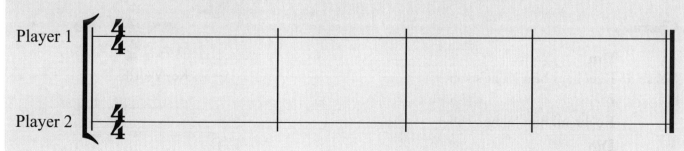

Chord of Dm

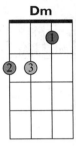

 The Dm Chord on ukulele and strumming pattern

Drunken Sailor is a sea shanty, traditionally sung by sailors as they worked on their ships. Like most songs from the **oral tradition**, the composer is unknown. Several versions of the lyrics exist. This song shares the same melody as well-known folk song *Óró, sé do 'bheatha abhaile*.

See the Ukulele Fingerings Cover Flap at the back of *Sounds Good 2* to check your fingerings.

'Drunken Sailor'

Verse 1

Dm
What shall we do with the drunken sailor?
C
What shall we do with the drunken sailor?
Dm
What shall we do with the drunken sailor?
Dm   C   Dm
Ear-ly in the morning

Chorus
Dm
Hooray, and up she rises
C
Hooray, and up she rises
Dm
Hooray, and up she rises
Dm   C   Dm
Ear-ly in the morning

       Dm
Verse 2   Put him in the long boat 'til he's sober
       C
       Put him in the long boat 'til he's sober
       Dm
       Put him in the long boat 'til he's sober
       Dm   C   Dm
       Ear-ly in the morning

Chorus

       Dm
Verse 3   Keel haul him 'til he's sober
       C
       Keel haul him 'til he's sober
       Dm
       Keel haul him 'til he's sober
       Dm   C   Dm
       Ear-ly in the morning

 Play along with the audio track

Chorus

Verse 4   That's what we do with the drunken sailor!
       C
       That's what we do with the drunken sailor!
       Dm
       That's what we do with the drunken sailor!
       Dm   C   Dm
       Ear-ly in the morning

Chorus

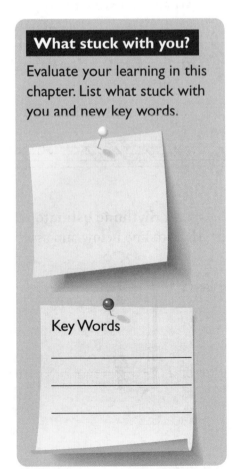

What stuck with you?

Evaluate your learning in this chapter. List what stuck with you and new key words.

Key Words

276

Bringing Together Our Skills

'Waltzing Matilda'

Indicate chords that are suitable to provide harmonic support to this melody line. Insert your chosen chords in the boxes provided.

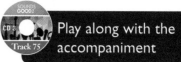

Play along with the accompaniment

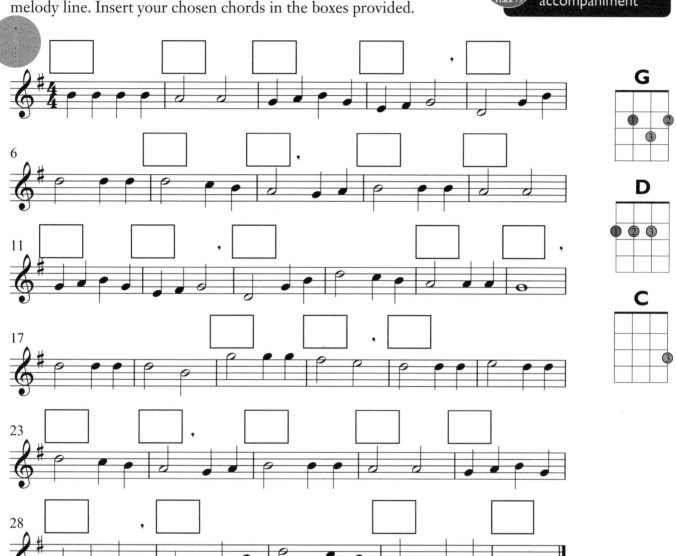

'Waltzing Matilda' is suitable to perform on recorder with ukulele accompaniment. In groups rehearse and perform this song using the chords you have chosen. You may decide to refine your chords in places.

'Waltzing Matilda' is an Australian folk song. Research and make notes on this song.

'Whiskey in the Jar'

Indicate chords that are suitable to provide harmonic support to this melody line. Insert your chosen chords in the boxes provided.

Play along with the accompaniment

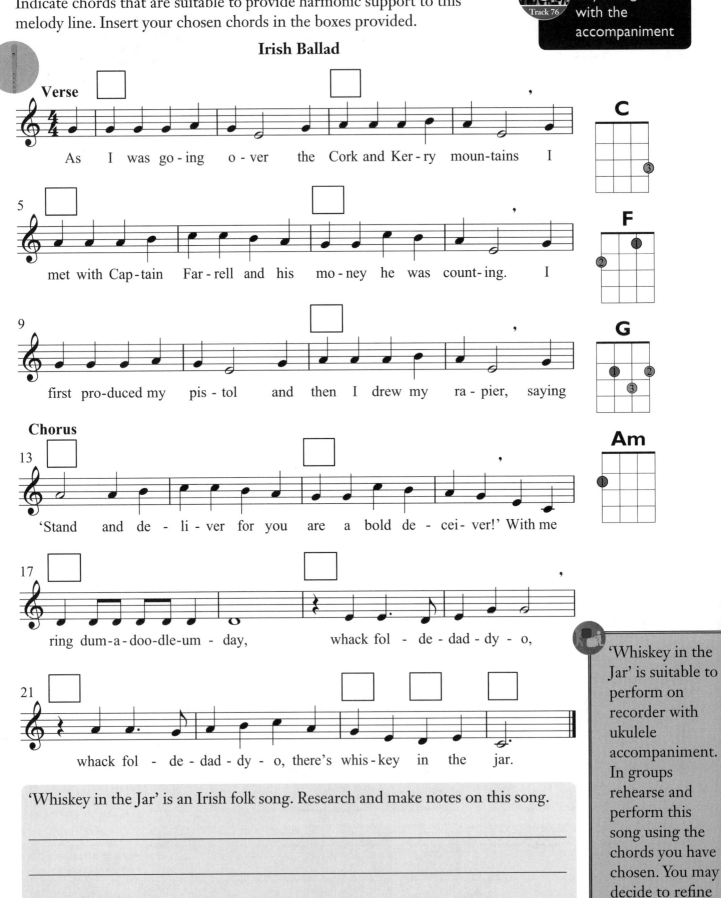

'Whiskey in the Jar' is an Irish folk song. Research and make notes on this song.

'Whiskey in the Jar' is suitable to perform on recorder with ukulele accompaniment. In groups rehearse and perform this song using the chords you have chosen. You may decide to refine your chords in places.

Songs for Performance

'Dirty Old Town' by Ewan MacColl

Verse 1

    C

I met my love by the gas works wall,

      F   C

Dreamed a dream by the old ca - nal.

    G   Am

Kissed my girl by the factory wall,

    G   Am

Dirty old town,   dirty old town.

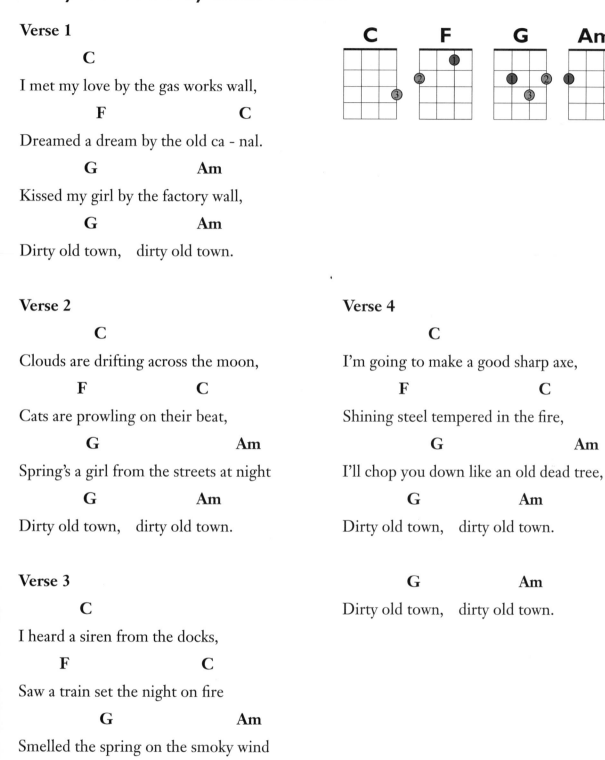

Verse 2

    C

Clouds are drifting across the moon,

    F   C

Cats are prowling on their beat,

    G   Am

Spring's a girl from the streets at night

    G   Am

Dirty old town,   dirty old town.

Verse 3

    C

I heard a siren from the docks,

    F   C

Saw a train set the night on fire

    G   Am

Smelled the spring on the smoky wind

    G   Am

Dirty old town,   dirty old town.

Verse 4

    C

I'm going to make a good sharp axe,

    F   C

Shining steel tempered in the fire,

    G   Am

I'll chop you down like an old dead tree,

    G   Am

Dirty old town,   dirty old town.

    G   Am

Dirty old town,   dirty old town.

'Danny Boy' words by Frederick Weatherly, music traditional

C   F   Am   G7   C7

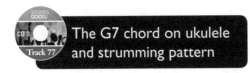

The G7 chord on ukulele and strumming pattern

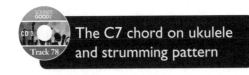

The C7 chord on ukulele and strumming pattern

Verse 1

G7   C   C7   F
Oh Danny boy, the pipes, the pipes are calling,

           C   C7   G7
From glen to glen, and down the mountainside,

           C   F
The summer's gone, and all the flowers are dying,

G7   C   G7   C
'Tis you, 'tis you must go and I must bide.

    G   C   F   C
But come ye back when summer's in the meadow,

    F   C F   G7
Or when the valley's hushed and white with snow,

       C   F
'Tis I'll be here in sunshine or in shadow.

    F   C   F G7   C
Oh Danny boy, oh Danny boy, I love you so.

Verse 2

G7   C   C7   F
And if you come, when all the flowers are dying,

           C   C7   G7
And I am dead, as dead I may well be,

           C   F
You'll come and find the place where I am lying,

G7   C   G7   C
And kneel and say an 'Ave' there for me.

    G   C   F   C
And I shall hear, tho' soft you tread above me,

    F   C F   G7
And all my dreams will warm and sweeter be,

       C   F
If you'll not fail to tell me that you love me,

    F   C   F G7   C
I'll simply sleep in peace, until you come to me.

'Somewhere Over the Rainbow' by E.Y. Harburg and Harold Arlen

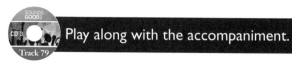 Play along with the accompaniment.
Track 79

Verse 1

C   Em   F   C

Somewhere over the rainbow, way up high

F   C   A7   Dm   G7 C

There's a land that I heard of once in a lullaby.

 The Fm chord and strumming pattern
Track 80

Verse 2

C   Em   F   C

Somewhere over the rainbow, skies are blue,

F   C   A7   Dm   C

And the dreams that you dare to dream really do come true.

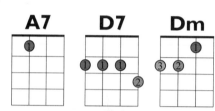

Middle

G   C   Dm   G7   C   G

Someday I'll wish upon a star and wake up where the clouds are far behind me,

      C   D7

Where troubles melt like lemon drops away above the chimney tops,

      Em   A7   Dm G7

that's where you'll find me.

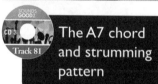 The A7 chord and strumming pattern
Track 81

Verse 3

C   Em   F   C

Somewhere over the rainbow, blue birds fly

F   Fm C   A7   D7   G7   C

Birds fly   over the rainbow, why then, oh why can't I?

 The D7 chord and strumming pattern
Track 82

C   Dm   G7   C

If happy little bluebirds fly beyond the rainbow, why oh why can't I?

Performance Questionnaire

1 What should musicians consider before choosing a piece of music for performance?

_____

2 *Identify* what performance skills you developed this year.

_____

3 *List* **two** pieces of music you have performed this year.

_____

_____

4 *Outline* difficulties you faced when learning to play the ukulele.

_____

_____

5 *Describe* how you felt after your performance.

_____

6 *Suggest* three benefits of performing with others.

_____

_____

_____

7 *Provide* a piece of advice for students learning the ukulele.

_____

_____

8 *Argue* why rehearsing music together is so important.

_____

_____

9 *Propose* what you consider makes a good performance.

_____

_____

Performance Appraisal Form

Title of piece _____

Composer _____

Performer _____

For each aspect of the performance, tick the first, second or third column.

	Consistently good	Good, but some mistakes	Could be improved
Musical qualities			
Correct notes			
Good rhythmically			
Good tempo			
Use of dynamics			
Use of articulation			
Control of instrument or voice			
Overall style			
Presentation			

Indicate **what you like best about this performance.**

_____

_____

_____

_____

Identify **what you have learnt from this performance that you can apply to your own performances.**

_____

_____

_____

_____

_____

Task 1

◆ *Propose* and *design* a list of criteria or a format for evaluating a **ukulele** performance. Write this in the space below.

◆ Invite a musician from your school to perform for you. *Use* your criteria to *evaluate* their performance or watch a performance on YouTube such as those we visited at the beginning of this unit.

◆ *Compare* your criteria to the Performance Appraisal Form. Would you make any changes to this format? If so, *outline* your reasons for doing so.

_____

_____

_____

_____

_____

_____

_____

_____

_____

_____

_____

_____

_____

_____

_____

_____

_____

_____

Task 2

In this unit we explored **chord progressions** to help us acquire important skills for coordinating strumming patterns and chord changes. Developing our skills also involved learning both **major** and **minor** chords. These chords can help to set a **mood** or create a certain feeling.

Incidental music is music which has been composed for use with a film, play or computer game. Its role is to reflect the narrative or enhance a particular atmosphere or mood.

Explore various combinations of the chords you have learnt and *compose* a piece of incidental music for a scene from one of the following:

a children's fairy-tale

a spooky computer game

a love story

Your composition should be at least eight bars long and use three or more chords in the progression.

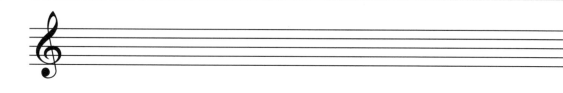

Task 3

1 *Use* recording software available to you to record a chord progression or short **harmonic ostinato**.

2 *Experiment* with your progression by applying **processing effects** to your work.

3 *Evaluate* and reflect on how these affect or change the sound, and assess whether any of the processes are effective in improving how your creation sounds.

4 *Present* your findings below.

Try adding reverb or distortion to your composition.

You may choose to add this to your Composition Portfolio.

Task 4

Looking back at the songs we have learnt, you will notice it doesn't take many chords to write a masterpiece.

Investigate songs which use three, four or five **chords**. You will find examples of these songs complied on YouTube tutorials for Ukulele. Search online for 'play songs with three ukulele chords'. Compile evidence of your research in the box below.

Songs using three chords

_____

_____

_____

_____

_____

Songs using four chords

_____

_____

_____

_____

_____

Songs using five chords

_____

_____

_____

_____

_____

Reflection and Evaluation Sheet

Learning

Unit title:

Learning Outcomes (LOs) I worked with:

Music I listened to:

_____

_____

Learning and exploring

I really enjoyed…

_____

Something interesting I learnt…

_____

My biggest challenge was…

_____

I overcame this by…

_____

One improvement I have made is…

_____

Traffic-light your learning

Learning Outcomes	☹	😐	🙂	✓
1.4				
1.7				
1.12				
2.1				
2.4				
2.5				
2.6				
2.8				
2.10				
3.5				
3.9				
3.10				

Key words	Action verbs
_____	_____
_____	_____

Key skills

_____

I got better at x skill by _____

_____

This unit reminded me of learning about… _____

_____

What still puzzles me is…

_____

_____

Feedback and goal setting…

_____

_____

_____

Rate your learning

287

Revision Lab

Strand One Activities

1.1	
a)	*Explain* the term **ostinato**. _____ _____
b)	*Compose* a four-bar musical phrase in 3/4 in the key of **D major**. Support this phrase by creating a one-bar **rhythmic ostinato** to accompany it. Musical phrase: *(empty staff with treble clef, D major key signature, 3/4 time, four bars)* Rhythmic ostinato: *(empty rhythm line, one bar)* Final draft: *(empty staff with treble clef, four bars)* *Indicate* the **instruments** chosen to perform this and *explain* why you have chosen them. _____ _____ _____ _____

c) *Compose* a four-bar musical phrase in **4/4** in the key of **F major**.

Support this phrase by creating a two-bar **harmonic ostinato** to accompany it.

Musical phrase:

Harmonic ostinato:

Final draft:

Indicate the **instruments** chosen to perform this and *propose* why you have chosen them.

_____

_____

_____

_____

d) *Compose* a four-bar musical phrase in **6/8** in the key of **B♭ major**.

Support this phrase by creating a two-bar **melodic ostinato** to accompany it.

Musical phrase:

Melodic ostinato:

Final draft:

Indicate the **instruments** chosen to perform this and *suggest* why you have chosen them.

_____

_____

_____

_____

1.2	
a)	*Explain* the term **stimulus**.

_____

_____

b) *Examine* how **composers** can be inspired by a stimulus and suggest some stimuli examples.

_____

_____

_____

_____

c) *Create* a four-bar melody in 4/4 in response to this image/stimulus.

◆ *Evaluate* the role of the **elements** of music and how they can help you create your melody e.g. pulse, timbre, mood, tempo and dynamics.

◆ *Identify* an **instrument** and the **key signature** for your melody.

◆ *Use* your whiteboard to *explore* and *experiment* with ideas/drafts.

◆ *Transcribe* your final draft below and input or **record** your composition using music software available to you.

Final draft:

1.3	
a)	*Explain* the term **improvisation**.

_____

_____

b) *List* two **genres** associated with improvisation.

(i) _____

(ii) _____

c) *Design* a **rhythmic ostinato** that can be improvised over.

Design a four-bar **harmonic** ukulele **accompaniment** based on the **chord progression** I–IV–vi–V in C major.

Complete the chord box below to help you to identify the chords in **C major**.

I	**ii**	**iii**	**IV**	**V**	**vi**	**vii**

Indicate your harmonic chord progression below and a strumming pattern for it. The first bar is completed for you.

Chord   C

Strums | / / / / | | | ‖

Strums

d) *Design* a four-bar **harmonic** piano **accompaniment** to accompany the first phrase of 'Twinkle Twinkle' below. Some notes of the tune are missing. Can you work these out together.

Complete the chord box below to help you to *identify* the chords in **F major**.

I	**ii**	**iii**	**IV**	**V**	**vi**	**vii**

Experiment and *devise* a **chord progression** using chords I, IV or V which suit this phrase. Indicate where the chords should change above the melody and insert a piano accompaniment on the **bass stave** below, using the **root** note of the chords you have chosen.

e) *Explain* the following terms; include a visual example of each on a stave

Block chords

_____

Pedal note

Broken chords

Pedal note

f) *Identify* and *describe* the **texture** of your completed arrangement of the opening phrase of 'Twinkle Twinkle'.

_____

_____

Identify and define two other textures we have learned about.

(i) _____

(ii) _____

1.4	

a) *Briefly explain* the difference between **melody** and **harmony**.

_____

_____

_____

_____

b) *Identify* and *indicate* suitable **chords** to provide harmonic support for the melody below.

Bingo

American folksong

Complete the chord box below to help you to *identify* the chords in **B♭ major**.

Use the chord box to help you *identify* a suitable **chord progression**.

I	ii	iii	IV	V	vi	vii

c) *Identify* and *indicate* suitable **chords** to provide harmonic support for the melody below.

Kä - ki se kuk - kuu kuu - si - kos sa, Ja koi - vi - koss' on pen - sä,
Listen to the coo - koo Singing so_ sweet - ly A -mong all the trees and mead - ows,

Taas - kin on tul - leet ne tuk - ki - po - jar Ja kau - nis,_ läm - min ken - sä.
Here come the log - gers through the woods, They are bring ing the_ sum - mer weath - er.

(chord box label: Em)

Use the chord box below to help you identify a **chord progression**.

Design a chord box to help you to identify the chords in **C major**.

I	ii	iii	IV	V	vi	vii

1.5	
a)	Explain the term **graphic score**.
b)	In groups of three, *read*, *interpret* and sing or play from the symbolic representation of a three-part performance below.

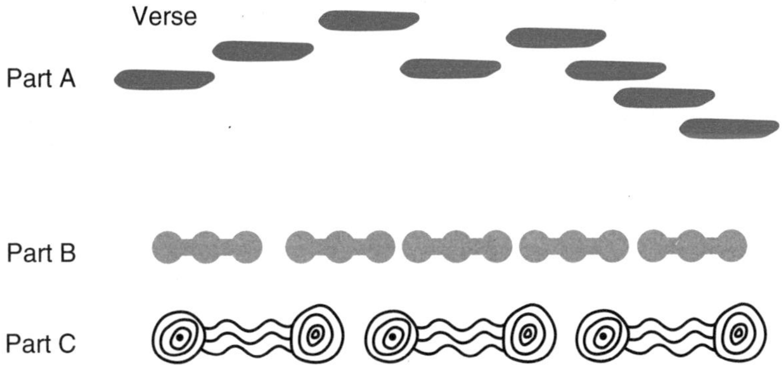

Verse

Part A

Part B

Part C

c) *Describe* how composers have used symbols to notate their creations and the impact this can have on performances of their work.

_____

_____

_____

_____

d) *Devise* four symbols that could be used to represent sound. Insert the images in the grid below with a detailed description of how you imagine they would sound or function within a graphic score.

Symbol	Description
1	
2	
3	
4	

1.6

a) Listen and *transcribe* the following four-bar **rhythmic patterns**.

Track 83
1. $\frac{2}{4}$

Track 84
2. $\frac{3}{4}$

Track 85
3. $\frac{4}{4}$

b) Listen and *transcribe* the following two-bar **melodic pattern in C major** that begins on the tonic.

Track 86
4. $\frac{4}{4}$

Track 87
5. $\frac{4}{4}$

c) Listen and *transcribe* the following two-bar **melodic patterns in G major** that begins on the tonic.

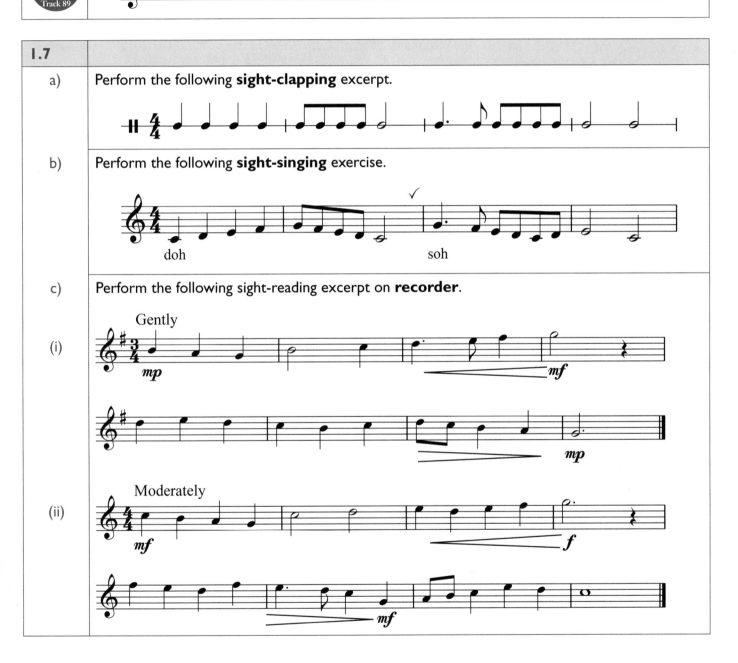

6.

7.

1.7

a) Perform the following **sight-clapping** excerpt.

b) Perform the following **sight-singing** exercise.

doh   soh

c) Perform the following sight-reading excerpt on **recorder**.

(i) Gently

mp   *mf*   *mp*

(ii) Moderately

mf   *f*   *mf*

d)

Perform the following sight-reading on ukulele.

(i)

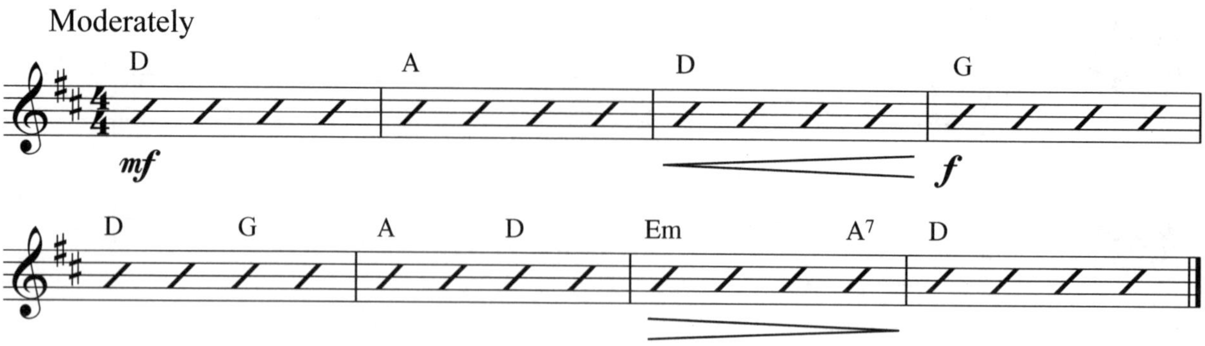

Moderately

(ii)

Moderately

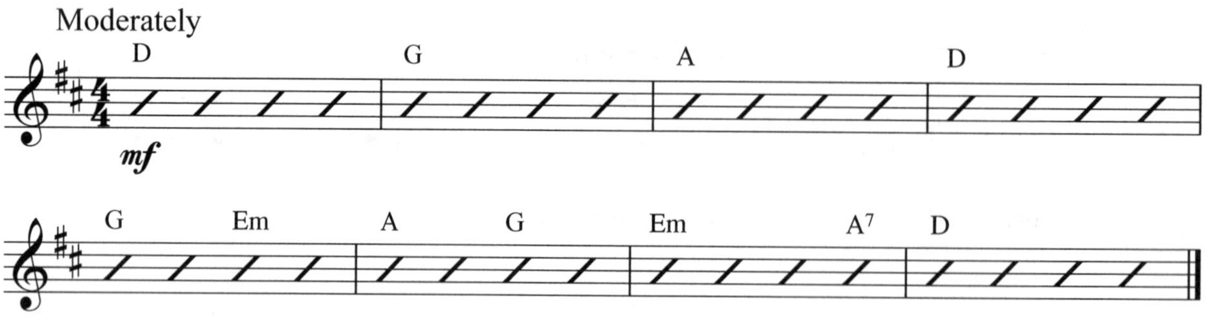

1.8

a) *Explain* the term **structure** or form.

_____

_____

_____

_____

b) *Explain* the term **texture**.

_____

_____

_____

_____

Devise a **visual representation** of the three **textures** used to describe music.

Texture			
Image			
Definition			
Musical example			

1.9	
a)	*Explain* the term **metre**.
	_____
	_____
b)	*Briefly explain* **body percussion**.
	_____
	_____
	Compose a two-bar rhythm pattern in **4/4**. *Create* a **body-percussion pattern** for performing this rhythm pattern and indicate the performance instructions under the rhythm pattern.
c)	*Propose* reasons for your choice of actions. How do they enhance the performance of the rhythm pattern?
	_____
	_____
	_____
	_____
d)	*List* four common body-percussion actions.
	(i) _____
	(ii) _____
	(iii) _____
	(iv) _____

1.10	
a)	*List* three **contrasting styles** of music represented in your school or community.
	(i) _____
	(ii) _____
	(iii) _____

b) *Compare* and contrast the characteristics and **defining features** of the three styles you have indicated above.

Style			
Characteristics			
Features			
Performers			

1.11

a) *Illustrate* the **structure** of a pop or folk song through a **visual representation**.

b) *Suggest* one way of illustrating the structure of **rondo** form through a **physical representation**.

c) Name a piece of music composed in **rondo form:**

d) Illustrate the structure of **rondo** form through a visual image or representation.

1.12	

a) Listen to a piano **accompaniment** for the **lyrics** printed below. *Use* a * symbol above the words to *indicate* where the **chords** change.

Amazing Grace, how sweet the sound,

That saved a wretch like me.

I once was lost, but now am found,

Was blind, but now I see.

This song is in **C major** and uses the three **major chords** – I, IV and V.

Complete the chord box below to help you to *identify* the chords in **C major**.

Use the chord box to help you identify the chords I – IV –V.

I	**ii**	**iii**	**IV**	**V**	**vi**	**vii**

b) *List* two other songs which use these three **major chords**.

1 _____

2 _____

c) *Identify* one other **chord** which is used to complete the most commonly used group of chords in popular music?

_____

d) *List* the **minor chords** in this key.

_____

1.13	
a)	*Identify* **two arrangements** of a piece of Irish traditional **folk music**.

Piece chosen:		
Arrangement	1	2
Composer		
Performer		

b) *Compare* them referring to the **elements of music**. Include other comparisons such as style, instrumentation and performing techniques used in each performence.

_____

_____

_____

_____

_____

_____

_____

_____

_____

_____

_____

1.14	
a)	*Identify* **two** pieces of music that are similar in period and style, composed by different **composers**, from two different countries.

Period:		
Composer	1	2
Country		
Piece of music		

b) *Compare* the two pieces of music referring to the **elements of music**, instrumentation and other features.

_____

_____

_____

_____

_____

_____

_____

_____

_____

_____

_____

Write a short note on the **composer** and period/style you have chosen.

Composer 1:

_____

_____

_____

_____

_____

_____

Composer 2:

_____

_____

_____

_____

_____

Strand Two Activities

2.1	
a)	*Explain* the term **sound source**.
	_____
	_____
b)	*Briefly describe* what is meant by the musical term **improvise**.
	_____
	_____
	_____

2.2	
a)	*Define* the term **rap**.
	_____
	_____
b)	*List* three **topical issues** rap artists deal with in their **lyrics**.
	1 _____
	2 _____
	3 _____
c)	*Create* a musical statement which deals with the topic of **homelessness**.

Compose a **rhythmic pattern** for your statement's lyrics and a **melody** to accompany your musical statement.

Insert your final draft on the staves below.

d) *Illustrate* the **purpose** of your musical statement and *explain* the steps involved in **developing** your statement from idea to reality.

_____

_____

_____

_____

_____

_____

_____

_____

e) Perform and record your rap using the software available to you.

2.3	

a) *Explain* the term **motif**.

_____

_____

b) *Identify* **three** short **motifs** with your teacher. *Transcribe* them on the staves below and *provide* the name of the pieces the motifs are taken from and their composers.

	1	2	3
Motif/theme			
Name of piece			
Composer			

c) In the case of **one** motif from those shown above, *adapt* the **melody** by changing its feel, style or harmony and *transcribe* your adapted motif on the staves below.

original excerpt/motif/theme   adapted excerpt/motif/theme

(i)

(ii)

d)	*Briefly describe* how you have *adapted* the **theme** or **motifs** you have been working with below.
	_____
	_____
	_____
	_____
	_____
	_____
	_____
	_____
	_____

2.4	
a)	*Analyse* and *evaluate* the **performance skills** and techniques necessary to *interpret* music for performance. Refer to your own performance of a song or instrumental piece as a **soloist** or part of a **group**.
	Identify a piece of music or song you have performed this year.

Piece:	Composer:
_____	_____
_____	
_____	
_____	
_____	
_____	
_____	
_____	

b)	*List* and *briefly explain* three **performing techniques**.
	1 _____
	2 _____
	3 _____

2.5	
a)	*Explain* the term **ensemble**.
	_____
b)	List and describe three ensembles you have learnt about.
	1 _____
	2 _____
	3 _____
c)	*Identify* a musical work you have performed with you class.

Piece:	Composer:

Evaluate the importance of the following elements for your performance.

Co-operation	
Communication	
Listening	
Intonation	
Interpretation	
Style	

Briefly *comment* on your role in this performance.

_____

_____

_____

2.6	
a)	Select a short **film clip** or **sequence of images** with your teacher. *Discuss* and *identify* a mood that is illustrated or the theme of your film clip or images. *Compose* a short piece inspired by your selected mood or theme. *Compose* a **melodic ostinato** and add four layers of sound over your **ostinato** as it repeats. Choose a **key signature** to work with and *use* the chord box below to help you compose your parts.

I	ii	iii	IV	V	vi	vii

2.6	
b)	*Comment* on the **texture** of your composition. _____ _____ _____

2.7	
a)	*Explain* the term **mood**. _____ _____
b)	*List* four **moods** that can be illustrated in music and *suggest* ways of illustrating your ideas in a composition. 1 _____ 2 _____ 3 _____ 4 _____

c)   *Describe* an example of a mood, illustrated by a **composer** in a piece of music you have listened to.

Mood	Composer	Piece

Description:

_____

_____

_____

_____

_____

_____

_____

d)   *Explain* the term **found sound**.

_____

_____

_____

e)   *Suggest* how found sounds can be used to *illustrate* a particular **mood** or feeling.

_____

_____

_____

f)   Choose a **newspaper article, short story** or **poem**. *Create* and *present* found sounds which help you to *illustrate* the mood/feelings of the material you have chosen to work with.

Describe the process below, making reference to the story, poem or article you chose and the **found sounds** you used. It may be helpful to read your chosen text and perform your found-sound composition along with it.

_____

_____

_____

_____

_____

_____

_____

_____

_____

2.8	
a)	In Unit 6 we explored the chordal structure of songs and identified the common use of the **chord progression I-V-vi-IV**. Adele's 'Someone Like You' and Ed Sheeran's 'Perfect' are two examples of songs that use this progression. List **five** more examples.

Song	Performer
1	
2	
3	
4	
5	

2.9	
a)	*Explain* the term **range**.
b)	*Explain* the term **timbre**.
c)	List two instruments which have a **contrasting timbre** and *describe* how they differ in sound.

Instrument	Timbre
1	
2	

d)	List the four **families of the orchestra**.

1 _____

2 _____

3 _____

4 _____

e) *List* the four **string** instruments in order of **pitch** lowest to highest.

1 _____

2 _____

3 _____

4 _____

f) *Indicate* the **range** of each of these instruments on the stave below.

g) *Describe* how sound is produced on string instruments.

_____

_____

_____

_____

h) *List* three **performing techniques** associated with string playing.

_____

_____

_____

i) *Explain* the term **pizzicato**.

_____

_____

j) *Identify* a well-known orchestral **conductor**.

_____

k) *Identify* an Irish orchestra.

_____

l) Vocal **ensembles** or **choirs** typically perform in four parts. Can you name these parts?

1 _____

2 _____

3 _____

4 _____

m) *Illustrate* the **range** of each of these voices on the stave below.

n) *Identify* and *describe* two **vocal techniques**.

1 _____

2 _____

o) *Identify* a community organisation which promotes singing in Ireland.

_____

2.10	

a) In pairs *develop* a set of **criteria** for evaluating live or recorded performances and complete an in-depth review of a performance.

b) Insert your criteria in the space below and include the information gathered from your review of a performance.

Performer/s:	Piece/Song:
Criteria	**Comments**

2.11	
a)	*Outline* how you access music day to day.
	_____
	_____
b)	*Evaluate* the impact technology is having on how we access music and *propose* ways in which the music you have created in class can be shared with a **global** audience.
	_____
	_____
	_____
	_____
	_____
	_____
	_____
	_____
	_____
	_____

Strand Three Activities

3.1	

a) Produce a **playlist** and a set of recordings to accompany a local historical event or community celebration.

Provide details of the event or celebration below.

_____

_____

_____

b) *Propose* what **genres** or styles of music would suit the event or celebration you have chosen.

_____

_____

_____

c) *Suggest* two reasons why one of the songs in your **playlist** was selected for this activity.

1 _____

2 _____

d) *Indicate* the songs you have chosen for your playlist in the grid below.

Identify an **aural signpost** for the listener in the case of each song you have chosen.

Track	Song title	Artist/Performer	Aural signpost for listener

e) *Suggest* reasons why playlists are a popular way of compiling and listening to music.

_____

_____

_____

f) *List* four scenarios where people will access and listen to a pre-prepared playlist such as the one you have created above.

1 _____

2 _____

3 _____

4 _____

Suggest ways in which we can make our playlists accessible to others.

_____

_____

3.2

Many composers have written music designed to depict characters, their relationships and their emotions. We explored examples of this in Unit 3 of *Sounds Good 1*.

◆ Tchaikovsky's 'The Blue Bird and Princess Florine' is an example of this **illustrative music** in the **Romantic period** (page 70).

◆ Scheidt's *Galliard Battaglia* illustrates two sides in a gallant battle using trumpets to echo and compete with each other. This is a piece from the **Baroque era** (page 64).

Listen and carefully *examine* both of these works using your *Sounds Good 1* CD. Write a detailed account on the impact the music has on the **depiction of the characters**, **relationships** or **emotions**. Refer to the composers, relevant genres and specific musical features in your answer.

_____

_____

_____

_____

_____

_____

_____

_____

_____

_____

_____

_____

_____

_____

_____

3.3	
a)	We have explored many contemporary and historical styles in *Sounds Good 1* and *2*. *List* six styles you have explored. 1 _____ 2 _____ 3 _____ 4 _____ 5 _____ 6 _____
b)	Choose one of these **styles** and make a study of it. Write a detailed account of this style, refer to the development of this style and the influences other styles had on its development. *Analyse* the structure and **form** of this music, *describe* common musical devices and features associated with it. Mention performers of this style and *provide* some **musical examples** for the listener to explore. _____ _____ _____ _____ _____ _____ _____ _____ _____ _____ _____ _____ _____ _____ _____ _____ _____ _____

3.4	
a)	*Explain* the term **jingle**.
	_____
	_____
b)	*Identify* two well-known advertising jingles, refer to the brand or product the jingle is used to advertise.
	1 _____
	2 _____
c)	*List* three must-have products currently on the market.
	1 _____
	2 _____
	3 _____
d)	*Outline* the process/stages involved in designing jingles to promote a product.
	_____
	_____
	_____
e)	*Evaluate* the role of advertising jingles in promotion of products such as those you have listed above.
	_____
	_____
	_____
	_____
	_____
	_____
f)	Choose a product from your list above and *compose* an original jingle for use in a radio advertisement to promote the product. Insert the jingle on the stave below and assign the **lyrics** to the **melody**.

g)   Record your jingle and *present* it to your classmates.

Comment on the purpose and *appraise* the development of your jingle.

_____

_____

_____

3.5

a)   *Define* the term **incidental music** and *explain* its purpose.

_____

_____

b)   *List* three situations in which incidental music is used.

1 _____

2 _____

3 _____

c)   *Identify* a piece of incidental music and *comment* on the context for which it was composed.

_____

_____

_____

d)   Choose a context or environment for a piece of incidental music.

Outline how you would create a suitable piece of music for it.

Refer to the style, instruments and musical features you would include in your composition.

_____

_____

_____

_____

_____

_____

_____

_____

_____

_____

3.6	

Listen to the following music excerpts and *associate* them with the appropriate image or text by drawing a line to connect the track and the image or text.

Track 1

SOUNDS GOOD2
CD 3
Track 90

Track 2

SOUNDS GOOD2
CD 3
Track 91

"It was a dark, gloomy day on Achill Island"

Track 3

SOUNDS GOOD2
CD 3
Track 92

Justify each connection you have just made by giving the reasons why you feel the music matches the image or words.

Track	Reason why this track matches the words or images you have associated it with
1	
2	
3	

3.7	
a)	*List* two Irish **composers**.

1 _____

2 _____

b) *List* two Irish **songwriters**.

1 _____

2 _____

c) Make a study which *compares* the compositions of two Irish composers <u>or</u> songwriters.

◆ *Investigate* and *describe* the differences and similarities between the two compositions below.

◆ Refer to the composers and try to *distinguish* their style and the musical features of their compositions.

◆ *Identify* **musical signposts** for the listener to discover.

Composer/Songwriter	Composition
1	1
2	2

_____

_____

_____

_____

_____

_____

_____

_____

_____

_____

_____

_____

_____

_____

_____

_____

_____

_____

3.8	

Select a particular advert which uses music. *Analyse* the role music plays in supporting the advertising message and promotes the product. Refer to the music used and the product being promoted in your answer.

Advert/brand	Product	Music used	Key message/theme

_____

_____

_____

_____

_____

_____

_____

_____

_____

_____

3.9	

a) *Explain* the term **processing effects**.

_____

_____

b) *List* and *describe* four processing effects used in the **recording process**. In each case *explain* how the music is affected by the change.

1 _____

2 _____

3 _____

4 _____

c) *Identify* a piece of music which uses two of the processing effects named above.

_____

d)	*Evaluate* the use and effectiveness of the processing effects in this piece of music.
	_____
	_____
	_____
	_____

3.10	
a)	*Explain* the term **copyright**.
	_____
	_____
b)	*Identify* and *explain* the **principles of music property rights**.
	_____
	_____
	_____
	_____
	_____
	Critique the impact **copyright** law has on the sharing and publishing of music.
	_____
	_____
	_____
	_____
	_____
	_____

3.11

Compose a newspaper article which *discusses* the time allocated to Irish artists and performers on a variety of local or national media. Refer to specific media formats, artists and performers in your article.

Today's blog title

_____

_____
_____
_____
_____
_____
_____
_____
_____
_____
_____
_____
_____
_____
_____
_____
_____
_____
_____
_____

Action Verbs

Action Verbs play a significant role in your learning journey. Each action verb has been specifically selected to communicate what you should be able to achieve. These are command words and will be referred to in your final assessment for Junior Cycle Music.

Adapt make something suitable for new condition, use or purpose

Analyse study or examine something in detail; break down in order to bring out the essential elements or structure; identify parts and relationships, and to interpret information to reach conclusions

Apply select and use information and/or knowledge and understanding to explain a given situation or real circumstances

Appraise evaluate, judge or consider a piece of work

Associate to connect or bring into relation; to fit together and cause to correspond

Argue challenge or debate an issue or idea with the purpose of persuading or committing someone else to a particular stance or action

Brief description/explanation give a short statement of only the main points

Classify group things based on common characteristics

Comment give an opinion based on a given statement or the result of a calculation

Compare give an account of the similarities or differences between two (or more) items or situations, referring to both/all of them throughout

Compose write or create a work of art, especially music or poetry

Create to bring something into existence; to cause something to happen as a result of one's actions

Critique state, giving reasons, the positive and negative aspects of, for example, an idea, artefact or artistic process

Define give the precise meaning of a word, phrase, concept

Demonstrate prove or make clear by reasoning or evidence, illustrating with examples or practical application

Describe tell or depict in written or spoken words; to represent or delineate by a picture or other figure

Design do or plan something with a specific purpose in mind

Develop bring to a later or more advanced stage; to elaborate or work out in detail

Devise plan, elaborate or invent something from existing principles or ideas

Discuss offer a considered, balanced review that includes a range of arguments, factors or hypotheses; opinions or conclusions should be presented clearly and supported by appropriate evidence

Distinguish make the differences between two or more concepts or items clear

Evaluate (information) collect and examine information to make judgments and appraisals; describe how evidence supports or does not support a conclusion in an inquiry or investigation; identify the limitations of information in conclusions; make judgements about ideas, solutions or methods

Evaluate (ethical judgement) collect and examine evidence to make judgments and appraisals; describe how evidence supports or does not support a judgement; identify the limitations of evidence in conclusions; make judgements about ideas, solutions or methods

Examine consider an argument, concept or object in a way that uncovers its assumptions, interrelationships or construction

Experiment to try and test, in order to discover something new or to prove something

Explain give a detailed account including reasons or causes

Explore systematically look into something closely; to scrutinise or probe

Find a general term that may variously be interpreted as calculate, measure, determine, etc.

Group identify objects according to characteristics

Identify recognise patterns, facts, or details; provide an answer from a number of possibilities; recognise and state briefly a distinguishing fact or feature

Illustrate use drawings or examples to describe something

Improvise create and perform music spontaneously or without prior preparation; to produce or make something from whatever is available

Indicate to point out or point to; to direct attention to

Infer use the results of an investigation based on a premise; read beyond what has been literally expressed

Investigate analyse, observe, study, or make a detailed and systematic examination, in order to establish facts or information and reach new conclusions

Interpret use knowledge and understanding to recognise trends and draw conclusions from given information

Justify give valid reasons or evidence to support an answer or conclusion

List provide a number of points, with no elaboration

Outline give the main points; restrict to essentials

Present to bring, offer or give in a formal way; to bring before or introduce to a public forum

Propose offer or suggest for consideration, acceptance or action

Provide evidence data, work and documentation that support inferences or conclusions

Recognise identify facts, characteristics or concepts that are critical (relevant/appropriate) to the understanding of a situation, event, process or phenomenon

Refine to improve by inserting finer distinctions or musical elements

Rehearse practise a play, piece of music, or other work for later public performance

Suggest propose a solution, hypothesis or other possible answer

Synthesise combine different ideas in order to create new understanding

Transcribe put thoughts, speech, data, into written or printed form; write out what is heard into characters or sentences

Use apply knowledge, skills or rules to put them into practice

Verify give evidence to support the truth of a statement

Classroom-Based Assessments (CBAs)

There are two Classroom-Based Assessments (CBAs) in Junior Cycle Music. Both are assessed at a common level and relate to specified learning outcomes set out in the Music Specification. CBAs are linked to the learning experiences provided over three years of study and are assessed at the end of Year 2 and Year 3 of Junior Cycle. Work presented for both CBAs will be monitored and supported by your teacher.

Classroom-Based Assessments	Format	Student preparation	Completed
Composition Portfolio	Two pieces chosen by the student from his/her portfolio	Compositions are produced over time with support and guidance from teacher	Towards the end of Year 2
Programme Note	Individual or group programme note in chosen format	During a maximum of 3 weeks, with support and guidance from teacher	Term 2 of Year 3

CBA1: Composition Portfolio

This is an opportunity for you to compile evidence of your creative accomplishments. The purpose of this assessment is to recognise and celebrate the musical compositions you create over the three years of junior cycle. These projects should reflect your musical ideas and creative expression across a variety of genres. Two pieces from your portfolio of compositions will be selected by you for assessment.

Some suggested creative projects set out in the Music Specification include:

◆ Responding to an auditory or visual stimulus

◆ Arranging an existing piece of music

◆ Creating an answering phrase to an existing phrase

◆ Adding music to a text

◆ Responding to a story or a literary text

◆ Creating an advertisement jingle

◆ Devising a piece of electro-acoustic music

◆ Creating an anthem or a musical piece for a school event

◆ Composing music in response to a personal experience

> **Relevant LOs include:**
> 1.1, 1.2, 1.3, 1.4, 1.12
> 2.1, 2.2, 2.3, 2.7
> 3.4, 3.5, 3.9

Some important information to consider when compiling your portfolio:

◆ You must include any draft work relating to your work

◆ The compositions you work with can be from any recognised musical style or genre

◆ It can be written for instrument or voice and for solo or group

◆ It can be presented in written, digital, visual or audio form, or any other suitable format

◆ A student reflection note must be included with each of the pieces submitted

◆ You may work in pairs or groups but it will be your individual role and contribution to the work that is assessed

A space has been provided for you to compile two samples of work for your Composition Portfolio on pages 328 and 330.

Success Criteria CBA1

Unit:	Date:
Learning goals:	**Learning Outcomes:**

Success criteria I can…				

Feedback:

Strengths:

Areas for improvement:

Goals:

CBA1 Composition Portfolio

Compiling evidence and reflecting on your learning experience.

Topic: _____
Task: _____
_____
_____

PORTFOLIO

Date _____ **Name** _____

Context

Where did you get ideas for this composition and what could this creation be used for?

_____

My Skills

My creation!

Evaluating and Reflecting

What did you learn from this process and what would you do differently next time?

Notes:

_____
_____
_____
_____

★★★★★

Success Criteria CBA1

Unit:	Date:
Learning goals:	**Learning Outcomes:**

Success criteria I can…				

Feedback:

Strengths:

Areas for improvement:

Goals:

CBA1 Composition Portfolio

Compiling evidence and reflecting on your learning experience.

PORTFOLIO

Date _____ Name _____

Topic: _____
Task: _____
_____
_____

Context

Where did you get ideas for this composition and what could this creation be used for?

_____

My Skills

My creation!

Evaluating and Reflecting

What did you learn from this process and what would you do differently next time?

Notes:

_____
_____
_____
_____

Classroom Based Assessment 2 (CBA2) – Programme Note Guidelines

The Programme Note is related to the three pieces you have decided to perform in your practical exam. It is intended to illuminate the content of the performance in an interesting and relevant way. It includes:

◆ a brief introduction to the composers/songwriters (if applicable)

◆ a description of the historical context of the pieces and the circumstances surrounding the composition

◆ one interesting musical point in each piece for the listener/audience to listen out for

◆ famous performers of the tune or on the instrument

◆ the student's role in a group performance.

The Programme Note can be presented in a written, digital, visual or audio form, or any other format that is deemed suitable. <u>There must be a reference to each of the three pieces in the Programme Note</u>. You will need to include some facts on the composer or the songwriter, some interesting points about the purpose behind the composition and some musical highlights so that the audience or the listener can be alerted to and be aware of the context of the pieces for your practical examination.

<u>Whether you are performing as a soloist or as part of group</u>, or a combination of both, <u>you will still need to provide an individual programme note</u>, but the note on the group performance should include a comment on your role and contribution to the group performance. If you are the composer of any of the pieces that comprise your programme for the practical examination, you should comment on and reflect upon these questions above in the same manner. The challenge is in creating a programme note which can interest both the well-informed listener and the novice listener.

This Programme Note will need to be completed <u>two weeks in advance of the practical</u> examination, and it is advised that you spend no more than three weeks on researching and completing it. You may find it easier to complete your Programme Note as you learn your pieces as this research will also inform your practising and refining of these pieces in preparation for the practical examination.

In considering what information to include you could ask yourself the following questions for each piece:

◆ Who is the composer/songwriter of this piece?

◆ Why did the composer/songwriter write this music?

◆ If the composer or songwriter is unknown (for example, in the case of some traditional music or folk music) what type of instrumental or vocal piece is this?

◆ Who are some famous exponents of this type of traditional or folk music?

◆ What was happening in the composer's country at the time of this composition?

◆ Is this piece typical of the time it was written or collected in?

◆ What is the most interesting moment in this piece for me?

◆ What do I want the attention of the listener to be guided towards?

◆ What is or where is my favourite section of this piece?

Relevant LOs include:
1.10, 1.11, 1.13, 1.14
2.4, 2.5, 2.10
3.2, 3.7

The structure of the Programme Note is left to your discretion, and you have the choice and the flexibility to present this in a format of your choosing, and in a way that allows you to focus on the aspects relevant to your upcoming performance. Programme notes are usually accessed by people with a wide variety of background knowledge.

Glossary

A capella	Vocal music that is performed without an instrumental accompaniment.
Absolute music	Abstract music, the opposite to programme music. It is not composed to represent or illustrate anything else.
Accent	Extra stress given to a note in a piece of music, indicated by the > symbol.
Accompaniment	A musical part (vocal or instrumental) which supports or provides the harmony for the main tune.
Aria	Italian word meaning 'air' or tune. A song for solo voice with or without accompaniment, usually from a larger work.
Arpeggio	A type of broken chord. The notes of the chord are played one by one in ascending or descending order.
Ascending	Music which moves from lower to higher notes.
Barbershop	A style of a cappella singing that typically uses four-part close harmony.
Baroque	The musical era from 1600 to 1750.
Basso continuo	An accompaniment made up of a continuous bass line over which chords are improvised.
Block chord	A chord in which the notes are played simultaneously
Body percussion	Sounds made using parts of the body (e.g. foot stamping, thigh slapping).
Broken chord	A chord whose notes are played in succession or in sequence.
Cadence	A short chord progression used at the end of a musical phrase to create a resting point in the music.
Call and response	A compositional technique in which a first musical phrase sounds as though it is answered by a second phrase performed by a different voice or group.
Canon	A form of strict imitation where one part leads and other parts follow with the same or closely related notes, at a distance.
Chance music	A modern style of composing where some elements of the performance are left to chance.
Chord	Two or more notes sounding simultaneously.
Chord progression	A series of chords sounding one after another, also known as a harmonic progression.
Chromatic music	Music in which the movement is by semitone. This often occurs when notes which do not belong to the chosen key are included in a piece of music.
Chromatic scale	A scale that moves in semitones.
Classical era	Generally considered as 1750 to 1830.
Clef	A symbol placed at the beginning of each stave, used to indicate pitches.
Common time	A time signature notated as a C, indicating four crotchet beats per bar or measure.
Gomposer	A person who creates and writes music.
Compression	Processing effect used to alter the volume of tracks. Increasing the gain (volume) without exceeding the limits of the sound
Concerto	A piece of music for solo instrument with orchestra.

Conductor	A person who, by means of gestures, leads an ensemble performance, indicating tempo, expression and other aspects of the music.
Consort	Instrumental ensemble, typical of the Renaissance and Baroque eras, e.g. recorder consort.
Copyright	A form of intellectual property, applicable to creative work including art, literature and music.
Countermelody	A melody which is secondary to the main melody. Also known as a countersubject.
Cover song	The performance or recording of a song that was performed by another artist when it was released.
Crescendo	Becoming louder. Or a dynamic marking instructing performers to gradually play louder.
Da Capo al Fine	Da Capo (DC) is Italian for 'from the beginning'. This marking instructs performers to return to the beginning of the music and play 'al Fine', which means to the end.
Descending	Music which moves from higher to lower pitches.
Dialogue	Music which is suggestive of a conversation taking place between instruments.
Dictation	Listening and transcribing a rhythm or melody onto a stave.
Diminuendo	Becoming quieter, or a dynamic marking instructing performers to play gradually quieter.
Dissonance	An interval or chord which creates tension or a discordant sound.
Distortion	Processing effect which overloads the sound, creating a harsh and fuzzy sound.
Duet	A musical ensemble of two singers or instruments, each playing an individual part.
Dynamics	The relative musical loudness or quietness of a performance.
Elements of music	The key components of music: pulse, duration, tempo, pitch, dynamics, timbre, texture, form, expression, tonality.
Ensemble	A group of musicians performing instrumental or vocal music
Fanfare	A short ceremonial piece of dramatic music played typically by brass instruments. Often used to announce the beginning of an important event or to welcome an important person.
Figured bass	Numbers printed beneath the continuo/bass line which indicate to the keyboard player which chords which they should improvise on.
Film score	Music composed for a film. Its purpose is to illustrate and enhance the story.
Folk music	Traditional songs which originate from a specific country or culture, passed on and preserved in the oral tradition. Many versions of such songs can exist.
Form	Describes the structure/layout of a piece of music.
Found sounds	Sounds created from everyday objects (e.g. pens, paper, water, etc.).
Fugue	A short melody or melodic phrase, heard in one part and successively taken up by other parts.
Fusion	The blending of contrasting musical styles or genres.

Genre	A category or classification of musical style.
Glissando	A glide up or down from one note to the next that includes all the pitches in between.
Graphic notation	A form of notation using shapes or lines or images instead of conventional music notation.
Harmony	When a combination of simultaneously played notes produce a sound that is pleasing to listen to.
Homophonic	A musical texture in which a main melody is supported by block chords.
Hymn	A religious song composed for congregations to sing together.
Illustrative music	See Programme music.
Improvisation	A creative performing technique where musicians create music in the moment.
Incidental music	Music composed for use with, for instance, a film, play, television programme, or computer game, as a background or to reflect a narrative, or to enhance a particular atmosphere.
Intermezzo	Music composed for performance between the scenes or acts of a play or between movements of a larger musical work.
Intertitles	A piece of printed text (such as dialogue in a silent movie or information about the context) that has been filmed and appears on-screen during a movie.
Interval	The distance in pitch between two notes.
Jingle	A short advertising slogan, verse or tune which is easily remembered.
Key signature	Sharps and flats indicated at the beginning of each stave to identify the key.
Lament	Song or poem which is an expression of grief or sorrow.
Leap	A jump in a melodic line of an interval greater than a 2nd.
Ledger line	Short lines used to extend the pitch above or below the five lines of the stave.
Libretto	The text of an opera.
Lullaby	A cradle song or instrumental piece, normally slow tempo and with a soothing, gentle rhythm.
Melody	A sequence of pitches, and the rhythm in which they occur, making a distinct entity.
Metronome	A device used to mark an exact tempo, to help performers to stay in time.
Monophonic	A musical texture consisting of one single unaccompanied melodic line.
Mood	A predominant emotion illustrated in a piece of music.
Motif	An important or recurring rhythmic or melodic idea in a piece of music.
Music map	A visual representation of the structure, form or content of a piece of music.
Nocturne	A piece of music with a dreamy, calming mood which illustrates night time.
Non-traditional feature	Musical features present in a piece of music which are not typically associated with the style or genre of the music.
Octave	From the Latin for 'eight', an interval of eight diatonic steps between pitches.
Open string	A string that is not stopped or pressed while being played.

Oral tradition	A form of communicating culture and traditions through word of mouth. Passing on historical traditions from one generation to the next without written instruction.
Orchestration	Conceiving and arranging music for an orchestra to perform.
Ornamentation	Adding notes to a melody to decorate the tune. Trills, rolls or grace notes are all examples of ornamentation.
Ostinato	A repeated rhythmic or melodic pattern used in the accompaniment, typically sustained throughout a piece of music.
Overdubbing	Recording technique where additional tracks are recorded and added to the main track.
Panning	Processing effect where the sound is split between speakers.
Patron	Someone (or an organisation) who employs or gives financial support. Composers often worked under patronage.
Pedal note	A sustained note, usually in the bass part, that is typically held over several bars while the harmony above changes.
Pitch	How high or low a sound or note is.
Pizzicato	A performing technique where string players pluck strings rather than bow them.
Planxty	An Irish harp tune composed in honour of a patron, associated with Turlough O'Carolan.
Playlist	A compiled list of recorded music, chosen for a particular reason or purpose.
Polymetre	Two or more time signatures being used simultaneously.
Polyphonic	A musical texture where two or more melodic lines are heard simultaneously.
Prepared piano	A modern technique where objects are placed within the piano to alter its sound.
Processing effects	Audio effects which artificially create or enhance sounds.
Programme music	Descriptive instrumental music composed to illustrate a picture, tell a story or create a mood.
Programme note	Written information for the benefit of listeners.
Quartet	An ensemble with four singers or instrumental performers.
Range	The distance between the lowest and highest pitches available on an instrument, or used in a piece of music.
Recitative	A vocal style that follows the rhythm of normal speech. It is usually used to narrate a story.
Renaissance era	In music, generally considered to be 1450 to 1600.
Rests	Musical symbols indicating the absence of sound.
Reverb (reverberation)	Also known as 'echo': the prolongation of a sound, acoustically or electronically. Sometimes used to recreate the natural effects of room reverberation.
Rhythm	A strong, regular or repeated pattern of sound.

Riff	A riff is an ostinato. It is typically a repeated chord progression or sequence of notes that accompanies a melody.
Romantic era	In music, generally considered to be 1830 to 1900.
Rondo	A musical form where a main melodic idea returns between other episodes, represented as ABACADA.
Round	A musical composition in which two or more voices or instruments perform the same melody with each part beginning at a different point.
Royalties	Royalties are paid to the owners of copyrighted music each time it is used.
Rubato	Flexibility in tempo, where time is 'robbed' from one note and given to another. It allows for expression in a performance.
Sampling	The reuse of a portion or sample of previously recorded sounds in the recording of a new composition.
Scale	Pitches organised in ascending or descending order. Common scales include major, minor and chromatic scales.
Score	Printed music which communicates a composition to performers.
Sight-reading	Reading and performing a piece of music from sheet music without prior knowledge of it.
Sight-singing	Singing a melody from sheet music without prior knowledge of it.
Silent movie	A silent film is a film with no synchronised recorded sound or spoken dialogue.
Sonata	Multi-movement instrumental work.
Songwriter	A person who writes the music and words of songs.
Sound source	Any object which can vibrate to produce a sound.
Soundwave	The vibrations in the air that carry sound from a sound source.
Step movement	When a melody moves from one note to an adjacent note, without leaping.
Suite	A set of instrumental pieces which are grouped together. Suites were originally made up of various dance forms.
Symphony	A substantial work, often multi-movement, written for orchestra.
Syncopation	A rhythmic feature where the emphasis is placed on the weak beats, creating a lively rhythmic pattern.
Tempo	The speed or pace of a piece of music.
Ternary form	A musical form in which the first section returns after a middle section, represented by the letters ABA.
Texture	Describes the density or layers present in a piece of music.
Theme	A musical motif or idea which is interwoven through a work, can form the basis of an entire composition.
Timbre	The unique tone, colour or quality of any sound or instrument.
Time signature	A pair of numbers, one above the other, showing how many beats there are in each bar, and what note value represents each beat.
Tonic	The keynote, or first note, of any scale and also the label given to the chord based on this note. In C major the tonic is C.

Tonic solfa	A system of naming pitches in a scale using syllables rather than letters.
Traditional feature	The musical elements that typically distinguish an established style or genre.
Trailer music	Background music that is heard during the preview of a film; it is not always taken from the soundtrack of the film itself.
Transpose	To rewrite a piece of music at a higher or lower pitch.
Triad	A three-note chord made up of the note itself and the notes an interval of a 3rd and a 5th above it.
Trio	A composition for three performers or in three parts.
Triplet	Three notes played in the time of two; in sheet music, the affected notes are bracketed together and labelled with the number three.
Unison	When all singers or instrumentalists perform the same melody together.
Upbeat	The beat before the first (strong, accented) beat of the bar. Also known as an anacrusis.
Variation	Changing a main theme or melody, developing it rhythmically, melodically or harmonically.